Trends in Functional Programming
Volume 8

Edited by
Marco T. Morazán
Seton Hall University

intellect Bristol, UK / Chicago, USA

First Published in the UK in 2008 by
Intellect Books, PO Box 862, Bristol BS99 1DE, UK

First published in the USA in 2008 by
Intellect Books, The University of Chicago Press, 1427 E. 60th Street, Chicago,
IL 60637, USA

A catalogue record for this book is available from the British Library.

Cover Design: Gabriel Solomons

ISBN 978-1-84150-196-3

Printed and bound by Gutenberg Press, Malta.

Contents

Preface

The 8th Symposium on Trends in Functional Programming (TFP 2007) was held in New York City, USA on April 2nd-4th, 2007. It followed the very successful previous editions held in Stirling (1999 and 2001), St. Andrews (2000), Edinburgh (2003), München (2004), Tallinn (2005), and Nottingham (2006). TFP 2007 was jointly co-hosted by the Department of Mathematics and Computer Science of Seton Hall University and the Department of Computer Science of The City College of New York. This was the first time the TFP symposium was held in the USA. It gathered 65 researchers, students, and industry professionals proudly making it the largest in TFP history surpassing previous versions by having at least 35 percent more participants. TFP 2007 brought together a truly international milieu representing a variety of countries that included Argentina, England, France, Germany, Ireland, Scotland, Spain, Sweden, The Netherlands, and the United States of America. It attracted individuals with interests in all aspects of functional programming ranging from the implementation of functional languages to the development of applications using functional languages. The success of TFP 2007 represents the growing importance of functional programming and the growing importance of the TFP policy to encourage new and veteran speakers to present their novel work at a friendly forum without first having to go through a strenuous review process. This policy has lead to a series of symposia with a rich diversity of talks from which a selection of publication-ripe articles are chosen for inclusion in a post-symposium peer-reviewed volume. Such has been the success of TFP 2007, that the TFP steering committee has decided in principle to alternate the TFP venue between the USA and Europe every year. In 2008 TFP will be held in Nijmegen, The Netherlands and in 2009 TFP is slated to return to the USA.

This volume contains the articles presented at TFP 2007 that were chosen by the program committee for publication in the *official* post-symposium proceedings according to prevailing academic reviewing standards. The program committee received 33 extended abstracts of which 30 were accepted for presentation at the symposium and for inclusion in the *draft* proceedings. The abstract screening phase ensured that all work presented at TFP 2007 was within scope, relevant, and not fundamentally flawed. After the symposium, all authors that had their work accepted for presentation were given the opportunity to revise their papers so that they could incorporate the feedback received during the symposium and the advancements they had made since the submission of their abstracts. The review of the revised manuscripts resulted in the acceptance of the ten articles included in this volume.

TFP, STUDENTS, AND THE BEST STUDENT PAPER AWARD

TFP recognizes two ways in which students play an important role in new trends. The first recognizes that students are likely to be the least experienced with the publication cycle. To enhance the quality of student papers (i.e. papers written by and describing work done mostly by students), the program committee offers these submissions extra feedback before the post-symposium review process. The reviewers are frank and direct informing student authors of the flaws and the strengths they perceive in each submission. The goal is to provide qualitative feedback and suggestions for improvements that will help student authors make their articles competitive in a review process in which all submissions are judged on an equal footing. This year the program committee offered extra feedback to fourteen draft student papers of which seven were ultimately accepted for publication in this volume. This acceptance rate among student papers is clear evidence that the extra feedback provided to student authors has a positive impact.

The second recognizes the exceptional role played by students in new trends by offering each year a *Best Student Paper Award*. As part of the review process every program committee member is encouraged to nominate papers for this award. Upon finalizing the review process, the program committee elects the recipient of the award. This award carries a cash prize, which is promptly given to the student authors, and a diploma which is traditionally conferred at the symposium dinner of the next edition of TFP. The article *Space-Efficient Gradual Typing* co-authored by students David Herman (Northeastern University) and Aaron Tomb (University of California at Santa Cruz) with Cormac Flanagan (University of California at Santa Cruz) was elected as the Best Student Paper presented at TFP 2007. My heart-felt congratulations go out to the authors for this well-deserved honor.

BEYOND TALKS AND LATEST RESULTS

In addition to fostering the presentation of the latest research results, TFP recognizes the importance of providing a lively environment that encourages social interactions and that fosters friendships and collaborations among participants. It is important to provide opportunities for participants to informally interact with colleagues outside their home institutions. To this end, TFP has historically included a series of social events with every version of the symposium. The goal is to create synergy among the participants that may lead to more joint work and joint projects.

TFP 2007 had several social events, including:

- Extensive coffee breaks throughout each day of the symposium.

- Three long lunches.

- A four-hour coach tour of Manhattan with several stops to visit places of interest.

- The symposium's dinner in Manhattan's Little Italy.

- Three extra dinners held at fun and well-known establishments in Manhattan.

It is my estimation that both the scientific program and the social events made TFP 2007 a big hit with participants. Allow me to share with you some of the unedited anonymous feedback TFP 2007 received:

- *I am quite satisfied with my first TFP experience. I particularly enjoyed the warmth and friendship that pervaded the symposium's atmosphere and dining experiences.*

- *Very nice conference! I like the many opportunities to speak individually with other participants. Talks were good.*

- *I liked the talks, the people who attended, the classroom, the NYC venue, and the banquet. Can't think of anything I didn't like.*

- *I think TFP 2007 was a resounding success: great programme, great location, great organization, great food! Of course, there must have been small things that could be improved, but nothing really springs to mind.*

- *I think this was one of the better organized conferences I have been to. I would be happy if the status quo is maintained in the next year.*

- *I have enjoyed very much this edition of TFP in NY City. I think that everything was very well organized and I have not any complain.*

- *I enjoyed this conference a lot. The meals were great. I was able to spend four hours at one point talking with experts in the field whom I'd long admired.*

- *I liked the program and the organization in general.*

TFP also recognizes the importance of bringing together the different generations of functional programmers. To this end, TFP strives to invite high-profile individuals that have had a great impact on the functional programming world to deliver a keynote address. TFP 2007 was proud to have Prof. John McCarthy (Stanford University) deliver the keynote address. The first part of his talk focused on the history of Lisp and was well-peppered with interesting personal anecdotes. The second part focused on his ideas on developing a programming language based on speech acts. Participants welcomed and enjoyed the opportunity to meet a "giant in Computer Science" – as one of the participants called John. On a more personal note, I would like to take this opportunity to thank John for everything – not just the talk and the time together. Many of us gather at different venues today to discuss the latest research results in the functional programming world, due in part to the first steps John took when he initially developed Lisp.

ARTICLE CATEGORIES AND REVIEW CRITERIA

TFP accepts submissions of articles in five different categories:

1. **Research Articles**: These articles describe new and relevant research results that are part of a new trend.

2. **Project Articles**: These articles describe the results obtained to date and the expected impact on students of recently started projects that are likely to be part of a new trend.

3. **Evaluation Articles**: These articles describe the goals, the academic results, the research results, and the impact on students of finished projects.

4. **Position Articles**: These articles present a convincing academic argument for what should be a new trend.

5. **Overview Articles**: These articles present a thorough review of recent work in a modern trend.

This year only articles in the research and project categories were accepted for publication by the program committee. All articles in this volume fall into the research category unless they are explicitly noted as a project paper.

The TFP 2007 program committee adopted the following guidelines to evaluate articles during the review process:

- **General Criteria for all Articles**:

  - The article is formatted according to the TFP-rules.
  - The number of pages is less or equal to sixteen (this criteria was relaxed to allow authors to incorporate changes the reviewers felt were important.).
  - The content is original, technically correct, unpublished, and not submitted elsewhere for publication.
  - The article is in English, well-written, well-structured, and well-illustrated.
  - The article contains an abstract, an introduction, and a conclusion.
  - The article properly sets its contribution in the context of related work.
  - The topic is clearly stated.
  - The article's category is clearly indicated when submitted.
  - The methodology used is well-motivated.
  - The article is clearly intended for a functional programming audience.
  - The article is self-contained (i.e. understanding the article is not too dependent on references to websites, authors' previously published articles, technical reports, etc.).

- **Research Paper Criteria**:

  - Topic is relevant to the state-of-the-art in the field.
  - Technical contribution is clearly stated.
  - Technical soundness is properly addressed.
  - There is convincing motivation for the relevance of the problem and the approach taken to solve it.
  - There is a clear outline of the approach taken to solve the problem, the solution, and how the solution solves the problem.
  - The conclusion summarizes the problem, the solution, and how the work presented solves the problem.

- **Project Paper Criteria**:

  - The article describes a recently started new project that is likely to be part of a new trend.
  - There is a convincing motivation for the relevance of the project.
  - The article contains an overview of the project's methodology.
  - The article states the expected research contributions.
  - The article states the expected academic benefits of the results.
  - Technical content is present and sound.
  - The article contains an overview of related work and related, current or previous, projects.
  - The article contains an overview of expected student involvement (i.e. a description, if applicable, of the role students can/will have in the project).
  - The article includes a description of the results obtained to date.
  - New projects, without new results to date, must describe and justify expectations.

- **Evaluation Paper Criteria**:

  - The article is an overview of a finished project, its goals, its academic results, and its research results.
  - The article describes and motivates the design choices made during the project and evaluates these choices.
  - The article includes reflections on the achieved results in relation to the aims of the project and the related work.
  - There is a clear and well-motivated description of the methodological lessons that can be drawn from the finished project.
  - There is a discussion on how this project and its results may influence new trends.
  - Technical content is present and sound.

 – The article contains an overview of the impact the project had on student participants (i.e. a description, if applicable, of how the project has impacted the careers of student participants).

 – The article contains an overview of future projects/work.

- **Position Paper Criteria**:

 – The article contains a convincing academic motivation for what should become a new trend.

 – The article includes academic arguments and convincing examples.

 – The article contains well-motivated academically realistic prospects.

 – Technical content is present and sound.

 – The article contains an overview of related work and the current state-of-the-art.

- **Overview Paper Criteria**:

 – The article contains a thorough review of recent work on a trendy subject.

 – The article contains a comparison of different approaches taken and their results on the same problem.

 – The article addresses the importance of the subject matter for the functional programming community.

ACKNOWLEDGEMENTS

TFP 2007 was most definitely a joint effort that brought together many talented people. I thank every single individual that contributed time and effort to making this year's symposium a success. A very special thank you goes out to each and every member of the program committee. In no small way, they had my back at all times. Each program committee member made incredibly conscientious contributions that lead to a strong program during the symposium and to the strong selection of articles that appear in this volume. I could have not assembled a better program committee and I personally thank them for their collective efforts.

TFP 2007 gratefully acknowledges the support of its sponsors: The Department of Mathematics and Computer Science and The College of Arts and Sciences of Seton Hall University, and The Department of Computer Science, The Center for Algorithms and Interactive Scientific Software (CAISS), and The Grove School of Engineering and the Division of Science of The City College of New York. Without their financial and logistical support, the registration fees would have been much higher and the organization would have not flowed as smoothly as it did. I would like to express my personal appreciation to Joan Guetti and Joseph Marbach from Seton Hall University and to Douglas R. Troeger and Gilbert Baumslag from The City College of New York for their efforts to guarantee the success of TFP 2007 and the enjoyment of the symposium by all participants. A heart-felt thank you goes out to Luis Camillo, Mary Tramel, Christopher J. Dutra, and Barbara Mucha for being there to cover all the last minute and unforeseen details that arose as the symposium progressed. Without them the day-to-day operations of TFP 2007 would have been a nightmare. I owe a great deal to Steve M. O'Brien for the wonderful job done developing and maintaining the TFP 2007 website. The job was probably more than he bargained for, but he carried out the duties he volunteered for with distinction. Heart-felt thanks also go out to Žanna Slaveniece for her invaluable artistic talents in developing the website and for her keen planning insights in choosing the venues for the social events. I dare to say that without her TFP 2007 would have just been another symposium. I would also like to express my personal gratitude to the 2007 symposium chair, Henrik Nilsson, for the timely guidance he provided which helped me stay on track and to Greg Michaelson – one of the kindest persons I have ever met – for all his assistance.

Last but not least, I thank the authors for writing, submitting, and presenting their work and I thank the participants for attending. It is these two groups that have always made TFP special and that made this year's symposium a true delight to lead. I thank them for the trust and confidence they placed in me to deliver a worthwhile event.

In closing, I would like to thank the TFP steering committee for electing me as the TFP 2007 program chair. It has truly been an honor and a pleasure to serve in this capacity. It meant a great deal to me to serve as the program chair to an edition of TFP. My first peer-reviewed publication appeared in *Trends in Functional Programming Volume 1*. In some very real sense, I am partly the product of the TFP philosophy to nurture newcomers to the field. As I mentioned in my welcoming remarks at TFP 2007, I hope this fact inspires one or more of the students that were present to chair a future edition of TFP. TFP works!

Marco T. Morazán
Program Committee Chair TFP 2007
Editor of Trends in Functional Programming Volume 8
New York, August 2007

TFP 2007 PROGRAM COMMITTEE

John Clements	California Polytechnic State University, USA
Marko van Eekelen	Radboud Universiteit Nijmegen, The Netherlands
Benjamin Goldberg	New York University, USA
Kevin Hammond	University of St. Andrews, UK
Patricia Johann	Rutgers University, USA
Hans-Wolfgang Loidl	Ludwig-Maximilians Universität München, Germany
Rita Loogen	Philipps-Universität Marburg, Germany
Greg Michaelson	Heriot-Watt University, UK
Marco T. Morazán	Seton Hall University, USA
Henrik Nilsson	University of Nottingham, UK
Chris Okasaki	United States Military Academy at West Point, USA
Rex Page	University of Oklahoma, USA
Ricardo Peña	Universidad Complutense de Madrid, Spain
Benjamin C. Pierce	University of Pennsylvania, USA
John Reppy	University of Chicago, USA
Ulrik P. Schultz	University of Southern Denmark, Denmark
Clara Segura	Universidad Complutense de Madrid, Spain
Jocelyn Sérot	Université Blaise Pascal, France
Zhong Shao	Yale University, USA
Olin Shivers	Georgia Institute of Technology, USA
Phil Trinder	Heriot-Watt University, UK
David Walker	Princeton University, USA

Sub-reviewers

Jost Berthold	Xiao Yan Deng	Lu Fan
Jonathan Grattage	Pieter Koopman	Manfred Minimair
Rinus Plasmeijer	Sjaak Smetsers	Abdallah Al Zain

TFP 2007 ORGANIZATION

Symposium Chair:	Henrik Nilsson	University of Nottingham
Program Chair:	Marco T. Morazán	Seton Hall University
Treasurer:	Greg Michaelson	Heriot-Watt University
Organization Chair:	Marco T. Morazán	Seton Hall University

TFP 2007 Local Organizing Committee

Gilbert Baumslag	City College of New York
Luis Camillo	City College of New York
Christopher J. Dutra	Seton Hall University
Joan Guetti	Seton Hall University
Marco T. Morazán	Seton Hall University
Steve M. O'Brien	Seton Hall University
Žanna Slaveniece	AXA Equitable
Mary Tramel	City College of New York
Douglas R. Troeger	City College of New York

Chapter 1

Space-Efficient Gradual Typing
– *Best Student Paper* –

David Herman[1], Aaron Tomb[2], Cormac Flanagan[2]

Abstract: Gradual type systems offer a smooth continuum between static and dynamic typing by permitting the free mixture of typed and untyped code. The runtime systems for these languages, and other languages with hybrid type checking, typically enforce function types by dynamically generating function proxies. This approach can result in unbounded growth in the number of proxies, however, which drastically impacts space efficiency and destroys tail recursion.

We present a semantics for gradual typing that is based on *coercions* instead of function proxies, and which combines adjacent coercions at runtime to limit their space consumption. We prove bounds on the space consumed by coercions as well as soundness of the type system, demonstrating that programmers can safely mix typing disciplines without incurring unreasonable overheads. Our approach also detects certain errors earlier than prior work.

1.1 GRADUAL TYPING FOR SOFTWARE EVOLUTION

Dynamically typed languages have always excelled at exploratory programming. Languages such as Lisp, Scheme, Smalltalk, and JavaScript support quick early prototyping and incremental development without the overhead of documenting (often-changing) structural invariants as types. For large applications, however,

---

[1]College of Computer and Information Science, Northeastern University, 360 Huntington Ave, Boston, MA 02115, E-mail: `dherman@ccs.neu.edu`

[2]Computer Science Department, School of Engineering, University of California at Santa Cruz, 1156 High Street MS: SOE3, Santa Cruz, CA 95064, E-mail: `atomb@soe.ucsc.edu, cormac@soe.ucsc.edu`

static type systems have proven invaluable. They are crucial for understanding and enforcing key program invariants and abstractions, and they catch many errors early in the development process.

Given these different strengths, it is not uncommon to encounter the following scenario: a programmer builds a prototype in a dynamically typed scripting language, perhaps even in parallel to a separate, official software development process with an entire team. The team effort gets mired in process issues and over-engineering, and the prototype ends up in production use. Before long, this hastily conceived prototype grows into a fully fledged production system, but without the structure or guarantees provided by static types. The system becomes unwieldy; QA cannot produce test cases fast enough and bugs start cropping up that no one can track down. Ultimately, the team decides to port the application to a statically typed language, requiring a complete rewrite of the entire system.

The cost of cross-language migration is huge and often insupportable. But the scenario above is avoidable. Several languages combine static and dynamic typing, among them Boo [8], Visual Basic.NET [20], Sage [17], and PLT Scheme [26]. This approach of *hybrid typing*, where types are enforced with a combination of static and dynamic checks, has begun to gain attention in the research community [2, 5, 17, 24, 20, 26]. Recently, Siek and Taha [24, 25] coined the slogan *gradual typing* for this important application of hybrid typing: the ability to implement both partially conceived prototypes and mature production systems in the same programming language by gradually introducing type discipline. Gradual typing offers the possibility of continuous software evolution from prototype to product, thus avoiding the huge costs of language migration.

Our recent experience in the working group on the JavaScript [9] language specification provides a more concrete example. JavaScript is a dynamically typed functional programming language that is widely used for scripting user interactions in web browsers, and is a key technology in Ajax applications [16]. The enormous popularity of the language is due in no small part to its low barrier to entry; anyone can write a JavaScript program by copying and pasting code from one web page to another. Its dynamic type system and fail-soft runtime semantics allow programmers to produce something that *seems* to work with a minimum of effort. The increasing complexity of modern web applications, however, has motivated the addition of a static type system. The working group does not intend to abandon the dynamically typed portion of the language—because of its usefulness and to retain backwards compatibility—but rather to allow typing disciplines to interact via a hybrid system that supports gradual typing.[3]

1.1.1   The Cost of Gradual Typing

Gradually typed languages support both statically typed and dynamically typed code, and include runtime checks (or type casts) at the boundaries between these two typing disciplines, to guarantee that dynamically typed code cannot violate

---

[3]The JavaScript specification is work in progress [10].

the invariants of statically typed code. To illustrate this idea, consider the following code fragment, which passes an untyped variable x into a variable y of type Int:

$$\text{let } x = \text{true in } \dots \text{ let } y : \text{Int} = x \text{ in } \dots$$

During compilation, the type checker inserts a dynamic type cast $\langle\text{Int}\rangle$ to enforce the type invariant on y; at runtime, this cast detects the attempted type violation:

$$\text{let } x = \text{true in } \dots \text{ let } y : \text{Int} = (\langle\text{Int}\rangle\, x) \text{ in } \dots$$
$$\longrightarrow^* \quad \text{Error} : \textit{"failed cast"}$$

Unfortunately, even these simple, first-order type checks can result in unexpected costs, as in the following example, where a programmer has added some type annotations to a previously untyped program:

$$\textit{even} : \text{Dyn} \to \text{Dyn} = \lambda n : \text{Int. if } (n = 0) \text{ then true else } \textit{odd } (n - 1)$$
$$\textit{odd} : \text{Int} \to \text{Bool} = \lambda n : \text{Int. if } (n = 0) \text{ then false else } \textit{even } (n - 1)$$

This program seems innocuous, but suffers from a space leak. Since *even* is dynamically typed, the result of each call to *even* $(n - 1)$ must be cast to Bool, resulting in unbounded growth in the control stack and destroying tail recursion.

Additional complications arise when first-class functions cross the boundaries between typing disciplines. In general, it is not possible to check if an untyped function satisfies a particular static type. A natural solution is to wrap the function in a proxy that, whenever it is applied, casts its argument and result values appropriately, ensuring that the function is only observed with its expected type. This proxy-based approach is used heavily in recent literature [12, 13, 17, 19, 24], but has serious consequences for space efficiency.

As a simple example, consider the following program in continuation-passing style, where both mutually recursive functions take a continuation argument k, but only one of these arguments is annotated with a precise type:

$$\textit{even} = \lambda n : \text{Int. } \lambda k : (\text{Dyn} \to \text{Dyn}). \quad \text{if } (n = 0) \text{ then } (k \text{ true}) \text{ else } \textit{odd } (n - 1)\, k$$
$$\textit{odd} = \lambda n : \text{Int. } \lambda k : (\text{Bool} \to \text{Bool}). \text{ if } (n = 0) \text{ then } (k \text{ false}) \text{ else } \textit{even } (n - 1)\, k$$

Here, the recursive calls to *odd* and *even* quietly cast the continuation argument k with higher-order casts $\langle\text{Bool} \to \text{Bool}\rangle$ and $\langle\text{Dyn} \to \text{Dyn}\rangle$, respectively. This means that k is wrapped in an additional function proxy at each recursive call!

These examples demonstrate that naïve gradual typing violates space safety of functional programming languages by incurring surprising and unnecessary changes in asymptotic space consumption of programs. The flexibility promised by gradual typing can only be achieved if programmers are free to decide how precisely to type various parts of a program. This flexibility is lost if adding type annotations accidentally triggers drastic changes in memory usage.

1.1.2 Space-Efficient Gradual Typing

We present a semantics for gradual typing that overcomes these problems. Our approach hinges on the simple insight that when proxies accumulate at runtime, they often contain redundant information. In the higher-order example above, the growing chain of function proxies contains only two distinct components, Bool → Bool and Dyn → Dyn, which could be merged to the simpler but equivalent Bool → Bool.

Type casts behave like *error projections* [11], which are closed under composition. However, the syntax of casts does not always compose; for example, there is no cast c such that $\langle c \rangle \, e = \langle \texttt{Int} \rangle \, \langle \texttt{Bool} \rangle \, e$. Furthermore, projections are idempotent, which should allow us to eliminate duplicate casts. For example, $\langle \texttt{Bool} \to \texttt{Bool} \rangle \, \langle \texttt{Bool} \to \texttt{Bool} \rangle \, e = \langle \texttt{Bool} \to \texttt{Bool} \rangle \, e$. But such transformations are inconvenient, if not impossible, with a representation of higher-order type casts as functions.

Our formalization instead leverages Henglein's *coercion calculus* [18], which provides a syntax for projections, called coercions, which are closed under a composition operator. This allows us to combine adjacent casts whenever they occur at runtime in order to eliminate redundant information and thus guarantee clear bounds on space consumption. The details of combining and simplifying coercions are presented in Section 1.5. By eagerly combining coercions, we can also detect certain errors immediately as soon as a function cast is applied; in contrast, prior approaches would not detect these errors until the casted function is invoked.

Our approach is applicable to many hybrid-typed languages [13, 14, 17] that use function proxies and hence are prone to space consumption problems. For clarity, we formalize our approach for the simply typed λ-calculus with references. Of course, gradual typing is not restricted to such simple type systems: the Sage language [17] incorporates gradual typing as part of a very expressive type system with polymorphic functions, type operators, first-class types, dependent types, general refinement types, etc. Concurrently, Siek and Taha [24] developed gradual typing for the simpler language $\lambda_{\to}^{?}$, which we use as the basis for this presentation.

The presentation of our results proceeds as follows. The following section reviews the syntax and type system of $\lambda_{\to}^{?}$. Section 3 introduces the coercion algebra underlying our approach. Section 4 describes how we translate source programs into a target language with explicit coercions. Section 5 provides an operational semantics for that target language, and Section 6 proves bounds on the space consumption. Section 7 extends our approach to detect errors earlier and provide better coverage. The last two sections place our work into context.

1.2   GRADUALLY TYPED LAMBDA CALCULUS

This section reviews the gradually typed λ-calculus $\lambda_{\to}^{?}$. This language is essentially the simply typed λ-calculus extended with the type Dyn to represent dynamic types; it also includes mutable reference cells to demonstrate the gradual typing of assignments. We refer the interested reader to Siek and Taha's work [24]

Figure 1.1: Source Language Type System

Consistency rules $\boxed{S \sim T}$

[C-REFL]   [C-DYNR]   [C-DYNL]   [C-FLOAT]

$$\frac{}{T \sim T} \qquad \frac{}{T \sim \text{Dyn}} \qquad \frac{}{\text{Dyn} \sim T} \qquad \frac{}{\text{Int} \sim \text{Float}}$$

[C-FUN]   [C-REF]

$$\frac{T_1 \sim S_1 \quad S_2 \sim T_2}{(S_1 \to S_2) \sim (T_1 \to T_2)} \qquad \frac{T \sim S \quad S \sim T}{\text{Ref } S \sim \text{Ref } T}$$

Type rules $\boxed{E \vdash e : T}$

[T-VAR]   [T-FUN]   [T-CONST]

$$\frac{(x : T) \in E}{E \vdash x : T} \qquad \frac{E, x : S \vdash e : T}{E \vdash (\lambda x{:}S.\, e) : (S \to T)} \qquad \frac{}{E \vdash k : ty(k)}$$

[T-APP1]   [T-APP2]

$$\frac{E \vdash e_1 : (S \to T) \quad E \vdash e_2 : S' \quad S' \sim S}{E \vdash (e_1 \; e_2) : T} \qquad \frac{E \vdash e_1 : \text{Dyn} \quad E \vdash e_2 : S}{E \vdash (e_1 \; e_2) : \text{Dyn}}$$

[T-REF]   [T-DEREF1]   [T-DEREF2]

$$\frac{E \vdash e : T}{E \vdash \text{ref } e : \text{Ref } T} \qquad \frac{E \vdash e : \text{Ref } T}{E \vdash !e : T} \qquad \frac{E \vdash e : \text{Dyn}}{E \vdash !e : \text{Dyn}}$$

[T-ASSIGN1]   [T-ASSIGN2]

$$\frac{E \vdash e_1 : \text{Ref } T \quad E \vdash e_2 : S \quad S \sim T}{E \vdash e_1 := e_2 : S} \qquad \frac{E \vdash e_1 : \text{Dyn} \quad E \vdash e_2 : T}{E \vdash e_1 := e_2 : \text{Dyn}}$$

for motivations regarding the design of this language and its type system.

$$
\begin{aligned}
\textit{Typing environments:} \quad & E \quad ::= \emptyset \mid E, x : T \\
\textit{Terms:} \quad & e \quad ::= k \mid x \mid \lambda x{:}T.\, e \mid e\; e \mid \text{ref } e \mid !e \mid e := e \\
\textit{Types:} \quad & S, T \quad ::= B \mid T \to T \mid \text{Dyn} \mid \text{Ref } T
\end{aligned}
$$

Terms include the usual constants, variables, abstractions, and applications, as well as reference allocation, dereference, and assignment. Types include the dynamic type Dyn, function types $T \to T$, reference types Ref T, and some collection of ground or base types B (such as Int or Float).

The $\lambda^?_\to$ type system is a little unusual in that it is based on an intransitive *consistency* relation $S \sim T$ instead of the more conventional transitive subtyping relation $S <: T$. Any type is consistent with the type Dyn, from which it follows that, for example, Bool $\sim$ Dyn and Dyn $\sim$ Int. However, booleans cannot be used directly as integers, which is why the consistency relation is not transitively closed. We do not assume the consistency relation is symmetric, since a language might, for example, allow coercions from integers to floats but not vice-versa.

The consistency relation is defined in Figure 1.1. The rules [C-DYNL] and

[C-DynR] allow all coercions to and from type Dyn. The rule [C-Float] serves as an example of asymmetry by allowing coercion from Int to Float but not the reverse. The rule [C-Fun] is reminiscent of the contravariant/covariant rule for function subtyping. We extend the invariant reference cells of $\lambda^?_\rightarrow$ to allow coercion from Ref S to Ref T via rule [C-Ref], provided S and T are symmetrically consistent. Unlike functions, reference cells do not distinguish their output ("read") type from their input ("write") type, so coercion must be possible in either direction. For example, the two reference types Ref Int and Ref Dyn are consistent.

Figure 1.1 also presents the type rules for the source language. Notice the presence of two separate procedure application rules. Rule [T-App1] checks statically-typed functions; in this case, the argument may have any type consistent with the function's domain. Since the consistency relation is intransitive, we cannot split out applications of this relation into a separate type rule, as is commonly done for subtyping via a subsumption rule. Rule [T-App2] handles the case where the operator is dynamically typed; in this case the argument may be of any type. The assignment rules follow an analogous pattern, accepting a consistent type when the left-hand side is known to have type Ref T, and any type when the left-hand side is dynamically typed. Similarly, dereferences only produce precise types for reference types.

1.3 COERCIONS

To achieve a space-efficient implementation, we elaborate source programs into a target language with explicit type casts, which allow expressions of one type to be used at any consistent type. Our representation of casts is based on *coercions*, drawn from Henglein's theory of dynamic typing [18]. The key benefit of coercions over prior proxy-based representations is that they are *combinable*; if two coercions are wrapped around a function value, then they can be safely combined into a single coercion, thus reducing the space consumption of the program without changing its semantic behavior.

The coercion language and its typing rules are both defined in Figure 1.2. The coercion judgment $\vdash c : S \rightsquigarrow T$ states that coercion c serves to coerce values from type S to type T (but may fail on some values of type S that are not coercible to type T). The identity coercion I always succeeds, and has type $\vdash c : T \rightsquigarrow T$ for any T. Conversely, the failure coercion Fail always fails, but can relate any two types S and T, and so $\vdash$ Fail $: S \rightsquigarrow T$. For each base type B, the coercion B? "downcasts" a value of type Dyn to type B, and so has type $\vdash B? : \text{Dyn} \rightsquigarrow B$. Conversely, the tagging coercion $B!$ has type $\vdash B! : B \rightsquigarrow \text{Dyn}$. Similarly, the function checking coercion Fun? converts a value of type Dyn to have the dynamic function type Dyn $\rightarrow$ Dyn. If a more precise function type is required, this value can be further coerced via a function coercion Fun c d, where c coerces function arguments and d coerces results. For example, the coercion (Fun Int? Int!) coerces from Dyn $\rightarrow$ Dyn to Int $\rightarrow$ Int, by untagging function arguments (via Int?) and tagging function results (via Int!). Conversely, the tagging coercion

Figure 1.2: Coercion Language and Type Rules

$$\textit{Coercions:} \quad c,d \;::=\; I \mid \texttt{Fail} \mid D! \mid D? \mid \texttt{IntFloat} \mid \texttt{Fun}\; c\; c \mid \texttt{Ref}\; c\; c \mid c;c$$
$$\textit{Dynamic tags:} \quad D \;::=\; B \mid \texttt{Fun} \mid \texttt{Ref}$$

<u>C</u>oercion rules $\qquad\qquad\qquad\qquad\qquad\qquad\qquad \boxed{\vdash c : S \rightsquigarrow T}$

[C-ID]
$$\overline{\vdash I : T \rightsquigarrow T}$$

[C-FAIL]
$$\overline{\vdash \texttt{Fail} : S \rightsquigarrow T}$$

[C-$B!$]
$$\overline{\vdash B! : B \rightsquigarrow \texttt{Dyn}}$$

[C-$B?$]
$$\overline{\vdash B? : \texttt{Dyn} \rightsquigarrow B}$$

[C-FUN!]
$$\overline{\vdash \texttt{Fun}! : (\texttt{Dyn} \rightarrow \texttt{Dyn}) \rightsquigarrow \texttt{Dyn}}$$

[C-FUN?]
$$\overline{\vdash \texttt{Fun}? : \texttt{Dyn} \rightsquigarrow (\texttt{Dyn} \rightarrow \texttt{Dyn})}$$

[C-FUN]
$$\frac{\vdash c_1 : T_1' \rightsquigarrow T_1 \qquad \vdash c_2 : T_2 \rightsquigarrow T_2'}{\vdash (\texttt{Fun}\; c_1\; c_2) : (T_1 \rightarrow T_2) \rightsquigarrow (T_1' \rightarrow T_2')}$$

[C-REF!]
$$\overline{\vdash \texttt{Ref}! : (\texttt{Ref}\; \texttt{Dyn}) \rightsquigarrow \texttt{Dyn}}$$

[C-REF?]
$$\overline{\vdash \texttt{Ref}? : \texttt{Dyn} \rightsquigarrow (\texttt{Ref}\; \texttt{Dyn})}$$

[C-REF]
$$\frac{\vdash c : T \rightsquigarrow S \qquad \vdash d : S \rightsquigarrow T}{\vdash (\texttt{Ref}\; c\; d) : (\texttt{Ref}\; S) \rightsquigarrow (\texttt{Ref}\; T)}$$

[C-COMPOSE]
$$\frac{\vdash c_1 : T \rightsquigarrow T_1 \qquad \vdash c_2 : T_1 \rightsquigarrow T_2}{\vdash (c_1;c_2) : T \rightsquigarrow T_2}$$

[C-FLOAT]
$$\overline{\vdash \texttt{IntFloat} : \texttt{Int} \rightsquigarrow \texttt{Float}}$$

Fun! coerces a dynamic function of type $\texttt{Dyn} \rightarrow \texttt{Dyn}$ to type $\texttt{Dyn}$. Like function coercions, reference coercions also contain two components: the first for coercing values put into the reference cell; the second for coercing values read from the cell. Finally, the coercion $c;d$ represents coercion composition, i.e., the coercion c followed by coercion d.

This coercion language is sufficient to translate between all consistent types: if types S and T are consistent, then the following partial function $coerce(S,T)$ is defined and returns the appropriate coercion between these types.

$$coerce : Type \times Type \quad \rightarrow \quad Coercion$$

$$
\begin{aligned}
coerce(T,T) &= I \\
coerce(B,\text{Dyn}) &= B! \\
coerce(\text{Dyn},B) &= B? \\
coerce(\text{Int},\text{Float}) &= \text{IntFloat}
\end{aligned}
$$

$$
\begin{aligned}
coerce(S_1 \rightarrow S_2, T_1 \rightarrow T_2) &= \text{Fun } coerce(T_1,S_1)\, coerce(S_2,T_2) \\
coerce(\text{Dyn}, T_1 \rightarrow T_2) &= \text{Fun?}; coerce(\text{Dyn} \rightarrow \text{Dyn}, T_1 \rightarrow T_2) \\
coerce(T_1 \rightarrow T_2, \text{Dyn}) &= coerce(T_1 \rightarrow T_2, \text{Dyn} \rightarrow \text{Dyn}); \text{Fun!}
\end{aligned}
$$

$$
\begin{aligned}
coerce(\text{Ref } S, \text{Ref } T) &= \text{Ref } coerce(T,S)\, coerce(S,T) \\
coerce(\text{Dyn}, \text{Ref } T) &= \text{Ref?}; coerce(\text{Ref Dyn}, \text{Ref } T) \\
coerce(\text{Ref } T, \text{Dyn}) &= coerce(\text{Ref } T, \text{Ref Dyn}); \text{Ref!}
\end{aligned}
$$

Coercing a type T to itself produces the identity coercion I. Coercing base types B to type Dyn requires a tagging coercion $B!$, and coercing Dyn to a base type B requires a runtime check $B?$. Function coercions work by coercing their domain and range types. The type Dyn is coerced to a function type via a two-step coercion: first the value is checked to be a function and then coerced from the dynamic function type $\text{Dyn} \rightarrow \text{Dyn}$ to $T_1 \rightarrow T_2$. Dually, typed functions are coerced to type Dyn via coercion to a dynamic function type followed by the function tag Fun!. Coercing a Ref S to a Ref T entails coercing all writes from T to S and all reads from S to T. Coercing reference types to and from Dyn is analogous to function coercion.

Lemma 1.1 (Well-typed coercions).

1. $S \sim T$ iff $coerce(S,T)$ is defined.

2. If $c = coerce(S,T)$ then $\vdash c : S \rightsquigarrow T$.

Proof. Inductions on the derivations of $S \sim T$ and $coerce(S,T)$. □

1.4   TARGET LANGUAGE AND CAST INSERTION

During compilation, we both type check the source program and insert explicit type casts where necessary. The target language of this cast insertion process is essentially the same as the source, except that it uses explicit casts of the form $\langle c \rangle\, t$ as the only mechanism for connecting terms of type Dyn and terms of other types. For example, the term $\langle \text{Int?} \rangle\, x$ has type Int, provided that x has type Dyn. The language syntax and type rules are defined in Figure 1.3, and are mostly straightforward. The language also includes addresses a which refer to a global store σ, and the store typing environment Σ maps addresses to types.

Figure 1.3: Target Language Syntax and Type Rules

$$
\begin{array}{rll}
\textit{Terms:} & s,t & ::= x \mid u \mid t\,t \mid \mathbf{ref}\ t \mid {!}t \mid t := t \mid \langle c \rangle\,t \\
\textit{Values:} & v & ::= u \mid \langle c \rangle\,u \quad (\text{if } c \notin \{I, \mathtt{Fail}, \mathtt{IntFloat}\}) \\
\textit{Uncoerced values:} & u & ::= \lambda x{:}T.\,t \mid k \mid a \\
\textit{Stores:} & \sigma & ::= \emptyset \mid \sigma[a := v] \\
\textit{Typing environments:} & E & ::= \emptyset \mid E, x : T \\
\textit{Store typings:} & \Sigma & ::= \emptyset \mid \Sigma, a : T
\end{array}
$$

Type rules $\boxed{E;\Sigma \vdash t : T \qquad E;\Sigma \vdash \sigma}$

[T-VAR]
$$\frac{(x:t) \in E}{E;\Sigma \vdash x : T}$$

[T-FUN]
$$\frac{E, x : S; \Sigma \vdash t : T}{E;\Sigma \vdash (\lambda x{:}S.\,t) : (S \to T)}$$

[T-APP]
$$\frac{E;\Sigma \vdash t_1 : (S \to T) \qquad E;\Sigma \vdash t_2 : S}{E;\Sigma \vdash (t_1\ t_2) : T}$$

[T-REF]
$$\frac{E;\Sigma \vdash t : T}{E;\Sigma \vdash \mathbf{ref}\ t : \mathtt{Ref}\ T}$$

[T-DEREF]
$$\frac{E;\Sigma \vdash t : \mathtt{Ref}\ T}{E;\Sigma \vdash {!}t : T}$$

[T-ASSIGN]
$$\frac{E;\Sigma \vdash t_1 : \mathtt{Ref}\ T \qquad E;\Sigma \vdash t_2 : T}{E;\Sigma \vdash t_1 := t_2 : T}$$

[T-CONST]
$$\frac{}{E;\Sigma \vdash k : ty(k)}$$

[T-CAST]
$$\frac{\vdash c : S \rightsquigarrow T \qquad E;\Sigma \vdash t : S}{E;\Sigma \vdash \langle c \rangle\,t : T}$$

[T-ADDR]
$$\frac{(a : T) \in \Sigma}{E;\Sigma \vdash a : \mathtt{Ref}\ T}$$

[T-STORE]
$$\frac{dom(\sigma) = dom(\Sigma) \qquad \forall a \in dom(\sigma).\ E;\Sigma \vdash \sigma(a) : \Sigma(a)}{E;\Sigma \vdash \sigma}$$

The process of type checking and inserting coercions is formalized via the *cast insertion judgment*:

$$E \vdash e \hookrightarrow t : T$$

Here, the type environment E provides types for free variables, e is the original source program, t is a modified version of the original program with additional coercions, and T is the inferred type for t. The rules defining the cast insertion judgment are shown in Figure 1.4, and they rely on the partial function *coerce* to compute coercions between types. For example, rule [C-APP1] compiles an application expression where the operator has a function type $S \to T$ by casting the argument expression to type S. Rule [C-APP2] handles the case where the operator is dynamically typed by inserting a $\langle \mathtt{Fun?} \rangle$ check to ensure the operator evaluates to a function, and casting the argument to type Dyn to yield a tagged value. Rules [C-REF] and [C-DEREF1] handle typed reference allocation and dereference. Rule [C-DEREF2] handles dynamically typed dereference by inserting a runtime $\langle \mathtt{Ref?} \rangle$ check. Rule [C-ASSIGN1] handles statically typed assignment, casting the right-hand side to the expected type of the reference cell, and [C-ASSIGN2] handles dynamically typed assignment, casting the left-hand side with a runtime $\langle \mathtt{Ref?} \rangle$

Figure 1.4: Cast Insertion Rules

Cast insertion rules $\boxed{E \vdash e \hookrightarrow t : T}$

[C-VAR]
$$\frac{(x:T) \in E}{E \vdash x \hookrightarrow x : T}$$

[C-CONST]
$$\frac{}{E \vdash k \hookrightarrow k : ty(k)}$$

[C-FUN]
$$\frac{E, x:S \vdash e \hookrightarrow t : T}{E \vdash (\lambda x{:}S.\, e) \hookrightarrow (\lambda x{:}S.\, t) : (S \to T)}$$

[C-APP1]
$$\frac{E \vdash e_1 \hookrightarrow t_1 : (S \to T) \qquad E \vdash e_2 \hookrightarrow t_2 : S' \qquad c = coerce(S', S)}{E \vdash e_1\, e_2 \hookrightarrow (t_1\, (\langle c \rangle\, t_2)) : T}$$

[C-APP2]
$$\frac{E \vdash e_1 \hookrightarrow t_1 : \mathsf{Dyn} \qquad E \vdash e_2 \hookrightarrow t_2 : S' \qquad c = coerce(S', \mathsf{Dyn})}{E \vdash e_1\, e_2 \hookrightarrow (((\langle \mathsf{Fun?} \rangle\, t_1)\, (\langle c \rangle\, t_2)) : \mathsf{Dyn}}$$

[C-REF]
$$\frac{E \vdash e \hookrightarrow t : T}{E \vdash \mathsf{ref}\, e \hookrightarrow \mathsf{ref}\, t : \mathsf{Ref}\, T}$$

[C-DEREF1]
$$\frac{E \vdash e \hookrightarrow t : \mathsf{Ref}\, T}{E \vdash !e \hookrightarrow !t : T}$$

[C-DEREF2]
$$\frac{E \vdash e \hookrightarrow t : \mathsf{Dyn}}{E \vdash !e \hookrightarrow !(\langle \mathsf{Ref?} \rangle\, t) : \mathsf{Dyn}}$$

[C-ASSIGN1]
$$\frac{E \vdash e_1 \hookrightarrow t_1 : \mathsf{Ref}\, S \qquad E \vdash e_2 \hookrightarrow t_2 : T \qquad c = coerce(T, S)}{E \vdash e_1 := e_2 \hookrightarrow (t_1 := (\langle c \rangle\, t_2)) : S}$$

[C-ASSIGN2]
$$\frac{E \vdash e_1 \hookrightarrow t_1 : \mathsf{Dyn} \qquad E \vdash e_2 \hookrightarrow t_2 : T \qquad c = coerce(T, \mathsf{Dyn})}{E \vdash e_1 := e_2 \hookrightarrow (((\langle \mathsf{Ref?} \rangle\, t_1) := (\langle c \rangle\, t_2)) : \mathsf{Dyn}}$$

check and the right-hand side with a tagging coercion to type Dyn.

Compilation succeeds on all well-typed source programs, and produces only well-typed target programs.

Theorem 1.2 (Well-typed programs compile). *For all E, e, and T, the following statements are equivalent:*

1. $E \vdash e : T$

2. $\exists t$ such that $E \vdash e \hookrightarrow t : T$

Theorem 1.3 (Compiled programs are well-typed). *For all E, e, t, and T, if $E \vdash e \hookrightarrow t : T$ then $E; \emptyset \vdash t : T$*

Proof. Inductions on the cast insertion and source language typing derivations. $\square$

1.5 OPERATIONAL SEMANTICS

We now consider how to implement the target language in a manner that limits the space consumed by coercions. The key idea is to combine adjacent casts at runtime to eliminate redundant information while preserving the behavior of programs.

Figure 1.5 provides the definitions and reduction rules for the target language, using a small-step operational semantics with evaluation contexts. The grammar of evaluation contexts C is defined in terms of contexts D, which cannot begin with a cast. This prevents nesting of adjacent casts and allows the crucial [E-CCAST] reduction rule to ensure that adjacent casts in the program term are always merged.

In order to maintain bounds on their size, coercions are maintained normalized throughout evaluation according to the following rules:

$$
\begin{array}{rclcrcll}
I;c & = & c & \qquad & D!;D? & = & I \\
c;I & = & c & \qquad & D!;D'? & = & \texttt{Fail} & \text{if } D \neq D' \\
\texttt{Fail};c & = & \texttt{Fail} & \qquad & (\texttt{Fun } c_1\ c_2);(\texttt{Fun } d_1\ d_2) & = & \texttt{Fun } (d_1;c_1)\ (c_2;d_2) \\
c;\texttt{Fail} & = & \texttt{Fail} & \qquad & (\texttt{Ref } c_1\ c_2);(\texttt{Ref } d_1\ d_2) & = & \texttt{Ref } (d_1;c_1)\ (c_2;d_2) \\
& & & \qquad & (c_1;c_2);c_3 & = & c_1;(c_2;c_3)
\end{array}
$$

This normalization is applied in a transitive, compatible manner whenever the rule [E-CCAST] is applied, thus bounding the size of coercions during evaluation. Normalized coercions satisfy the following grammar:

$$
\begin{aligned}
nc \quad ::= \quad & I \mid \texttt{Fail} \mid D? \mid D! \mid D?;D! \\
& \mid \ [\texttt{Int}?;]\,\texttt{IntFloat}\,[;\texttt{Int}!] \\
& \mid \ [\texttt{Fun}?;]\,\texttt{Fun } nc\ nc\,[;\texttt{Fun}!] \\
& \mid \ [\texttt{Ref}?;]\,\texttt{Ref } nc\ nc\,[;\texttt{Ref}!]
\end{aligned}
$$

Most of the remaining reduction rules are straightforward. Rules [E-BETA], [E-NEW], [E-DEREF], and [E-ASSIGN] are standard. The rule [E-PRIM] relies on a function $\delta : Term \times Term \rightarrow Term$ to define the semantics of constant functions. For simplicity, we assume each δ to be defined for all constants k and arguments v. Rule [E-CBETA] applies function casts by casting the function argument and result. Rule [E-CDEREF] casts the result of reading a cell and [E-CASSIGN] casts the value written to a cell and casts the value again to the expected output type. Rules [E-ID] and [E-FCAST] respectively perform the identity and float coercions, and are restricted to non-cast contexts to prevent overlap with [E-CCAST].

Evaluation satisfies the usual preservation and progress lemmas.

Theorem 1.4 (Soundness of evaluation). *If* $\emptyset;\emptyset \vdash t : T$ *then either*

1. $t,\emptyset$ diverges,

2. $t,\emptyset \longrightarrow^* C[\langle\texttt{Fail}\rangle\ u],\sigma$ or

3. $t,\emptyset \longrightarrow^* v,\sigma$ and $\exists\Sigma$ such that $\emptyset;\Sigma \vdash v : T$ and $\emptyset;\Sigma \vdash \sigma$.

Proof. Via standard subject reduction and progress lemmas in the style of Wright and Felleisen [24]. □

Figure 1.5: Operational Semantics

$$Evaluation\ Contexts: \quad C ::= D \mid \langle c \rangle\ D$$
$$Non\text{-}cast\ Contexts: \quad D ::= \bullet \mid (C\ t) \mid (v\ C) \mid \texttt{ref}\ C \mid !C \mid C := t \mid v := C$$

$$
\begin{array}{rcll}
C[(\lambda x{:}S.\ t)\ v], \sigma & \longrightarrow & C[t[x := v]], \sigma & [\text{E-BETA}] \\
C[\texttt{ref}\ v], \sigma & \longrightarrow & C[a], \sigma[a := v] & \quad\text{for } a \notin dom(\sigma) \quad [\text{E-NEW}] \\
C[!a], \sigma & \longrightarrow & C[\sigma(a)], \sigma & [\text{E-DEREF}] \\
C[a := v], \sigma & \longrightarrow & C[v], \sigma[a := v] & [\text{E-ASSIGN}] \\
C[k\ v], \sigma & \longrightarrow & C[\delta(k, v)], \sigma & [\text{E-PRIM}] \\
C[(\langle \texttt{Fun}\ c\ d \rangle\ u)\ v], \sigma & \longrightarrow & C[\langle d \rangle\ (u\ (\langle c \rangle\ v))], \sigma & [\text{E-CBETA}] \\
C[!(\langle \texttt{Ref}\ c\ d \rangle\ a)], \sigma & \longrightarrow & C[\langle d \rangle\ !a], \sigma & [\text{E-CDEREF}] \\
C[(\langle \texttt{Ref}\ c\ d \rangle\ a) := v], \sigma & \longrightarrow & C[\langle d \rangle\ (a := \langle c \rangle\ v)], \sigma & [\text{E-CASSIGN}] \\
C[\langle I \rangle\ u], \sigma & \longrightarrow & C[u], \sigma & \quad\text{if } C \neq C'[\langle c \rangle\ \bullet] \quad [\text{E-ID}] \\
C[\langle \texttt{IntFloat} \rangle\ n], \sigma & \longrightarrow & C[nearestFloat(n)], \sigma & \quad\text{if } C \neq C'[\langle c \rangle\ \bullet] \quad [\text{E-FCAST}] \\
C[\langle c \rangle\ (\langle d \rangle\ t)], \sigma & \longrightarrow & C[\langle d; c \rangle\ t], \sigma & [\text{E-CCAST}]
\end{array}
$$

1.6 SPACE EFFICIENCY

We now consider how much space coercions consume at runtime, beginning with an analysis of how much space each individual coercion can consume.

1.6.1 Space Consumption

The size of a coercion $size(c)$ is defined as the size of its abstract syntax tree representation. When two coercions are sequentially composed and normalized during evaluation, the size of the normalized, composed coercion may of course be larger than either of the original coercions. In order to reason about the space required by such composed coercions, we introduce a notion of the *height* of a coercion:

$$height(I) = height(\texttt{Fail}) = height(D!) = height(D?) = 1$$
$$height(\texttt{Ref}\ c\ d) = height(\texttt{Fun}\ c\ d) = 1 + max(height(c), height(d))$$
$$height(c; d) = max(height(c), height(d))$$

Notably, the height of a composed coercion is bounded by the maximum height of its constituents. In addition, normalization never increases the height of a coercion. Thus, the height of any coercion created during program evaluation is never larger than the height of some coercion in the original elaborated program.

Furthermore, this bound on the height of each coercion in turn guarantees a bound on the coercion's size, according to the following lemma. In particular, even though the length of a coercion sequence $c_1; \ldots; c_n$ does not contribute to its height, the restricted structure of well-typed, normalized coercions constrains the length (and hence size) of such sequences.

Lemma 1.5. *For all well-typed normalized coercions* c, $size(c) \leq 5(2^{height(c)} - 1)$.

Proof. Induction on c. Assume $c = c_1; \ldots; c_n$, where each c_i is not a sequential composition.

Suppose some $c_i = \text{Ref } d_1 \ d_2$. So $\vdash c_i : \text{Ref } S \rightsquigarrow \text{Ref } T$. Hence c_i can be preceded only by Ref?, which must be the first coercion in the sequence, and similarly can be followed only by Ref!, which must be the last coercion in the sequence. Thus in the worst case $c = \text{Ref?}; \text{Ref } d_1 \ d_2; \text{Ref!}$ and $size(c) = 5 + size(d_1) + size(d_2)$. Applying the induction hypothesis to the sizes of d_1 and d_2 yields:

$$size(c) \leq 5 + 2(5(2^{height(c)-1} - 1)) = 5(2^{height(c)} - 1)$$

The case for $\text{Fun } d_1 \ d_2$ is similar. The coercions I and Fail can only appear alone. Finally, coercions of the form $D?; D!$ are valid. However, composition of a coercion c matching this pattern with one of the other valid coercions is either ill-typed or triggers a normalization that yields a coercion identical to c. □

In addition, the height of any coercion created during cast insertion is bounded by the height of some type in the typing derivation (where the height of a type is the height of its abstract syntax tree representation).

Lemma 1.6. *If* $c = coerce(S, T)$, *then* $height(c) \leq max(height(S), height(T))$.

Proof. Induction on the structure of $coerce(S, T)$. □

Theorem 1.7 (Size of coercions). *For any* e_0, c *such that*

1. $\emptyset \vdash e_0 \hookrightarrow t_0 : T$ *and*

2. $t_0, \emptyset \longrightarrow^* t, \sigma$ *and*

3. c *occurs in* (t, σ),

$\exists S$ *in the derivation of* $\emptyset \vdash e_0 \hookrightarrow t_0 : T$ *such that* $height(c) \leq height(S)$ *and* $size(c) \leq 5(2^{height(S)} - 1)$.

Proof. Induction on the length of the reduction sequence. The base case proceeds by induction on the derivation of $\emptyset \vdash e_0 \hookrightarrow t_0 : T$. In cases [C-APP1], [C-APP2], [C-DEREF2], [C-ASSIGN1], and [C-ASSIGN2], the new coercions are introduced by applications of $coerce(S, T)$ for types S and T in the derivation. In each such case, Lemma 1.6 guarantees that $height(c) \leq max(height(S), height(T))$, and by Lemma 1.5, $size(c) \leq 5(2^{max(height(S), height(T))} - 1)$. The remaining cases are trivial inductions.

If the reduction sequence is non-empty, we have $t_0, \emptyset \longrightarrow^k t', \sigma' \longrightarrow t, \sigma$. If c occurs in t', σ' then by induction, there exists an S in the derivation of $\emptyset \vdash e_0 \hookrightarrow t_0 : T$ such that $height(c) \leq height(S)$ and $size(c) \leq 5(2^{height(S)} - 1)$. Otherwise, the only reduction rules that produce fresh coercions are [E-CBETA], [E-CDEREF], [E-CASSIGN], all of which produce strictly smaller coercions, and [E-CCAST]. In the latter case, the fresh coercion $c = c_1; c_2$ is synthesized from coercions c_1 and c_2

in the redex. By induction, there are types S_1 and S_2 in the derivation of $\emptyset \vdash e_0 \hookrightarrow t_0 : T$ such that $height(c_i) \leq height(S_i)$ and $size(c_i) \leq 5(2^{height(S_i)} - 1)$ for $i \in 1,2$. Since $height(c) = max(height(c_1), height(c_2))$, let S' be the taller of the two types. Then $height(c) \leq height(S')$ and by Lemma 1.5, $size(c) \leq 5(2^{height(c)} - 1)$, so $size(c) \leq 5(2^{height(S')} - 1)$. $\square$

We now bound the total cost of maintaining coercions in the space-efficient semantics. We define the size of a program state inductively as the sum of the sizes of its components. In order to construct a realistic measure of the store, we count only those cells that an idealized garbage collector would consider live by restricting the *size* function to the domain of reachable addresses.

$$size(t, \sigma) = size(t) + size(\sigma|_{reachable(t)})$$
$$size(\sigma) = \sum_{a \in dom(\sigma)}(1 + size(\sigma(a)))$$
$$size(k) = size(a) = size(x) = 1$$
$$size(\lambda x{:}T.\,t) = 1 + size(T) + size(t)$$
$$size(\mathtt{ref}\ t) = size(!t) = 1 + size(t)$$
$$size(t_1 := t_2) = size(t_1\ t_2) = 1 + size(t_1) + size(t_2)$$
$$size(\langle c \rangle\ t) = 1 + size(c) + size(t)$$

To show that coercions occupy bounded space in the model, we compare the size of program states in reduction sequences to program states in an "oracle" semantics where coercions require no space. The oracular measure $size_{OR}$ is defined similarly to *size*, but without a cost for maintaining coercions; that is, $size_{OR}(c) = 0$. The following theorem then bounds the fraction of the program state occupied by coercions in the space-efficient semantics.

Theorem 1.8 (Space consumption). *If $\emptyset \vdash e \hookrightarrow t : T$ and $t,\emptyset \longrightarrow^* t',\sigma$, then there exists some S in the derivation of $\emptyset \vdash e \hookrightarrow t : T$ such that $size(t',\sigma) \in O(2^{height(S)} \cdot size_{OR}(t',\sigma))$.*

Proof. During evaluation, the [E-CCAST] rule prevents nesting of adjacent coercions in any term in the evaluation context, redex, or store. Thus the number of coercions in the program state is proportional to the size of the program state. By Theorem 1.7 the size of each coercion is in $O(2^{height(S)})$ for the largest S in the typing of e. $\square$

1.6.2 Tail Recursion

Theorem 1.8 has the important consequence that coercions do not affect the control space consumption of tail-recursive programs. For example, the *even* and *odd* functions mentioned in the introduction now consume constant space. This important property is achieved by always combining adjacent coercions on the stack via the [E-CCAST] rule. This section sketches three implementation techniques for this rule.

Coercion-passing style   This approach is similar to security-passing style [27], which adds an extra argument to every procedure representing its security context; in this case, the argument represents the result coercion. Tail calls coalesce but do not perform this coercion, instead passing it along to the next function.

Trampoline   A trampoline [15] is a well-known technique for implementing tail-recursive languages where tail calls are implemented by returning a thunk to a top-level loop. Tail-recursive functions with coercions return both a thunk and a coercion to the driver loop, which accumulates and coalesces returned coercions.

Continuation marks   Continuation marks [7, 6] allow programs to annotate continuation frames with arbitrary data. When a marked frame performs a tail call, the subsequent frame can inherit and modify the destroyed frame's marks. Coercions on the stack are stored as marks and coalesced on tail calls.

1.7   EARLY ERROR DETECTION

Consider the following code fragment, which erroneously attempts to convert an $(\text{Int} \to \text{Int})$ function to have type $(\text{Bool} \to \text{Int})$:

$$\text{let } f : \text{Dyn} = (\lambda x : \text{Int}.\, x) \text{ in}$$
$$\text{let } g : (\text{Bool} \to \text{Int}) = f \text{ in } \dots$$

Prior strategies for gradual typing would not detect this error until g is applied to a boolean argument, causing the integer cast to fail.

In contrast, our coercion-based implementation allows us to detect this error as soon as g is defined. After cast insertion and evaluation, the value of g is

$$\langle \text{Fun Fail } I \rangle \, (\lambda x : \text{Int}.\, x)$$

where the domain coercion Fail explicates the inconsistency of the two domain types Int and Bool. We can modify our semantics to halt as soon as such inconsistencies are detected, by adding the following coercion normalization rules:

$$\begin{array}{llll}
\text{Fun } c \text{ Fail} & = & \text{Fail} & \qquad \text{Ref } c \text{ Fail} & = & \text{Fail} \\
\text{Fun Fail } c & = & \text{Fail} & \qquad \text{Ref Fail } c & = & \text{Fail}
\end{array}$$

Using these rules, our implementation strategy halts as soon as g is defined, resulting in earlier error detection and better test coverage, since g may not actually be called in some test runs.

1.8   RELATED WORK

There is a large body of work combining static and dynamic typing. The simplest approach is to use reflection with the type Dyn, as in Amber [3]. Since case dispatch cannot be precisely type-checked with reflection alone, many languages provide statically typed `typecase` on dynamically typed values, including Simula-67 [1] and Modula-3 [4].

For dynamically typed languages, *soft typing* systems provide type-like static analysis for optimization and early error reporting [28]. These systems may provide static type information but do not allow explicit type annotations, whereas enforcing documented program invariants (i.e. types) is a central feature of gradual typing.

Similarly, Henglein's theory of dynamic typing [18] provides a framework for static type optimizations but only in a purely dynamically typed setting. We use Henglein's coercions instead for structuring the algebra of our cast representation. Our application is essentially different: in the gradually typed setting, coercions serve to enforce explicit type annotations, whereas in the dynamically typed setting, coercions represent checks required by primitive operations.

None of these approaches facilitates the *migration* between dynamically and statically typed code, at best requiring hand-coded interfaces between them. The gradually typed approach, exemplified by Sage [17] and $\lambda^{?}_{\rightarrow}$ [24], lowers the barrier for code migration by allowing mixture of expressions of type Dyn with more precisely typed expressions. Our work improves gradual typing by eliminating the drastic effects on space efficiency subtly incurred by crossing the boundary between typing disciplines. Siek and Taha's subsequent work on gradual typing for objects [25] merges some casts at runtime, but they do not address tail recursion and so the remaining casts may still occupy unbounded space. In particular, our Space Consumption Theorem does not hold in their setting.

In earlier work in this area, Ou et al. [23] explored similar ideas in the context of dependent type systems. Their approach uses function proxies to support clean interoperation and hence migration between simply typed code and dependently typed code. Several other systems employ dynamic function proxies, including hybrid type checking [13], software contracts [12], and recent work on software migration by Tobin-Hochstadt and Felleisen [26]. We believe our approach to coalescing redundant proxies could improve the efficiency of all of these systems.

Minamide and Garrigue [21] address a similar issue with unbounded proxies but in the context of specialization of polymorphic functions rather than general type conversions. Their approach does not handle tail calls correctly and only addresses runtime complexity. Our work presents a representation of casts as coercions in order to improve the memory guarantees of gradual typing. Nevertheless, our representation appears to improve the runtime efficiency similarly to Minamide and Garrigue's work. We intend to explore the runtime improvements of our approach as well.

1.9 CONCLUSION AND FUTURE WORK

We have presented a space-efficient implementation strategy for the gradually-typed λ-calculus. For simplicity, we have presented a semantics based on substitution rather than environments and closures. We would like to extend this work to more realistic models of space consumption for functional languages [22]. Our preliminary results in this direction are promising. More work remains to demonstrate the applicability of this technique in the setting of more advanced type systems. In particular, recursive types and polymorphic types may present a challenge for maintaining constant bounds on the size of coercions. We intend to explore techniques for representing these infinite structures as finite graphs.

Another useful feature for runtime checks is *blame annotations* [12], which pinpoint the particular expressions in the source program that cause coercion failures at runtime by associating coercions with their source locations. Blame-tracking improves the error messages for gradually typed programming languages by pinpointing the culprit of failed casts, and also leads to a stronger and more practical type soundness theorem [26]. It should be possible to track the minimum amount of source location information required for assigning blame, combining space-efficient gradual typing with informative error messages.

ACKNOWLEDGMENTS

David Herman is supported by a grant from the Mozilla Corporation. Cormac Flanagan is supported by a Sloan Fellowship and by NSF grant CCS-0341179. Aaron Tomb is also supported by NSF grant CCS-0341179.

REFERENCES

[1] G.M. Birtwhistle et al. *Simula Begin*. Chartwell-Bratt Ltd., 1979.

[2] Gilad Bracha. Pluggable type systems. In *Workshop on Revival of Dynamic Languages*, October 2004.

[3] Luca Cardelli. Amber. In *Spring School of the LITP on Combinators and Functional Programming Languages*, pages 21–47, 1986.

[4] Luca Cardelli, James Donahue, Lucille Glassman, Mick Jordan, Bill Kalsow, and Greg Nelson. Modula-3 report (revised). Technical Report 52, DEC SRC, 1989.

[5] Craig Chambers. *The Cecil Language Specification and Rationale: Version 3.0*. University of Washington, 1998.

[6] John Clements. *Portable and high-level access to the stack with Continuation Marks*. PhD thesis, Northeastern University, 2005.

[7] John Clements and Matthias Felleisen. A tail-recursive machine with stack inspection. *TOPLAS*, 26(6):1029–1052, 2004.

[8] Rodrigo B. de Oliveira. The Boo programming language, 2005.

[9] Ecma International. *ECMAScript Language Specification*, 3rd edition, 1999.

[10] Ecma International. *ECMAScript Edition 4 group wiki*, 2007.

[11] Robert Bruce Findler and Matthias Blume. Contracts as pairs of projections. In *FLOPS*, pages 226–241, 2006.

[12] Robert Bruce Findler and Matthias Felleisen. Contracts for higher-order functions. In *ICFP*, pages 48–59, October 2002.

[13] Cormac Flanagan. Hybrid type checking. In *POPL*, pages 245–256, 2006.

[14] Cormac Flanagan, Stephen N. Freund, and Aaron Tomb. Hybrid types, invariants, and refinements for imperative objects. In *FOOL/WOOD*, 2006.

[15] Steven E. Ganz, Daniel P. Friedman, and Mitchell Wand. Trampolined style. In *ICFP*, pages 18–27, 1999.

[16] Jesse J. Garrett. Ajax: A new approach to web applications, 2005.

[17] Jessica Gronski, Kenneth Knowles, Aaron Tomb, Stephen N. Freund, and Cormac Flanagan. Sage: Hybrid checking for flexible specifications. In *Scheme and Functional Programming Workshop*, September 2006.

[18] Fritz Henglein. Dynamic typing: Syntax and proof theory. *Science of Computer Programming*, 22(3):197–230, 1994.

[19] Jacob Matthews and Robert Bruce Findler. Operational semantics for multi-language programs. In *POPL*, 2007.

[20] Erik Meijer and Peter Drayton. Static typing where possible, dynamic typing when needed. In *Workshop on Revival of Dynamic Languages*, 2005.

[21] Yasuhiko Minamide and Jacques Garrigue. On the runtime complexity of type-directed unboxing. In *ICFP*, pages 1–12, 1998.

[22] Greg Morrisett, Matthias Felleisen, and Robert Harper. Abstract models of memory management. In *FPCA*, pages 66–77, 1995.

[23] Xinming Ou, Gang Tan, Yitzhak Mandelbaum, and David Walker. Dynamic typing with dependent types. In *IFIP TCS*, pages 437–450, 2004.

[24] Jeremy G. Siek and Walid Taha. Gradual typing for functional languages. In *Scheme and Functional Programming Workshop*, September 2006.

[25] Jeremy G. Siek and Walid Taha. Gradual typing for objects. In *ECOOP*, Berlin, Germany, July 2007.

[26] Sam Tobin-Hochstadt and Matthias Felleisen. Interlanguage migration: From scripts to programs. In *Dynamic Languages Symposium*, October 2006.

[27] Dan S. Wallach. *A New Approach to Mobile Code Security*. PhD thesis, Department of Computer Science, 1999.

[28] Andrew K. Wright. *Practical Soft Typing*. PhD thesis, Rice University, August 1998.

Chapter 2

A Metalanguage for Structural Operational Semantics

Matthew Lakin[1], Andrew Pitts[1]

Abstract: This paper introduces MLSOS, a functional metalanguage for declaring and animating definitions of structural operational semantics. The language provides a general mechanism for resolution-based search that respects the α-equivalence of object-language binding structures, based on nominal unification. It combines that with a FreshML-style generative treatment of bound names. We claim that MLSOS allows animation of operational semantics definitions to be prototyped in a natural way, starting from semi-formal specifications. We outline the main design choices behind the language and illustrate its use.

2.1 INTRODUCTION

There is currently a great deal of interest in (partially) automating various tasks in the field of programming language metatheory. While there are many aspects to this research effort (see [1] for a survey), the work reported here focuses on animating definitions of type systems and operational semantics. This typically involves generating a reference or prototype implementation from a high-level description of the desired semantics. General-purpose functional programming languages such as Objective Caml and Haskell are usually the first choice for such an implementation. However, such languages do not provide built-in support for representing object-language binders up to α-equivalence or for "proof-search" style computations of the validity of some judgement (such as the type inference problem) given a rule-based inductive definition of that judgment. Hence, the

---

[1]University of Cambridge Computer Laboratory, William Gates Building, 15 JJ Thomson Avenue, Cambridge, CB3 0FD, UK, E-mail:
`Matthew.Lakin@cl.cam.ac.uk`, `Andrew.Pitts@cl.cam.ac.uk`.

programmer must "reinvent the wheel" and re-implement this basic functionality every time they want to implement a language. This takes up time and increases the potential for bugs to appear. Furthermore, in the early stages of language design, the ability to play with a toy implementation of the language can be invaluable. It can provide useful feedback on test cases and guide the evolution of the language, with only a fraction of the effort required for a full formal verification of the language metatheory.

Our long-term aim is to automatically generate correct, efficient, executable code from a high-level specification of the intended behavior, such as the inference rules for inductively defined relations. The first thing that we need, however, is a programmable metalanguage that allows the user to succinctly specify that behavior. An important issue that must be faced in programming language support for computing instances of inductively defined relations is how to implement bound names in the object-language in a way that deals with issues of α-equivalence automatically. To that end we make use of *nominal unification* [23]—a generalization of first-order unification that solves equations modulo α-equivalence by taking into account *freshness* of names for object-language terms.

We propose an eager functional programming language for resolution-based computations on abstract syntax up to α-equivalence of object-language bound names, based on a mild generalization of nominal unification. We call this language MLSOS (**M**eta**L**anguage for **S**tructural **O**perational **S**emantics). One of the main contributions of the design is to show how to combine, in a well-behaved way, nominal unification's logical treatment of freshness with a dynamic approach to freshness derived from the FreshML programming language [19]. The "Barendregt variable convention" [3] expresses (informally) that bound names should be mutually distinct and distinct from other names appearing in the mathematical context. Hence, when it attempts to unify against a pattern containing binders, MLSOS automatically enforces the user's expectation that the Barendregt variable convention holds by replacing bound names with freshly generated names as the pattern is analyzed. This "generative unbinding" of binders is the characteristic feature of FreshML. On the other hand, when it encounters names in a pattern that are not bound, MLSOS uses unification variables, since it would be premature to commit to any particular name in this case. Hence our motto is "implement bound names generatively, and free names with unification variables". We claim that this leads to a style of programming which, compared to the logic programming language αProlog [5] that also makes use of nominal unification, relieves the user of the need to specify much information about the freshness of names in operational semantics specifications. (See §2.3.1 and §2.5 for evidence of this.)

The rest of this paper is organized as follows. §2.2 provides a brief overview of nominal unification. §2.3 gives an extended informal example of the use of MLSOS. §2.4 goes into the formalities, defining the grammar and operational semantics of the core MLSOS language. §2.5 discusses related work; we describe future work and conclude in §2.6.

2.2   BACKGROUND: NOMINAL UNIFICATION

Our method of specifying binding is the *nominal signature* of [23], which consists of a finite set of *atom sorts* α (types of object-language names) and a finite set of *data sorts* δ (types of α-equivalence classes of object-language terms). We build up a set of *arities* σ by the grammar

$$\sigma ::= \alpha \mid \delta \mid 1 \mid \sigma_1 \star \cdots \star \sigma_n \mid \langle\langle\alpha\rangle\rangle\sigma.$$

The arity $\sigma_1 \star \cdots \star \sigma_n$ is for *n*-tuples of terms, $(t_1,\ldots,t_n)$. The arity $\langle\langle\alpha\rangle\rangle\sigma$ is where binding is specified—it is inhabited by terms $\langle\langle a\rangle\rangle t$ representing the object-language binding of a *single* name a of atom sort α in a term t of arity σ. Given this grammar of arities, the specification of a nominal signature is completed by giving a finite set of typed *constructors*, $\mathsf{K} : \sigma \to \delta$, which allows us to construct terms $\mathsf{K}t$ of data sort δ from terms t of arity σ. By way of an example, here is a nominal signature for untyped λ-terms, as it is declared in MLSOS:

```
nametype var ; ;
datatype lam = Var of var
             | Lam of ⟨⟨var⟩⟩lam
             | App of lam ⋆ lam ; ;
```

Atom sorts (such as var) are declared using the nametype keyword; whereas data sorts (such as lam) and constructors (such as Var, Lam and App) are declared with an ML-like datatype declaration.

The *nominal terms* of the various arities over a given nominal signature are built up using the term-forming operations mentioned above, starting from a unit value () of arity 1, from countably many *atoms* a of each atom sort, and from countably many *suspensions* πX for each arity; the latter consist of a unification variable X and a finite permutation π of atoms waiting to be applied to whatever will be substituted for X. (See §2.4.1 and [23] for the need for such suspended permutations.)

Nominal unification is an algorithm for unifying nominal terms up to α-equivalence. As shown in [23], to make sense of α-equivalence for nominal terms, one needs to consider *freshness conditions* of the form $a \# X$ (read "a fresh for X") whose intended meaning is that a should not occur free in any term substituted for X. Thus given a unification problem $t =:= t'$ (where t and t' are nominal terms of the same arity over a given nominal signature), the nominal unification algorithm computes both a solving substitution of nominal terms for unification variables and a set of freshness conditions under which the required α-equivalence is valid (or fails finitely if no such solution exists). For example, it solves the problem $\langle\langle a\rangle\rangle X =:= \langle\langle b\rangle\rangle Y$ with the substitution $[Y \mapsto (a\,b)X]$ and the freshness condition $b \# X$. This means that the unification variable Y should be instantiated to the result of *swapping* all occurrences of a and b throughout the term eventually substituted for X. The freshness constraint that b may not occur free in X prevents name capture. We refer the reader to [23] for more details.

$$(\text{beta}_1) \ \overline{\ \text{beta}\ (t,\ t)\ } \qquad\qquad (\text{beta}_2) \ \frac{\text{beta}\ (t_1,\ t_1')\qquad \text{beta}\ (t_2,\ t_2')}{\text{beta}\ (t_1\ t_2,\ t_1'\ t_2')}$$

$$(\text{beta}_3) \ \frac{\text{beta}\ (t,\ t')}{\text{beta}\ (\lambda x.t,\ \lambda x.t')} \qquad\qquad (\text{beta}_4) \ \frac{\text{beta}\ (t_1,\ t_1')\qquad \text{beta}\ (t_2,\ t_2')}{\text{beta}\ ((\lambda x.t_1)\ t_2,\ t_1'[t_2'/x])}$$

FIGURE 2.1: Parallel Reduction Relation

```
1   let rec sub x t t′ = narrow t′ as
2     Var y → ((x =:= y); t) or ((x =/= y); t′)
3     | Lam ⟨⟨a⟩⟩t″ → Lam ⟨⟨a⟩⟩(sub x t t″)
4     | App (t₁, t₂) → App ((sub x t t₁), (sub x t t₂)) ;;

5   let rec beta (t₁, t₂) = narrow (t₁, t₂) as
6     (t, t) → yes
7     | (Lam ⟨⟨a⟩⟩t₁, Lam ⟨⟨a⟩⟩t₁′) → beta (t₁, t₁′)
8     | (App (t₁, t₂), App (t₁′, t₂′)) → beta (t₁, t₁′); beta (t₂, t₂′)
9     | (App ((Lam ⟨⟨a⟩⟩t₁), t₂), t′) → some t₁′, t₂′ : lam in
10        beta (t₁, t₁′); beta (t₂, t₂′); ((sub a t₂′ t₁′) =:= t′) ;;
```

FIGURE 2.2: MLSOS Parallel Reduction Program

Nominal unification has polynomial complexity [4] and produces most general unifiers [23]. That the latter exist depends upon the fact that nominal terms only allow abstractions over concrete atoms, $\langle\langle a\rangle\rangle t$, but not abstractions over unification variables, $\langle\langle X\rangle\rangle t$. As we shall see, this restriction greatly simplifies constraint solving. Without it, we would need to use a more powerful but **NP**-complete *equivariant* unification algorithm due to Cheney [8, 6].

2.3 PROGRAMMING EXAMPLE: PARALLEL REDUCTION

Figure 2.1 gives inference rules defining the beta relation of "parallel reduction" (that is, reducing several β-redexes within a λ-term in one go). This relation is used in the Tait/Martin-Löf proof of the Church-Rosser property of β-reduction in the untyped λ-calculus [3, Definition 3.2.3].

Using the nominal signature from the previous section, Figure 2.2 gives ML-SOS functions sub : var → lam → lam → lam and beta : lam ⋆ lam → ans, where ans is the MLSOS built-in type for proof-search computations—it is a copy of the unit type whose only value, yes, indicates success. The first implements capture-avoiding substitution for λ-terms and the second implements the parallel reduction relation. This section provides a brief explanation of how the code from Figure 2.2 would evaluate. This code uses various syntactic sugars which are implemented by translation into a small core language described later in this paper (§2.4).

2.3.1 Capture-Avoiding Substitution

Evaluating sub x t t' (Figure 2.2, lines 1–4) computes the *capture avoiding* substitution of (the α-equivalence class of) t for all free occurrences of the name x in (the α-equivalence class of) t'.

The narrow syntax is syntactic sugar for a non-deterministic branch, which here generates three branches of computation. The patterns in the individual clauses are expanded out into expressions which generate fresh atoms and unification variables as required: as discussed in the Introduction, we use fresh atoms to implement bound names and unification variables to stand for all other unknowns.

Each branch generates a constraint that t' should unify with the patterns on the left-hand sides of lines 2–4 to decide whether to proceed, instantiating unification variables in t' if necessary. The variable clause (line 2) also has an explicit branch (using the or keyword) which is used to encode the standard name equality test. We use a definable syntactic sugar $(e;\ e')$ for sequencing, to simulate a conjunction.

The nominal unification algorithm [23] is used to decide satisfiability of equality constraints, along with some extra rules to cope with name inequality constraints. These are largely straightforward, except for the case when two unknown names are constrained to be distinct (discussed in §2.4).

The clause for λ-abstractions (Figure 2.2, line 3) highlights the different behavior of value identifiers and atom identifiers in patterns in MLSOS: in line 2, y becomes a new unification variable, whereas in line 3, a is replaced with a *fresh* atom, because it appears in binding position. This means that the informal "Barendregt variable convention" [3] is handled implicitly at the language level, and hence we do not need to decorate the code with assertions that a must not appear free in t (or be equal to x).

2.3.2 Parallel Reduction

The beta function declared in lines 5–10 of Figure 2.2 implements the relation inductively defined in Figure 2.1. Line 6 expresses the base case (beta$_1$) of the definition, line 7 the rule (beta$_3$), line 8 the rule (beta$_2$) and lines 9–10 the rule (beta$_4$). Again, the atom identifier a in the pattern (App ((Lam $\langle\langle a \rangle\rangle t_1$), t_2), t') in line 9 refers to a *fresh* atom—this, along with the behavior of the sub function, ensures that the substitution involved in the MLSOS version of rule (beta$_4$) is not capturing. Note the use of the some syntax in line 9 to generate unification variables standing for unknown intermediate terms, and the use of sequencing to model a conjunction.

? fresh a : var ;;
— : var $=$ var_0

? fresh b : var ;;
— : var $=$ var_1

? let t_1 $=$ App ((Lam $\langle\langle a \rangle\rangle$Lam $\langle\langle b \rangle\rangle$Var a), Var b) ;;
— : lam $=$ App (Lam $\langle\langle var_0 \rangle\rangle$Lam $\langle\langle var_1 \rangle\rangle$Var var_0, Var var_1)

? let t_2 $=$ Lam $\langle\langle a \rangle\rangle$Var b ;;
— : lam $=$ Lam $\langle\langle var_0 \rangle\rangle$Var var_1

? beta (t_1, t_2) ;;
— : ans $=$ yes

? let t $=$ App ((Lam $\langle\langle a \rangle\rangle$Var a), Var b) ;;
— : lam $=$ App (Lam $\langle\langle var_0 \rangle\rangle$Var var_0, Var var_1) ;;

? some x : lam ;;
— : lam $=$ unknown

? beta (t, x) ;;
— : ans $=$ yes $[\, x = $ Var $var_1\,]$
— : ans $=$ yes $[\, x = $ App (Lam $\langle\langle var_2 \rangle\rangle$Var var_2, Var var_1)$\,]$
— : ...

FIGURE 2.3: Command-Line Example

2.3.3   Command-Line Example

Figure 2.3 illustrates a typical interaction with the MLSOS interpreter. We assume here that the nominal signature for λ-terms from §2.1 and the functions from Figure 2.2 have already been declared earlier in the session.

The first two interactions generate (distinct) fresh atoms a and b, to stand for variables in the λ-calculus. In all cases, the responses from the interpreter include tags such as var_0, to allow the user to identify the atoms generated internally during expression evaluation. We then construct two λ-terms t_1 and t_2, corresponding to $(\lambda a.\lambda b.a)$ b and $\lambda a.b$ respectively, and ask the system whether beta $(((\lambda a.\lambda b.a)$ $b)$, $\lambda a.b)$ is derivable using the rules from Figure 2.2. This is clearly the case (using the final rule (beta$_4$) of the definition of beta), and indeed the interpreter responds `yes`, as we would expect.

We then define a term t corresponding to $(\lambda a.a)$ b, and generate a new unification variable (which we bind to the value identifier x). The final command instructs the interpreter to find all instantiations of x for which beta $((\lambda a.a)$ b, $x)$ holds. This produces numerous answers: the standard β-reduction to Var b, the trivial case arising from the clause allowing any term to β-reduce to itself, and duplicate results caused by redundancies in the rules defining the beta relation. The var_2 tags appearing in the results of this computation are due to the dynamic generation of atoms during proof-search.

These examples give a flavor of how MLSOS might be used. In particular, the final example illustrates the use of unification variables to search for terms (up to α-equivalence) for which some judgement can be derived.

2.4 MLSOS CORE LANGUAGE AND OPERATIONAL SEMANTICS

This section defines the MLSOS "core" language and its operational semantics. We restrict ourselves to the core language since it is small and elegant and the various syntactic sugars employed in Figure 2.2 may be defined in it.

We fix countably infinite sets $\mathbb{V}$ of value identifiers (ranged over by x, y etc.), $\mathbb{A}$ of atoms (ranged over by a, b etc.) and $\mathbb{U}$ of unification variables (ranged over by X). These stand for metalanguage values, object-language names and unknown object-language terms respectively. The grammar of MLSOS types τ is

$$\tau ::= \sigma \mid \text{ans} \mid \tau \to \tau$$

where σ ranges over nominal arities as defined in §2.1. The type ans is a version of ML's unit type that we use for proof-search computations when only the success of the search rather than some final value is important. For example, semi-decidable relations of arity σ are typically implemented in MLSOS as functions of type $\sigma \to$ ans.

2.4.1 Permutations

Nominal logic [14] is based on the fundamental operation of *permuting* atoms. One only needs to consider finite permutations, that is, bijections on the set of atoms that only move finitely many atoms. We use a concrete representation for such permutations as finite lists of atom-swappings, which are written $(a\,a')$. Such a finite list represents the composition of the individual swappings, and it can be shown that every finite permutation can be represented in this way. We write Perm for the set of all *well-formed* atom-permutations, ranged over by π. A permutation is well-formed if, for every swapping $(a\,a')$ in π, the atoms a and a' are of the same atom-sort.

Unknown object-language terms are represented by *suspensions*, written πX. These represent a permutation π waiting to be applied to all atoms appearing in whatever term gets grafted in place of the unification variable X. These suspended permutations are used to ensure that α-conversion behaves correctly in the presence of unification variables: see [23].

2.4.2 Values and Expressions

Figure 2.4 gives grammars for the values and expressions of the MLSOS core language. The values are as one would expect from a functional language, with the addition of suspensions (to stand for unknown object-language terms), atoms

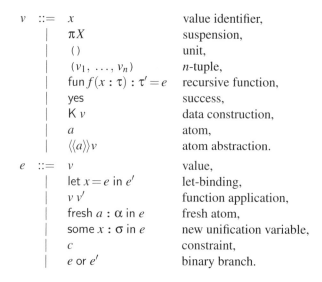

$$
\begin{array}{lll}
v & ::= & x & \text{value identifier,} \\
  & | & \pi X & \text{suspension,} \\
  & | & () & \text{unit,} \\
  & | & (v_1, \ldots, v_n) & n\text{-tuple,} \\
  & | & \mathsf{fun}\, f(x:\tau):\tau'=e & \text{recursive function,} \\
  & | & \mathsf{yes} & \text{success,} \\
  & | & \mathsf{K}\,v & \text{data construction,} \\
  & | & a & \text{atom,} \\
  & | & \langle\!\langle a\rangle\!\rangle v & \text{atom abstraction.} \\
e & ::= & v & \text{value,} \\
  & | & \mathsf{let}\, x = e\, \mathsf{in}\, e' & \text{let-binding,} \\
  & | & v\,v' & \text{function application,} \\
  & | & \mathsf{fresh}\, a:\alpha\, \mathsf{in}\, e & \text{fresh atom,} \\
  & | & \mathsf{some}\, x:\sigma\, \mathsf{in}\, e & \text{new unification variable,} \\
  & | & c & \text{constraint,} \\
  & | & e\, \mathsf{or}\, e' & \text{binary branch.}
\end{array}
$$

FIGURE 2.4: MLSOS Values And Expressions

and atom abstractions, and the yes value (which reports success in a proof-search computation).

The expression grammar is structured so that MLSOS core programs must be in A-normal form [10]—that is, evaluation is driven by let-bindings and all results of intermediate computations must be named. Programs written in a more liberal language can be translated into this format by the insertion of additional let-bindings. This restriction further simplifies the presentation of the operational semantics (see §2.4.4). The expression grammar includes constructs for generating fresh atoms (fresh $a : \alpha$ in e) and new unification variables (some $x : \sigma$ in e), branching (e or e') and testing constraints for satisfiability (c). Note that the programmer has no direct access to unification variables and atoms: like the treatment of mutable reference cells in traditional functional programming languages, unification variables and atoms are created dynamically by evaluating some and fresh expressions respectively (and may dynamically escape their lexical scopes).

As well as the usual let-binding and recursive function constructs which bind value identifiers, the some construct, some $x : \sigma$ in e, binds free occurrences of the value identifier x in the expression e. The fresh atom generation construct fresh $a : \alpha$ in e binds all free occurrences of the atom a in e. As usual, substitution of MLSOS values for value identifiers is capture-avoiding: we identify MLSOS expressions up to α-conversion of bound value identifiers and atoms and write $e[v/x]$ for the capture-avoiding substitution of v for all free occurrences of x in e. These meta-level notions of α-equivalence and substitution for MLSOS should not be confused with the object-level notions that can be implemented in MLSOS. Object-level binding is represented with the $\langle\!\langle a\rangle\!\rangle(-)$ construct, but the latter is not itself a meta-level binding construct; for example, $\langle\langle a \rangle\rangle a$ and $\langle\langle b \rangle\rangle b$ are distinct MLSOS values when a and b are distinct atoms. The object-level substitution of nominal terms for unification variables that is part of the MLSOS dynamics may involve capture of free atoms within the scope of the $\langle\langle a \rangle\rangle (-)$ construct. The only form of substitution needed for atoms is renaming via a permutation (see §2.4.1).

2.4.3 Constraints

We use a slightly richer language of constraints c than [23] to guide execution of MLSOS programs. They may be of the following forms:

$$
\begin{array}{llll}
c & ::= & v =:= v' & \text{equality constraint,} \\
  & | & a \mathbin{\#} v & \text{freshness constraint,} \\
  & | & v =/= v' & \textit{name inequality constraint.}
\end{array}
$$

where v stands for a value (of some nominal arity σ). Equality constraints really mean equality of the appropriate α-equivalence classes, and a freshness constraint $a \mathbin{\#} v$ expresses that a may not occur *free* in v. Note that, as emphasized by the typing rule for inequality constraints in Figure 2.6, these are only permitted between *names*, that is, atoms or suspensions of the same atom sort α. (Our name inequality constraints are similar to, but less general than, those described in [7, Chapter 7], since we place more restrictions on where suspensions may appear in the term syntax.) The only non-trivial cases are for inequalities between two suspensions: either

1. $\pi X =/= \pi' X'$, where X and X' are distinct unification variables—this constraint is left untouched as part of the "solution"; or

2. $\pi X =/= \pi' X$— this causes a finitely wide branch, which tries to instantiate X with every atom a for which $\pi(a) \neq \pi'(a)$.

We can give a simple semantics to this constraint language in terms of instantiations of the unification variables contained in the constraints by *ground* values, that is, by ones not containing unification variables. Then, it can be shown that *satisfiability* of a finite set $\bar{c}$ of such constraints (which we write $\models \bar{c}$) is *decidable*, using an algorithm that extends nominal unification [23] to deal with name inequality constraints. This allows us, to a large extent, to factor constraint solving out of the operational semantics of the metalanguage, leading to a rather elegant presentation (see §2.4.4). In particular, the presentation does not need to use the meta-operation of substitution for unification variables, which is left implicit as part of constraint solving.

2.4.4 Operational Semantics

Conceptually, evaluation of an MLSOS program consists of finitely many computation branches. During evaluation of a program, new branches may be spawned, each of which may return a result, or may fail finitely (which corresponds to where

1. $\mathsf{N}\bar{a}\,\exists\overline{X}\,(\bar{c};(S\circ(x.e))(v)) \longrightarrow_M \mathsf{N}\bar{a}\,\exists\overline{X}\,(\bar{c};S(e[v/x]))$

2. $\mathsf{N}\bar{a}\,\exists\overline{X}\,(\bar{c};S(\mathsf{let}\ x\!=\!e\ \mathsf{in}\ e')) \longrightarrow_M \mathsf{N}\bar{a}\,\exists\overline{X}\,(\bar{c};(S\circ(x.e'))(e))$

3. $\mathsf{N}\bar{a}\,\exists\overline{X}\,(\bar{c};S(v\ v')) \longrightarrow_M \mathsf{N}\bar{a}\,\exists\overline{X}\,(\bar{c};S(e[v,v'/f,x]))$
   if $v = (\mathsf{fun}\ f(x:\tau):\tau'\!=\!e)$

4. $\mathsf{N}\bar{a}\,\exists\overline{X}\,(\bar{c};S(c)) \longrightarrow_M \mathsf{N}\bar{a}\,\exists\overline{X}\,((\bar{c}\cup\{c\});S(\mathsf{yes}))$
   if $\models \bar{c}\cup\{c\}$

5. $\mathsf{N}\bar{a}\,\exists\overline{X}\,(\bar{c};S(\mathsf{fresh}\ a:\alpha\ \mathsf{in}\ e)) \longrightarrow_M \mathsf{N}\bar{a},a:\alpha\,\exists\overline{X}\,(\bar{c}';S(e))$
   if $a\notin dom(\bar{a})$ and $\bar{c}' \triangleq \{a\ \#\ X\mid X\in dom(\overline{X})\}\cup\bar{c}$

6. $\mathsf{N}\bar{a}\,\exists\overline{X}\,(\bar{c};S(\mathsf{some}\ x:\sigma\ \mathsf{in}\ e)) \longrightarrow_M \mathsf{N}\bar{a}\,\exists\overline{X},X:\sigma\,(\bar{c};S(e[\iota X/x]))$
   if $X\notin dom(\overline{X})$

7. $\mathsf{N}\bar{a}\,\exists\overline{X}\,(\bar{c};S(e_1\ \mathsf{or}\ e_2)) \longrightarrow_M \mathsf{N}\bar{a}\,\exists\overline{X}\,(\bar{c};S(e_i))$
   where $i\in\{1,2\}$

FIGURE 2.5: $\longrightarrow_M$ Transition Rules

one would backtrack in Prolog), or may diverge. The operational semantics presented here is abstract in the sense that it does not specify any particular search strategy or treatment of failed computations. This is a succinct and elegant means of developing the theory of the language, but is obviously not intended as the basis of an implementation.

The operational semantics takes the form of a *non-deterministic* single-step transition relation $\longrightarrow_M$ between abstract machine configurations C, defined in Figure 2.5. Our configurations make use of *frame-stacks*, S, which are either empty (*Id*) or of the form $S\circ(x.e)$, in which any free occurrences of the value identifier x in the expression e (which is on top of the stack) become bound. The frame-stack $S\circ(x.e)$ encodes an evaluation context where the value (if any) resulting from evaluation in the current evaluation position will be substituted for all free occurrences of x in e and the result evaluated in the context S. Non-empty frame-stacks are built up by let-bindings appearing in the program (see rule 2 in Figure 2.5, which reflects the fact that MLSOS is an *eager* language). Configurations are of the form $\mathsf{N}\bar{a}\,\exists\overline{X}\,(\bar{c};S(e))$, where S is a frame-stack, e is the expression currently being evaluated, and $\bar{c}$ is a finite set of constraints which serve to guide proof-search. Here $\bar{a}$ and $\overline{X}$ are finite environments of sorting information about the atoms and unification variables appearing in the configuration. (The quantifier symbols N and $\exists$ appearing in a configuration are merely punctuation, but suggest expected logical behavior.)

Rule 5 in Figure 2.5 implements fresh atom generation. As we identify expressions up to α-renaming of atoms, the "freshness" side-condition of this rule $(a\notin dom(\bar{a}))$ can always be satisfied. In this rule, the constraint set is updated

$$\frac{a \in dom(\Gamma) \qquad \Gamma \vdash v : \sigma}{\Gamma \vdash a \; \# \; v : \text{ans}} \qquad \frac{\Gamma \vdash v_1 : \sigma \qquad \Gamma \vdash v_2 : \sigma}{\Gamma \vdash v_1 \; =:= \; v_2 : \text{ans}}$$

$$\frac{\Gamma \vdash v_1 : \alpha \qquad \Gamma \vdash v_2 : \alpha}{\Gamma \vdash v_1 \; =/= \; v_2 : \text{ans}} \qquad \frac{\Gamma(x) = \tau}{\Gamma \vdash x : \tau} \qquad \frac{\Gamma(X) = \sigma}{\Gamma \vdash \pi X : \sigma} \qquad \frac{\Gamma(a) = \alpha}{\Gamma \vdash a : \alpha}$$

$$\frac{\Gamma(a) = \alpha \qquad \Gamma \vdash v : \sigma}{\Gamma \vdash \langle\!\langle a \rangle\!\rangle v : \langle\!\langle \alpha \rangle\!\rangle \sigma} \qquad \frac{}{\Gamma \vdash (\,) : 1} \qquad \frac{}{\Gamma \vdash \text{yes} : \text{ans}}$$

$$\frac{\Gamma \vdash v_1 : \sigma_1 \qquad \cdots \qquad \Gamma \vdash v_n : \sigma_n}{\Gamma \vdash (v_1, \ldots, v_n) : \sigma_1 \star \cdots \star \sigma_n} \qquad \frac{(\mathsf{K} : \sigma \to \delta) \in \Sigma \qquad \Gamma \vdash v : \sigma}{\Gamma \vdash \mathsf{K} \, v : \delta}$$

$$\frac{\Gamma, f : \tau \to \tau', x : \tau \vdash e : \tau' \qquad f, x \notin dom(\Gamma)}{\Gamma \vdash \text{fun} \, f(x : \tau) : \tau' = e : \tau \to \tau'} \qquad \frac{\Gamma \vdash v_1 : \tau \to \tau' \qquad \Gamma \vdash v_2 : \tau}{\Gamma \vdash v_1 \, v_2 : \tau'}$$

$$\frac{\Gamma \vdash e : \tau \qquad \Gamma, x : \tau \vdash e' : \tau' \qquad x \notin dom(\Gamma)}{\Gamma \vdash \text{let} \, x = e \, \text{in} \, e' : \tau'}$$

$$\frac{\Gamma, a : \alpha \vdash e : \tau \qquad a \notin dom(\Gamma)}{\Gamma \vdash \text{fresh} \, a : \alpha \, \text{in} \, e : \tau} \qquad \frac{\Gamma, x : \sigma \vdash e : \tau \qquad x \notin dom(\Gamma)}{\Gamma \vdash \text{some} \, x : \sigma \, \text{in} \, e : \tau}$$

$$\frac{\Gamma \vdash e_1 : \tau \qquad \Gamma \vdash e_2 : \tau}{\Gamma \vdash e_1 \, \text{or} \, e_2 : \tau}$$

FIGURE 2.6: Typing Rules For Core MLSOS: Constraints, Values And Expressions

with new freshness constraints between the freshly generated atom and all unification variables that have been generated so far. Similarly, rule 6 generates a new unification variable and binds it to a value identifier. (In the suspension ιX, ι denotes the identity permutation.) Rule 7 is a non-deterministic branch.

The rules defining the MLSOS type system are quite standard and are presented in Figure 2.6. Constraint expressions (§2.4.3) are assigned type ans. We say that a configuration $C = \mathsf{V}\bar{a} \; \exists \overline{X} \; (\bar{c}; S(e))$ is *well-typed* at type τ and write $\vdash C : \tau$ iff the sorting information contained in $\bar{a}$ and $\overline{X}$ is sufficient to infer that $\bar{c}$ is a finite set of well-formed constraints of type ans, and to assign types $\tau' \to \tau$ and τ' to the frame-stack S and expression e respectively (for some τ'). We also say that C is *satisfiable* if its constituent set of constraints is satisfiable, that is, if $\models \bar{c}$ holds (see §2.4.3). The following results (whose proofs are omitted) show that the MLSOS type system ensures for well-typed configurations that the only possibility for a computation branch to get stuck is when an unsatisfiable constraint is encountered.

Theorem 2.1 (Type Preservation). *For all configurations C, C' and for all types τ, if $\vdash C : \tau$ and $C \longrightarrow_M C'$ then $\vdash C' : \tau$. Furthermore, C is satisfiable if and only if C' is.*

Theorem 2.2 (Progress). *For all configurations C and for all types τ, if $\vdash C : \tau$, then either*

1. *C is of the form $\mathsf{V}\bar{a}\,\exists\overline{X}\,(\bar{c}; Id(v))$, i.e. this branch has terminated, or*

2. *there exists a configuration C' such that $C \longrightarrow_M C'$ holds, or*

3. *C is not satisfiable (i.e. C is of the form $\mathsf{V}\bar{a}\,\exists\overline{X}\,(\bar{c}; S(c))$, where i.e. $\models \bar{c} \cup \{c\}$ does not hold).*

Proof. These proofs are both by case analysis on C. □

2.5 RELATED WORK

FreshML [19, 21] is the immediate ancestor of MLSOS. It provides support for functional programming with binders up to α-equivalence, but without the proof-search facilities of MLSOS. Object-language names are represented by atoms, which are generated freshly when required (and never named directly). An abstraction $\langle\langle x \rangle\rangle e$ is deconstructed using *generative unbinding* [16]—a fresh name y is generated and *swapped* for x throughout e.

In FreshML, names may be represented using normal value identifiers such as x because everything is ground, i.e. there are no unknown names present. Shinwell and Pitts [20, 16] prove that this approach leads to correct representation of object-language syntax up to α-equivalence (in the sense that terms representing objects in the same α-equivalence class are contextually equivalent). FreshML can be thought of as a ground subset of MLSOS, in that FreshML does not include unification variables or proof-search facilities at the language level. In FreshML, the first clause in the definition of the capture-avoiding substitution function from Figure 2.2 can be implemented using a *name equality test* (syntax if $x = y$ then t else t'), since x and y are always concrete atoms. Our work aims to discover whether the FreshML-style treatment of binders can be successfully extended to a language with unification variables representing unknown terms.

FreshML is an *impure* functional language, in that the generation of atoms is an observable side-effect. The earlier FreshML-2000 language [15] had a *freshness inference* system for statically rejecting programs where freshly generated names were returned unabstracted (and hence were observable as a side-effect). This was dropped from the version of FreshML in [21], because it rejected too many reasonable-looking programs. However, recent work by Pottier [17] describes a tractable and practical decision procedure for rejecting impure programs in a FreshML-like language with user-supplied freshness assertions. That paper

```
1    func subst (var, lam, lam) = lam.
2    subst (X, E, (Var X)) = E.
3    subst (X, E, (Var Y)) = (Var Y) :− X # Y.
4    subst (X, E, App (E₁, E₂)) = App (subst (X, E, E₁), subst (X, E, E₂)).
5    subst (X, E, (Lam ⟨⟨a⟩⟩E′)) = Lam ⟨⟨a⟩⟩(subst (X, E, E′)) :− a # (X, E).

6    pred beta (lam, lam).
7    beta (E, E).
8    beta ((Lam ⟨⟨a⟩⟩E), (Lam ⟨⟨a⟩⟩E′)) :− beta (E, E′).
9    beta (App (E₁, E₂), App (E′₁, E′₂)) :− beta (E₁, E′₁), beta (E₂, E′₂).
10   beta (App ((Lam ⟨⟨a⟩⟩E₁), E₂), E₃) :−
        beta (E₁, E′₁), beta (E₂, E′₂), E₃ = subst (a, E′₂, E′₁).
```

FIGURE 2.7: αProlog Parallel Reduction Program

employs a system of *binding specifications* which is richer than our nominal signatures. These originate from work on Cαml [18], a tool which auto-generates
Objective Caml code from such a binding specification.

The language most closely related to MLSOS in terms of functionality is Cheney and Urban's αProlog [5, 7]. This is a logic programming language based on
nominal logic [14], which uses nominal unification to perform back-chaining.

Figure 2.7 presents a parallel reduction program in αProlog that mirrors the
MLSOS code from Figure 2.2. For consistency we have adopted the MLSOS
syntax for abstractions (⟨⟨a⟩⟩E as opposed to a\E from [5]), and re-ordered the
arguments to agree with the MLSOS program from Figure 2.2. In the base case of
capture-avoiding substitution (Figure 2.7, lines 2-3) the αProlog program uses two
clauses to implement the name equality test, and the freshness constraint X # Y
corresponds to our name inequality constraint. In the λ case of capture-avoiding
substitution (Figure 2.7, line 5) note that a freshness side-condition (a # (X, E))
is necessary. This is because the atom a has not been generated freshly in the
pattern, and hence the system cannot guarantee that a does not occur free in X or E
unless the user makes this explicit. This highlights a difference between αProlog
and MLSOS concerning the interpretation of the syntax a for an object-language
name. Although both programming languages make use of nominal unification, in
MLSOS the metavariable a stands for an atom to be generated freshly at runtime,
whereas in αProlog it stands for *one particular atom* from the countably infinite
set of atoms.

We would like to abstract away from the internal implementation of object-
language names and binding as much as possible. In MLSOS we cannot write programs whose meaning depends upon particular atoms and the behavior of MLSOS
programs does not depend on which concrete atom is chosen to implement a particular object-language bound name. This relates to the *equivariance* property of
nominal logic [14]—Cheney notes that "because of equivariance, resolution based

on nominal unification is incomplete for nominal logic" [5]. That paper proposes replacing nominal unification by equivariant unification, in order to achieve completeness with respect to nominal logic, at the cost of **NP**-completeness [6]. An alternative is to impose a syntactic criterion on αProlog programs which restricts to a subset of nominal logic formulae for which nominal unification is complete [8]. This is related to the problem discussed in §2.6.1.

Of course, there are alternative techniques for encoding binders, such as higher-order abstract syntax, which uses metalanguage binders to model object-language binders, and nameless de-Bruijn representations. The relative merits of the "nominal" techniques used in MLSOS and αProlog compared to such representations have been discussed elsewhere (see [23] for a survey). Broadly speaking, implementations using nameless representations are not easily readable and can be inefficient, whereas higher-order abstract syntax systems such as Twelf [13] and Bedwyr [2] make it hard to use what is often the natural style of "nominal" programming in which concrete bound names are manipulated. They also suffer from a kind of incompleteness (due to their restriction to higher order pattern unification) similar to that discussed in §2.6.1.

Systems such as PLT Redex [12], which were designed specifically for the purpose of producing step-by-step reduction tools from a description of a language semantics, clearly bear comparison to MLSOS. A downside of PLT Redex is that it does not seem to provide automated support for α-equivalence of object-level binders, in the same way as MLSOS. Furthermore, in PLT Redex one is restricted to the operation of reducing a subterm in place, whereas in MLSOS one can write more liberal programs, for example to find all inhabitants of a particular type. However, PLT Redex does have a graphical visualization toolkit.

There also exist mature, high-performance, general-purpose functional logic programming languages such as Curry [11] and Mercury [22]. However, these also lack built-in support for binders and α-equivalence and hence they are not such an attractive choice for the kind of applications we are targeting.

2.6   FUTURE WORK AND CONCLUSIONS

We have outlined some of the design decisions and motivations behind the development of MLSOS, a metalanguage designed for prototyping structural operational semantics definitions. In this section we mention some directions for future work.

2.6.1   Badly Behaved Inductive Definitions

MLSOS takes a "nominal" approach to expressing object-language binding syntax. As we have seen, it adopts a hybrid approach to implementing names in an object-language—they are represented by unification variables wherever possible, and by fresh atoms wherever essential (that is, whenever they appear in binding position). One might hope that any rule-based inductive definition could be implemented in MLSOS (along the lines of the example in §2.3) in a way that is complete—in the sense that MLSOS computes all and only correct solutions to user queries about the definition. (We hope that this notion of completeness is intuitively clear—we defer a formalization to a future paper for reasons of space.)

However, there exist certain inductive definitions whose natural encoding in MLSOS is not complete. The same phenomenon occurs in αProlog (§2.5) and we can adapt to MLSOS an example from [9, Example 5.3]. Consider the set S defined by the single inference rule

$$\overline{R\,(x,t,\lambda x.t)}$$

which gives the graph of λ-abstraction on (α-equivalence classes) of untyped λ-terms. For example, the term $(a,a,\lambda b.b)$ is manifestly in S, since $\lambda a.a$ and $\lambda b.b$ are α-equivalent. However, the natural MLSOS encoding of S as a function of type var $\star$ lam $\star$ lam $\rightarrow$ ans (using the nominal signature from §2.3), which we omit here for reasons of space, will fail to compute this solution. This is because the bound name x in the pattern $\lambda x.t$ in the conclusion of the rule must be modeled by a freshly generated atom; however this name also appears free in the conclusion and hence its identity matters to the semantics of the rule. Thus, it seems that generating fresh atoms for bound names during pattern-matching prevents us from computing all members of S.

The problem with this and similar definitions is that it allows us to inspect the identity of a name that appears in binding position by unbinding without any freshening. We would ideally like to rule out such badly behaved definitions, as they violate the assumption that we can represent a bound name with *any* freshly chosen atom. We aim to find some restricted class of inductively defined sets of α-equivalence classes of nominal terms for which MLSOS is powerful enough to give natural, yet complete encodings. Cheney and Urban [9, §5.2] consider such a restriction for the language αProlog which is discussed in §2.5, but it does not seem immediately applicable to MLSOS.

2.6.2 Correctness Properties

We conjecture that the dynamics of the language (§2.4.4) is such that MLSOS representations of α-equivalent object-language terms are contextually equivalent. This form of correctness has been proved for FreshML [20, 16], but has yet to be established for MLSOS.

2.6.3 Conclusion

MLSOS provides a simple yet expressive medium for computing with abstract syntax trees identified up to α-conversion. A prototype implementation of the language exists, and a more efficient implementation is in the pipeline. This could be useful not only to programming language designers, but also as an educational tool for teaching operational semantics to students. The syntax and programming style should be familiar to people who are comfortable with functional, as opposed to logic, programming languages. MLSOS has the benefit of the full expressive power of functional programming—we have only scratched the surface of what can be done in terms of optimizing the code that one would naïvely write. It is possible that further refinements to the system, such as mode and determinism annotations, could allow us to automatically generate reasonable implementations of systems with minimal input from the user, and provide some degree of verification of certain metatheoretic properties of their definitions.

ACKNOWLEDGEMENTS

This work was supported by UK EPSRC grant EP/D000459/1.

REFERENCES

[1] B. E. Aydemir, A. Bohannon, M. Fairbairn, J. N. Foster, B. C. Pierce, P. Sewell, D. Vytiniotis, G. Washburn, S. Weirich, and S. Zdancewic. Mechanised metatheory for the masses: The POPLmark challenge. In J. Hurd and T. Melham, editors, *18th International Conference on Theorem Proving in Higher Order Logics: TPHOLs 2005*, volume 3603 of *Lecture Notes in Computer Science*, pages 50–65. Springer-Verlag, 2005.

[2] D. Baelde, A. Gacek, D. Miller, G. Nadathur, and A. Tiu. The Bedwyr system for model checking over syntactic expressions. Submitted to CADE 2007.

[3] H. P. Barendregt. *The Lambda Calculus: Its Syntax and Semantics*. North-Holland, revised edition, 1984.

[4] Christophe Calvès and Maribel Fernández. Implementing nominal unification. In *3rd Int. Workshop on Term Graph Rewriting (TERMGRAPH'06), Vienna*, Electronic Notes in Theoretical Computer Science, 2006.

[5] J. Cheney and C. Urban. Alpha-Prolog: A logic programming language with names, binding and alpha-equivalence. In *Proc. 20th Int. Conf. on Logic Programming (ICLP 2004)*, number 3132 in LNCS, pages 269–283, 2004.

[6] James Cheney. The complexity of equivariant unification. In *Proceedings of the 31st International Colloquium on Automata, Languages and Programming (ICALP 2004)*, volume 3142 of *LNCS*, pages 332–344. Springer-Verlag, 2004.

[7] James Cheney. *Nominal Logic Programming*. PhD thesis, Cornell University, Ithaca, NY, August 2004.

[8] James Cheney. Equivariant unification. In *Proceedings of the 2005 Conference on Rewriting Techniques and Applications (RTA 2005)*, number 3467 in LNCS, pages 74–89, 2005.

[9] James Cheney and Christian Urban. Nominal logic programming. Preprint available from http://arxiv.org/abs/cs.PL/0609062, 2006.

[10] Cormac Flanagan, Amr Sabry, Bruce F. Duba, and Matthias Felleisen. The essence of compiling with continuations. *SIGPLAN Not.*, 39(4):502–514, 2004.

[11] M. Hanus, H. Kuchen, and J.J. Moreno-Navarro. Curry: A truly functional logic language. In *Proc. ILPS'95 Workshop on Visions for the Future of Logic Programming*, pages 95–107, 1995.

[12] J. Matthews, R. B. Findler, M. Flatt, and M. Felleisen. A visual environment for developing context-sensitive term rewriting systems. In *Proceedings of the International Conference on Rewriting Techniques and Applications (RTA) 2004*, 2004.

[13] F. Pfenning and C. Schürmann. System description: Twelf—a meta-logical framework for deductive systems. In *Proceedings of the 16th Conference on Automated Deduction (CADE 1999)*, volume 1632 of *Lecture Notes in Artificial Intelligence*, Trento, Italy, July 1999.

[14] A. M. Pitts. Nominal logic, a first order theory of names and binding. *Information and Computation*, 186:165–193, 2003.

[15] A. M. Pitts and M. J. Gabbay. A metalanguage for programming with bound names modulo renaming. In R. Backhouse and J. N. Oliveira, editors, *Mathematics of Program Construction. 5th International Conference, MPC2000, Ponte de Lima, Portugal, July 2000. Proceedings*, volume 1837 of *Lecture Notes in Computer Science*, pages 230–255. Springer-Verlag, Heidelberg, 2000.

[16] A. M. Pitts and M. R. Shinwell. Generative unbinding of names. In *34th Annual ACM SIGPLAN-SIGACT Symposium on Principles of Programming Languages (POPL 2007), Nice, France*, pages 85–95. ACM Press, January 2007.

[17] F. Pottier. Static name control for FreshML. In *Twenty-Second Annual IEEE Symposium on Logic In Computer Science (LICS'07)*, Wroclaw, Poland, July 2007. To appear.

[18] François Pottier. An overview of Cαml. In *ACM Workshop on ML*, volume 148 of *Electronic Notes in Theoretical Computer Science*, pages 27–52, March 2006.

[19] M. R. Shinwell. *The Fresh Approach: functional programming with names and binders*. PhD thesis, Cambridge University, 2006.

[20] M. R. Shinwell and A. M. Pitts. On a monadic semantics for freshness. *Theoretical Computer Science*, 342:28–55, 2005.

[21] M. R. Shinwell, A. M. Pitts, and M. J. Gabbay. FreshML: Programming with binders made simple. In *Eighth ACM SIGPLAN International Conference on Functional Programming (ICFP 2003), Uppsala, Sweden*, pages 263–274. ACM Press, August 2003.

[22] Zoltan Somogyi, Fergus Henderson, and Thomas Conway. The execution algorithm of Mercury, an efficient purely declarative logic programming language. *J. Log. Program.*, 29(1-3):17–64, 1996.

[23] C. Urban, A. M. Pitts, and M. J. Gabbay. Nominal unification. *Theoretical Computer Science*, 323:473–497, 2004.

Chapter 3

AHA: Amortized *H*eap Space Usage *A*nalysis
– *Project Paper* –

Marko van Eekelen, Olha Shkaravska, Ron van Kesteren,
Bart Jacobs, Erik Poll, Sjaak Smetsers[1]

Abstract: This paper introduces **AHA**, an NWO-funded[2] 344K Euro project involving research into an amortized analysis of heap-space usage by functional and imperative programs. Amortized analysis is a promising technique that can improve on simply summing worst case bounds. The project seeks to combine this technique with type theory in order to obtain non-linear bounds on heap-space usage for functional languages and to adapt the results for the lazy functional case and for imperative languages.

3.1 INTRODUCTION

Estimating heap consumption is an active research area as it becomes more and more an issue in many applications. This project seems to be part of an upcoming trend since a growing number of projects are addressing this as a research topic (see section 3.6 on related work). Examples of possible application areas include programming for small devices, e.g. smart cards, mobile phones, embedded systems and distributed computing, e.g. GRID. It is important to give as accurate bounds for heap consumption as possible to avoid unnecessarily expensive and even unpractical estimates for small devices and high integrity real-time applications.

---

[1] All authors are members of the Security of Systems Department, Institute for Computing and Information Sciences, Radboud University Nijmegen, Toernooiveld 1, Nijmegen, 6525 ED, The Netherlands; Project leader E-mail: marko@cs.ru.nl.

[2] This project is sponsored by the Netherlands Organization for Scientific Research (NWO) under grant nr. 612.063.511.

A promising technique to obtain accurate bounds of resource consumption and gain is amortized analysis. An amortized estimate of a resource does not target a single operation but a sequence of operations. One assigns to an operation some amortized cost that may be higher or lower than its actual cost. For the sequence considered it is important that its overall amortized cost covers its overall actual cost. An amortized cost of the sequence lies between its actual cost and the simple multiplication of the worst-case of one operation by the length of the sequence. An amortized cost of the sequence is in many cases easier to compute than its actual cost and it is obviously better than the worst-case estimate.

Combining amortization with type theory allows the inference of linear heap consumption bounds for functional programs with explicit memory deallocation [10]. The **AHA** project aims to adapt this method for *non-linear* bounds within (lazy) functional programs and transfer the results to the object-oriented programming. In this way the project both enhances fundamental theory and practical impact.

3.1.1 Relevance

Accurate estimates of heap space consumption are directly relevant for robustness, execution time and safety of programs. For instance, memory exhaustion may cause abrupt termination of an application or invoke garbage collection. In the latter case, heap management can indirectly slow down execution and hence influence time complexity. A better heap space analysis will therefore enable a more accurate estimation of time consumption. This is relevant for time-critical applications. Analyzing resource usage is also interesting for optimizations in compilers for functional languages, in particular optimizations of memory allocation and garbage collection techniques. A more accurate estimation of heap usage enables allocation of larger memory chunks beforehand instead of allocating memory cells separately when needed, leading to a better cache performance.

Resource usage is an important aspect of any safety or security policy for programs downloaded from external sources. It is one of the most important properties that one wants to specify and verify for Java programs meant to be executed on (embedded) Java-enabled devices with limited amounts of memory, such as smart cards implementing the Java Card platform and MIDP mobile phones implementing the Java 2 Micro Edition (J2ME) platform.

3.1.2 Research Questions

The **AHA** project investigates the possibilities for analyzing heap usage for both functional and imperative object-oriented languages, more specifically Clean and Java. It aims to answer the following research questions:

– How can the existing type-based linear heap consumption analysis of functional programs [10] be improved such that a wider class of resource usage bounds can be guaranteed? The question is how complex the type-checking and inference procedures may be. In particular, which arithmetic and constraint solvers will be needed for which classes of function definitions?

– Can heap space analysis be done for lazy functional languages? Heap space analysis for lazy functional languages is clearly more complicated than for strict languages, because the heap space is also used for unevaluated expressions (closures). The amount of memory that is used at a certain moment depends on the evaluation order of expressions, which in its turn is influenced by the strictness analyzer in the code generating compiler.

– How successfully can one adapt the approach for object-oriented imperative languages? The aim here is to be able to prove – or, better still, derive – properties about the heap space consumption of Java programs. The plan is to start with a functional subset of Java that encompasses classes admitting algebraic data type operations, like constructors and get-field methods (corresponding to nondestructive pattern matching) and generalize from there.

3.1.3 Outline of the Paper

Amortization for resource-aware program analysis is explained in section 3.2. In section 3.3 we give an overview of the existing amortization-related type system which is used to infer linear heap-consumption bounds for first-order functional programs. The research questions from section 3.1.2, which concern generalizations of the type system, are to be answered according to the project plan from section 3.4. The motivation and more detailed generalization of the type system for non-linear heap bounds for strict languages and related results on size inference are presented in section 3.5. We finish the paper with the overview of related projects devoted to quantitative resource analysis and define the place of **AHA** amongst this variety in section 3.6.

3.2 INTRODUCTION TO AMORTIZATION

The term "amortization" came to computer science from the financial world. There it denotes a process of ending a debt by regular payments into a special fund. In computer science, amortization is used to estimate time and heap consumption of programs. "Payments" in a program are done by its operations or by the data structures that participate in the computation, see [15]. These payments must cover the overall resource usage. Methods of distribution of such "payments" across operations or data structures form the subject of amortized analysis.

3.2.1 Amortization of Resources in Program Analysis

To begin with, consider amortized time costing. Given a sequence of operations, one often wants to know not the costs of the individual operations, but the cost of the entire sequence. One assigns to an operation an *amortized cost*, which can be greater or less than its actual cost. All one is interested in is that the sum of the amortized costs is large enough to cover the overall time usage. Thus, one redistributes the runtime of the entire sequence over the operations. The simplest way to arrange such redistribution is to assign to each operation the average cost $T(n)/n$, where $T(n)$ is the overall runtime and n is the number of operations. A *rich* operation is an operation for which its amortized cost, say, $T(n)/n$, exceeds its actual cost. Rich operations pay for "poor" ones.

Consider the Haskell-style version of the function multipop from [8] that, given a stack S and a counter k, pops an element from the top of the stack till the stack is empty or the counter is zero:

```
multipop :: Int → Stack Int  → Stack Int
multipop k []     = []
multipop 0 (x:xs) = x:xs
multipop k (x:xs) = multipop (k-1) xs
```

To construct a stack one needs a function push:

```
push :: Int → Stack Int → Stack Int
push x s = x:s
```

If the actual costs of each function call (such as multipop and push) is 1 time unit, then the actual cost of the program multipop k S is $min(s,k) + 1$ time units, where s is the size of the stack S.

Assigning amortized costs for multipop and push one may think in the following way. Each operation push has actual cost 1, but it "takes care" of the future of the element it pushes on the stack. This element may be popped out. So push obtains the amortized cost 2 to pay for itself and for the corresponding part of a call of multipop. Thus, the complete cost of multipop k S is paid while constructing the input S using push. *After construction of the stack S, the amortized cost for* multipop is just 1 for the call of multipop k []. Hence, the amortized cost of the construction of S followed by multipop is $2s + 1$, which is an upper bound for the actual cost being $s + min(s,k) + 1$.

The correctness of an amortized analysis for a sequence of n operations is defined by $\Sigma_{i=1}^{j} a_i \geq \Sigma_{i=1}^{j} t_i$, for all $j \leq n$, a_i is the amortized cost of the ith operation, and t_i is its actual cost. In this way one ensures that, at any moment of the computation, the overall amortized cost covers the overall actual cost.

3.2.2   Amortization Views

A general understanding of amortization [17] is based on a graph representation of programs. A program is viewed as a directed graph with *states* (i.e. data structures) as nodes and *edges* (i.e. basic operators or constructs) as transitions between them. A possible *computation* is a path in the graph. Branching in the graph appears due to non-determinism or due to replacing *if-then-else* by non-deterministic choice.

In the *physicist's view* of amortization one assigns to any state s a real number $\Phi(s)$ called the *potential* of the state s. We consider only non-negative potentials. Negative potentials can never be introduced since the typing rules insist that the potential is kept non-negative (see section 3.5.3). The first intuition behind the potential function is that it reflects the number of resources (heap units, time ticks) that may be discharged during a computation, starting from the state s. In the physicist's approach the amortized cost of an *any* path between some s and s' is the difference $\Phi(s') - \Phi(s)$.

To introduce a *banker's view* we first note the following. Each edge $e(s_1, s_2)$ has its actual cost $t(s_1, s_2)$ defined by the corresponding basic command or the construct. Let it have an amortized cost $a(s_1, s_2)$. The difference $a(s_1, s_2) - t(s_1, s_2)$ for the edge $e(s_1, s_2)$ is called a *surplus*. If the difference $a(s_1, s_2) - t(s_1, s_2)$ is positive, it is called a *credit*, it may be used to cover the actual costs of further computations. The actual/amortized cost of a path π, between some s and s', is the sum of actual/amortized costs of edges. In principle, the costs of two paths π and π' between the same vertices may differ. If for any two states s and s' it holds that $a(s, s') = t(s, s') + \Phi(s') - \Phi(s)$, then the analysis is called *conservative*.

It is clear that for any physicist's view one can find a corresponding banker's view. The opposite transformation is more complicated. The banker's approach is more general than the physicist's one, because one considers particular paths instead of their initial and end points. However, it has been shown [17] that for any banker's amortization distribution a there is a "better" conservative distribution a' and a potential function Φ for it, such that $a'(s, s') = t(s, s') + \Phi(s') - \Phi(s)$ (a conservative analysis), and $a'(s_1, s_2) \leq a(s_1, s_2)$ for any edge $e(s_1, s_2)$. Thus, without loss of generality one can consider *conservative* amortized analysis only.

3.2.3 Amortization for Heap Consumption Gives Size of Live Data

Now we interpret amortization for heap consumption analysis. A potential of a structure is a number of free heap units associated with this structure. An initial potential is the potential of an input structure before the program runs. Any data structure, which exists during the computation of a function, may be constructed either from heap units taken from the initially allocated units (defined by the initial potential function) or taken from reused heap cells (for a language with destructive pattern matching).

If heap management is performed via maintaining a free list, then the heap layouts before and after the computations are presented by the scheme in Figure 3.1. One can view maintaining a free list as an ideal garbage collector: once a location is destructed it is put on the top of the free list. A fresh cell is taken from the top of the free list. Thus, a potential function and the size of input data define an upper bound on the size of the live data at any moment of computation. In general, we have the following dependency:

$$size(input) + \Phi_{in} = size(data\_current) + \Phi_{current} = size(output) + \Phi_{out}$$

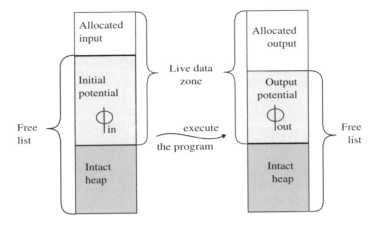

FIGURE 3.1: Heap layouts before and after the computations

3.3 STATE OF THE ART: A TYPE SYSTEM FOR LINEAR BOUNDS

One can implement a heap-aware amortized analysis via an annotated type system. In this section we consider an annotated type system introduced by Hofmann and Jost [10] for linear bounds on heap consumption. Given a first-order function definition this system allows us to infer an upper bound (if it exists and is linear) on the number of freshly allocated heap units.

The operations that affect heap consumption are constructors and pattern matching. The coefficients of linear bounds appear in the form of numerical annotations (constants) for types. For instance, a function that creates a fresh copy of a list of integers

```
copy :: [Int] → [Int]
copy []     = []
copy (x:xs) = x : copy xs
```

has the annotated signature $[\texttt{Int}]_1 \ _0 \!\to_0 [\texttt{Int}]_0$ (we adapted the notation of [10]). It reflects the fact that for each element of an input list 1 extra heap unit (credit) must be supplied to fix the space for its copy. Furthermore, it indicates via a 0-annotated arrow that it is not necessary to add extra heap cells for evaluating the function. Also, no cells at all will be released: nor a number of cells depending on the size of the result (since a 0 is assigned to the result), nor independent of that (since a 0 is assigned to the function arrow).

In general, the heap consumption by a function $\texttt{f}$ with the credit-annotated type $[\texttt{Int}]_k \ _{k_0}\!\to_{k'_0} [\texttt{Int}]_{k'}$ does not exceed $k \cdot n + k_0$ heap units and at the end of the computation at least $k' \cdot n' + k'_0$ heap units are available, with n and n' the sizes of the input and output lists, respectively. The potential of a list $[\texttt{Int}]_k$ of length n is $k \cdot n$. In fact, the type system above infers two (linear) potentials of a given function: the potential of an input and the potential of an output. The potential of the input may be discharged during evaluation of the program expression and the potential of the output may be used in further computations. Non-zero arrow annotations typically appear due to destructive pattern-matching.

It is possible to extend this approach for non-linear bounds. One of the aims of the **AHA** project is to study such extensions.

3.4 AHA PROJECT PLAN

To answer the three research questions posed in section 3.1.2, the project is partitioned into an initial step followed by two parallel research lines. The initial step serves as a prerequisite for the two lines and will establish the foundations of amortized analysis with non-linear bounds for strict languages. After that, a fundamental theoretical research line will extended this analysis to a lazy language. A parallel practical line will transfer the theoretical results to an imperative object-oriented setting.

In view of the breadth of the proposed research, which looks both at functional and imperative languages, the project will use the funding for two positions, a three year post-doc and a four year Ph.D. student. Cooperating with the post-doc the Ph.D. student will not only study the more fundamental issues but the Ph.D. student will also be responsible for creating prototypes demonstrating the effectiveness of the developed analysis. Master students will be actively encouraged to participate in creating these demonstrators.

Ultimately, we want to implement the type systems for heap space usage to obtain prototypes that can check whether a given (functional or imperative) program, augmented with resource-aware type annotations, meets a given bound on heap space usage. Ideally, we will be able to infer such bounds in many cases.

3.4.1 Amortized Analysis with Non-Linear Bounds

There are many interesting examples that require non-linear heap space, for instance matrix multiplication and the Cartesian product. Also, e.g. the generation of a sports competition programme, in which every team plays a home and an away match against every other team, needs a non-linear amount of heap space. The sports competition has $n \cdot n - n$ matches, where n is the number of teams. So, the program will require at least $n \cdot n - n$ heap space.

Arguments and results of functions are represented as (intermediate) structures in the heap. Sizes of results depend generally on the sizes of the arguments. For example, the number of matches (the size of the result) in an implemented sports competition[3] depends on the number of teams (the size of the argument). So, deriving such size dependencies is an important first step before computing amortized bounds that take temporary structures into account.

---

[3]Using amortization in section 3.5 it is shown that for a specific sports competition programme implementation that it actually requires $n \cdot (3 \cdot n + 3)$ heap space.

Methodology. To begin with, we tackle the derivation of size relations separately from heap-space usage to keep both systems as simple as possible. The results from the derivation of the size relations are input for the amortized analysis. The amortized analysis will be an extension of the existing linear analysis in [10].

3.4.2   Amortized Heap Analysis of a Lazy Language

Applying a strict semantic-based type system to a lazy evaluation strategy may lead to significant mis-evaluations of heap consumption. Indeed, one may count heap cells for a structure that are not actually allocated or allocated in a "zipped" form, or one counts a heap consumed/released by a function that is not called.

Consider, for instance, a lazy list of integers `lazy_list` n containing integers from n to 1. An element of this list is a record (n, r) which consist of the integer field for n, and a reference field with r, where r is the address a of the closure computing tail, if $n > 0$, and $r = $ nil otherwise. The closure is the function `tail` $t = \lambda$ i. **if** i>1 **then** (i-1, a) **else** (0, nil). So, the size of this structure is *constant: the size of integer + the size of a pointer + the size of the closure*, whereas the size of the corresponding strict list is *(the size of integer + the size of a pointer)*$\times n$. The lazy list is unfolded once it is needed (and may be memoized after that).

One of the ways to provide a transition from a strict semantics to a lazy one is to augment a strict language with an explicit suspension constructor S and force operator, as it is done in [15]: datatype α susp = S α. Then for the example above one has:

val l=S(lazy_list 1000) (*the constant heap is allocated*)
...
val x=force l (*proportional to 1000 cells are allocated*)

One may consider typing rules for explicit suspensions and forces, like

$$\frac{\Gamma \vdash_\Sigma e : \tau}{\Gamma \vdash_\Sigma force(Se) : \tau} \text{ FORCE}$$

Amortized time analysis for call-by-need[4] languages is considered in [15]. Instead of credits it uses *debts* to cover costs of suspensions. A closure is allowed to be forced only after its debt is "payed off" by the operations preceding the operation which forces the closure.

Choice of Programming Language. To consider heap usage analysis for lazy functional programming languages, we will begin with a strict version of core-Clean. We have chosen Clean since Clean's uniqueness typing [3] makes Clean more suited as a starting point than e.g. Haskell, since with uniqueness

---

[4]Following [15] we associate *call-by-value* with strict languages, *call-by-name* with lazy languages without memoization, and *call-by-need* with lazy languages with memoization.

typing reuse of nodes can be analyzed in a sophisticated manner. For this strict core-Clean language we will define an alternative operational semantics which will take heap usage into account, and then formulate a type system in which annotations in types express costs.

Methodology. Camelot [13] is an ML-like strict functional language with polymorphism and algebraic data types. To enable analysis of heap usage, in Camelot one can syntactically make the distinction between destructive and non-destructive pattern matching, where destructive pattern matching allows a node of heap space to be reclaimed. It is expected to be relatively easy to transfer such a distinction to a language that has uniqueness typing, as this can enforce the safe use of destructive pattern matching. Therefore, we expect that the results achieved for Camelot will be quickly transferred to the strict version of core-Clean.

Then, we will change the strict semantics into a mixed lazy/strict semantics and require that suspensions and forces are explicit in our input language. This corresponds to assuming that compiler optimizations and program transformations have been performed before the analysis starts. We will investigate the consequences for the operational semantics and for the type system. This is not a big step in the dark since the heap-aware inference system from [10] already has some flavor of the call-by-need semantics. *Shared* usage of variables by several expressions is treated, for instance, in the MATCH-rule given below in Section 3.5.3 and in the SHARE-rule in [10].

3.4.3 Adaptation to Object-Orientation

Choice of Programming Language. As the object-oriented programming languages to be studied we have chosen Java. We will use the Java semantics developed in the LOOP project [11], which includes an explicit formalization of the heap. This will first require accurate accounting of heap usage in the type-theoretic memory model underlying the LOOP tool [5].

The Java Modeling Language (JML), a specification language tailored to Java, already provides a syntax for specifying heap usage, but this part of JML is as of yet without any clear semantics. We want to provide a rigorous semantics for these properties about heap space usage and then develop an associated program logic for proving such properties.

Methodology. We will start to adjust the analysis of Section 3.5.3 by applying it to classes that admit a functional *algebraic data-type (ADT) interface*. These classes possess "basic" methods that have counterparts in functional programming. Constructors correspond to functional constructors and get-field methods ("observers") correspond to non-destructive pattern matching. Heap-aware program-logic rules are to be defined for these basic methods and the language constructs such as if-branching, sequencing and while-repetition (*a-la* "recursive function call"). Then, a field assignment, for example, may be presented as a composition of the destructive match and a constructor.

Next, research will be done to alleviate the restrictions. For that purpose, we will investigate the possibility of introducing amortized variants of existing specific analyzes (such as the non-recursive [6] and the symbolic [7] which treats aliasing). One of the main problems for heap space analysis is aliasing. Aliasing-aware type systems and logics presented in [1, 12] may be considered separately from the resource-aware typing system and are to be combined with it at the very last stage of the design of the proof system.

3.5   FIRST STEPS: NON-LINEAR BOUNDS AND SIZED TYPES

In this section we show why a more general treatment of credits (generalizing from constants to functions) is required for non-linear heap consumption analysis. We give examples, one of which illustrates the advantage of combination amortization with types and the other one is about non-linear heap consumption. Further, we present an experimental type system that combines sizes and amortization. Sizes are needed to determine generalized credits and may be considered independently. Finally, we give a summary of the first results of the project dealing with strictly sized types.

3.5.1   Towards Non-Linear Upper Bounds on the Size of Live Data

It is convenient to measure the potentials of data structures in terms of their sizes. For instance, the potential of a list of length n may be a function of n, that is $\Phi(n)$. In general, one assigns a potential to an *overall data structure*. In other words, a potential is assigned to the abstract state that is the collection of the sizes of the structures existing in a given concrete state. Now, consider a function of type $([\texttt{String32}]^n, [\texttt{String32}]^m) \to [(\texttt{Int}, \texttt{Int})]^{n \cdot m}$ that creates an initial table from input lists of length n and m of strings of fixed length (say 32). We use superscripts for sizes and subscripts for credits. It is natural to assume that for the input of type $([\texttt{String32}]^n, [\texttt{String32}]^m)$ the potential $\Phi(n, m)$ depends on n and m.

The system assigns a credit to each constructor of a data structure. For instance, in [10] each constructor of a list of type $[\alpha]_k$ has a constant credit k, and thus the potential of the list is $k \cdot n$, where n is its length.

In general the credit of a node may be a function. It may depend on the position of the node in the list, and/or on the size of the list, as well as on the size of "neighboring" data structure, etc. For instance, in the table-creating function the annotated type of its input may be $([\texttt{String32}]_k^n, [\texttt{String32}]_0^m)$, where $k(position, n, m) = m$.

In the linear heap-consumption analysis of [10] these dependencies are not taken into account. This makes the analysis very simple, because it reduces to solving a linear programming task. It covers a large class of functional programs with linear heap consumption, where coefficients of linear functions are credits of constructors.

Introducing dependencies will significantly increase the complexity of type checking and inference. We will study classes of function definitions for which type checking and inference of non-linear bounds are decidable.

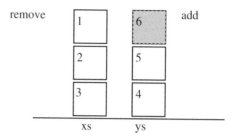

FIGURE 3.2: Adding to the queue.

3.5.2   Examples: Going on with Amortization-and-Types

The linear heap-consumption analysis shows that amortization and types can be combined naturally. In this section we consider 2 examples. One example illustrates the advantages of this combination. The other one motivates the study of annotated types for non-linear heap consumption.

Type Systems Bring Modularity to Amortized Analysis

In the following example the näive worst-case analysis significantly overestimates the real heap consumption and the precise analysis is relatively complicated. We show that with the help of types annotated with credits, one obtains a very good upper bound for a "reduced price": types make the analysis modular and, thus, simpler and more suitable for automated checking or inference.

Consider queues ("first-in-first-out" lists) presented as pairs of lists in the usual way. A queue q is represented by a pair (xs, ys), such that q is $xs + +(reverse\ ys)$. The head of the list xs is the first element of the queue, and the head of ys is the last element of the queue. For instance, the queue $[1, 2, 3, 4, 5]$ may be presented as $([1, 2, 3], [5, 4])$. One adds elements to the queue by pushing them on the head of ys; see Figure 3.2 below. After adding 6 the resulting queue is presented by $([1, 2, 3], [6, 5, 4])$. The function "remove from the queue", will pop 1 from xs. Consider the code for remove, where reverse creates a *fresh copy* of the reversed list:

```
remove :: ([Int], [Int]) → (Int, ([Int], [Int]))
remove ([],    []) = error
remove ([],    ys) = remove (reverse ys, [])
remove (x:xs, ys) = (x,   (xs, ys))
```

We assume that input pairs and output triples are *not boxed*, that is, two input pointer values are taken from the operand stack and in the case of normal termination three values will be pushed on the operand stack. (This helps to avoid technical overhead with heap consumption for pairs and triples creation.)

Let n denote the length of remove's first argument and m denote the length of the second argument. If $n = 0$, then remove consumes m heap cells, otherwise remove does not consume cells at all.

The annotated type for remove looks as follows:

$$([\texttt{Int}]_0^n, [\texttt{Int}]_1^m) \; {}_0{\to}_0 \; (\texttt{Int}, ([\texttt{Int}]_0^{p_1}, [\texttt{Int}]_1^{p_2}))$$

where p_1 and p_2 are defined piece-wise: if $n = 0$ then $p_1 = m - 1$, $p_2 = 0$; otherwise $p_1 = n - 1$, $p_2 = m$. As for the credits: if $n = 0$ then the potential of the second argument $1 \cdot m$ is spent by reverse and the potential of the second list on the r.h.s. is $0 = 1 \cdot p_2$. If $n > 0$ then the second argument and its potential $1 \cdot m$ are intact, and the potential of the second list on the r.h.s. is $m = 1 \cdot p_2$.

So, amortization keeps track of the resources that are left after computation and that may be used afterwards. The effect of combining amortization with types may be seen at the composition of remove with copy3 that returns a fresh copy of the third argument. The type of copy3 is $(\texttt{Int}, [\texttt{Int}]_0^n, [\texttt{Int}]_1^m) \; {}_0{\to}_0 \; [\texttt{Int}]_0^m$.

The naïve worst-case analysis consists in summation of two worst-case heap consumption estimations: for remove it is m, and for copy3 it is m. So, the naïve worst-case for copy3(remove(xs, ys)) is $2 \cdot m$.

The precise worst-case analysis requires detailed abstract program analysis of the *entire composition* and leads to a piecewise definition of the consumption function, which is later simplified to a linear function $p(n, m) = m$:

n	m	remove consumes	p_2	copy3 consumes	copy3(remove(−)) consumes
0	m	m	0	$p_2 = 0$	$m + 0 = m$
> 0	m	0	m	$p_2 = m$	$0 + m = m$

The type $(\texttt{Int}, [\texttt{Int}]_0^n, [\texttt{Int}]_1^m) \; {}_0{\to}_0 \; [\texttt{Int}]_0^m$ of copy3(remove(−)) is easily obtained by composition. It means that the composition consumes $1 \cdot m$ heap units. Type derivation for remove is done once and forever and the type is applicable for any other composition yielding a modular amortized analysis.

Example of the Use of Non-linear Bounds

We illustrate the kind of types we plan to derive by the following small example.

Consider the function definition that given two lists of strings, of length n and m respectively, creates the initial $n \times m$ table of pairs of integer numbers filled with $(-1, -1)$. This function is used for creating the initial table for a tournament, like a round in a soccer championship.

The initial table is used as follows. During a round, each team plays two games – at home and as a guest. Let, for instance, "PSV Eindhoven" be number 1 in the list and play in Eindhoven with "AZ Alkmaar" being number 3 withe result $2 - 1$. Then one places $(2, 1)$ in the position $(1, 3)$ in the table. This may be done in non-destructive or destructive (in-place update) way. At the end of the round the table, except the diagonal, is filled with the results.

We need an auxiliary initializing function init_row. Note, that a node of a list of pairs of integers allocates three heap units: one per each integer and one for the reference to the next element. The main "working" function is init_table. Finally, the function init_round creates the initial tournament table.

```
init_row :: [String32]₃ⁿ 0→0 [(Int, Int)]₀ⁿ
init_row []    = []
init_row (h:t) = (-1, -1) : init_row t
```

$$\text{init\_row} :: [\text{String32}]_3^n \;_0\!\to_0\; [(\text{Int}, \text{Int})]_0^n$$
$$\text{init\_row}\;[] = []$$
$$\text{init\_row}\;(h{:}t) = (-1, -1) : \text{init\_row}\;t$$

$$\text{init\_table} :: ([(\text{Int}, \text{Int})]_0^n, [\text{String32}]_{3n}^m) \;_0\!\to_0\; [[(\text{Int}, \text{Int})]_0^n]_0^m$$
$$\text{init\_table}\;\text{row}\;[] = []$$
$$\text{init\_table}\;\text{row}\;(h{:}t) = \text{copy row} : \text{init\_table}\;t$$

$$\text{init\_round} :: [\text{String32}]_{3n+3}^n \;_0\!\to_0\; [[(\text{Int}, \text{Int})]_0^n]_0^n$$
$$\text{init\_round}\;\text{teams} = \text{init\_table}\;(\text{init\_row teams})\;\text{teams}$$

The size dependency (superscripts in types) indicates that the result is of size $n \cdot n$. One might have expected size $n \cdot (n-1)$ but the program does not remove the superfluous diagonal. Taking into account credits (subscripts in types) for the intermediate structure produced by init_row we derived that the heap consumption of init_round is: $n \cdot (3n+3)$.

3.5.3 Experimental Type System

We start with a type system for a first-order call-by-value functional language over integers and polymorphic lists. First we consider only *shapely* function definitions, that is definitions for which the size of the output (polynomially) depends on the sizes of input lists. Below, we sketch the basic ideas of such a type system.

Language and Types

The *abstract* syntax of the language is defined by the following grammar, where c ranges over integer constants, x and y denote zero-order program variables, and f denotes a function name:

$$\begin{aligned}
\textit{Basic} \quad b \quad &::= \quad c \mid \text{nil} \mid \text{cons}(x,y) \mid f(x_1,\dots,x_n) \\
\textit{Expr} \quad e \quad &::= \quad \text{letfun } f(x_1,\dots,x_n) = e_1 \text{ in } e_2 \\
&\qquad \mid b \mid \text{let } x = b \text{ in } e \mid \text{if } x \text{ then } e_1 \text{ else } e_2 \\
&\qquad \mid \text{match } x \text{ with } \mid \text{nil} \Rightarrow e_1 \mid \text{cons}(x_{\text{hd}}, x_{\text{tl}}) \Rightarrow e_2
\end{aligned}$$

We have been studying a type and effect system in which types are annotated with size expressions and *credit functions*.

Size expressions that annotate types are polynomials representing lengths of finite lists and arithmetic operations over these lengths (at a later stage this may be extended to piecewise-defined polynomial functions):

$$\textit{SizeExpr} \quad p \quad ::= \quad \mathbb{N} \mid n \mid p+p \mid p-p \mid p*p$$

where n, possibly decorated, denotes a size variable, which ranges over integer numbers. Semantics for lists with negative sizes is not defined: these lists are ill-formed.

In the simplest case, the intuition behind a credit function $k : \mathbb{N} \to \mathcal{R}^+$ is that $k(i)$ is the credit, that is, a number of free heap units, assigned to the ith cons-cell of a given list. Note that we count cons-cells from nil, that is the head of a list of length n has credit $k(n)$. Fractional credits may be used to achieve more flexibility in defining distribution of extra heap cells across an overall data structure.

As we have noticed in 3.5.1, credits may depend not only on the position of a cons-cell, but also on other parameters, like the length of the outer list or the sizes of "neighboring" lists. In general, a credit function is of type $\mathbb{N} \times \ldots \times \mathbb{N} \to (\mathbb{N} \to \mathcal{R}^+)$. However here, for the sake of simplicity, we consider typing rules with the simplest credits of type $k : \mathbb{N} \to \mathcal{R}^+$, and k denotes a parametric credit function.

Zero-order types are assigned to program values, which are integers and annotated finite lists:

$$Types \quad \tau \quad ::= \quad \texttt{Int} \mid \alpha \mid [\tau]_k^p \qquad \alpha \in TypeVar$$

where α is a type variable. For now, lists represent matrix-like structures and must have size expressions at every position in the "nested-list" type.

First-order types are assigned to shapely function definitions over zero-order types. Let τ° denote a zero-order type where all the size annotations are size variables. First-order types are defined by:

$$FTypes \quad \tau^f \quad ::= \quad \tau_1^\circ \times \ldots \times \tau_n^\circ \to \tau_{n+1}$$
$$\text{such that } FVS(\tau_{n+1}) \subseteq FVS(\tau_1^\circ) \cup \cdots \cup FVS(\tau_n^\circ)$$

where $FVS(\tau)$ denotes free size variables of a type τ and K, K' are non-negative rational constants. Here, we abstracted from a few technical details concerning the equivalence of empty lists, like $[[\alpha]^p]^0 \equiv [[\alpha]^q]^0$. Full definitions are in [18].

Typing Rules

Consider a few typing rules that generalize the type system of Hofmann and Jost [10] using credit functions in stead of credit constants.

A typing judgment is a relation of the form $D; \Gamma; K \vdash_\Sigma e : \tau; K'$, where D is a set of *Diophantine equations* (i.e. equations with integer coefficients with variables varying over natural numbers) used to keep track of the size information. The signature Σ contains the type assumptions for the functions to be checked.

In the typing rules, $D \vdash p = p'$ means that $p = p'$ is derivable from D in first-order logic. $D \vdash \tau = \tau'$ is a shorthand that means that τ and τ' have the same underlying type and equality of their credit and size annotations is derivable.

The type system allows non-negative potentials only. The credit functions k and the constants K and K' are always non-negative. Due to the side conditions (like $K \geq K' + 1 + k(p' + 1)$ below) the typing rules guarantee that potentials fully cover the cost of computation. For the rule below the side condition guarantees that there will be enough heap cells to evaluate CONS.

$$K \geq K' + 1 + k(p' + 1)$$
$$D \vdash p = p' + 1$$

$$\frac{\qquad\qquad\qquad\qquad\qquad\qquad\qquad}{D;\ \Gamma,\ hd\!:\!\tau,\ tl\!:\![\tau]_k^{p'};\ K\ \vdash_\Sigma \mathsf{cons}(hd, tl)\!:\![\tau]_k^{p};\ K'}\ \text{Cons}$$

The non-destructive pattern-matching rule takes into account that a list and its tail are shared and, therefore, they share the potential. In the simplified version below all potential, but that of the head-cell, is transferred to the tail. The head-cell's credit is "opened" for usage:

$$p = 0,\ D;\ \Gamma,\ x\!:\![\tau']_k^{p};\ K\ \vdash_\Sigma e_{\mathsf{nil}}\!:\!\tau;\ K'$$
$$D;\ \Gamma, hd\!:\!\tau',\ x\!:\![\tau']_0^{p},\ tl\!:\![\tau']_k^{p-1};\ K + k(p)\ \vdash_\Sigma e_{\mathsf{cons}}\!:\!\tau;\ K'$$

$$\frac{\qquad\qquad\qquad\qquad\qquad\qquad\qquad\qquad}{\begin{array}{l} D;\ \Gamma,\ x\!:\![\tau']_k^{p};\ K\ \vdash_\Sigma \mathsf{match}\ x\ \mathsf{with}\ |\ \mathsf{nil} \Rightarrow e_{\mathsf{nil}} \qquad\qquad :\tau;\ K' \\ \qquad\qquad\qquad\qquad\qquad\qquad\quad |\ \mathsf{cons}(hd, tl) \Rightarrow e_{\mathsf{cons}} \end{array}}\ \text{Match}$$

The function application rule for a function f may be viewed as a generalization of the Cons-rule with f instead of cons and the function's arguments instead of hd, tl. Note that the precondition requires the information $\Sigma(\mathtt{f})$ about the type of the function. In this way, one achieves the finiteness of the derivation tree if the function is recursive. The information may be not complete, that is, the type may have unknown parameters in annotations. Type inference for the annotated types consists in finding these parameters.

To deal with inter-structural exchange of resources, one needs rules like

$$D \vdash K \geq \Sigma_{i=1}^{p} k'(i)$$
$$D;\ \Gamma, x\!:\![\tau]_k^{p};\ K\ \vdash_\Sigma e\!:\!\tau';\ K'$$

$$\frac{\qquad\qquad\qquad\qquad\qquad\qquad\qquad}{D;\ \Gamma, x\!:\![\tau]_{k+k'}^{p};\ K - \Sigma_{i=1}^{p} k'(i)\ \vdash_\Sigma e\!:\!\tau';\ K'}\ \text{ShuffleIn}$$

This rule is non-syntax driven and increases complexity of type-checking. We plan to establish conditions that define how such inference rules must be applied.

3.5.4   First Results: Sized Types

Whilst exploring possible research directions, it became clear that an important aspect of any advanced amortized analysis is static derivation of the sizes of data structures. More specifically, the relation between the sizes of the argument and the size of the result of a function has to be known. The size of a data structure, for now, is the number of nodes it consists of.

As a first result we have designed a pure size-aware type system, which is obtained from the one presented in section 3.5.3 by erasing credit functions and resource constants [18]. This type system treats *non-monotonic* polynomial size dependencies. We have shown that, in general, type-checking for this system is undecidable. Indeed, consider the matching rule. Its nil-branch contains the Diophantine equation that reflects the fact that the list is empty. At the end of type checking one may need to determine if a branch is going to be entered or not. To check this, the Diophantine equations have to be solved. So, type-checking is reducible to *Hilbert's tenth problem* (i.e. existence of an algorithm which given any Diophantine equation decides if it has roots or not). Hilbert's tenth problem is shown to be undecidable [14]. Thus, type checking is undecidable in general.

We have identified a syntactical restriction such that the equations to solve are trivially decidable: let-expressions are not allowed to contain pattern matching as a subexpression.

It is not known whether type inference is decidable for the size-aware system. Technically, it amounts to solving systems of polynomial equations that may be non-linear. So, to infer types we propose an altogether different approach [18]. The idea is simple. First, note that the size dependencies are exact and polynomial. From interpolation theory it is known that any polynomial of finite degree is determined by a finite number of data points. Hence, if a degree of the polynomial is assumed and enough pairs of input-output sizes are measured by running the function on test-data a hypothesis for the size equations can be determined. If size dependency has indeed the type assumed, checking the hypothesis in the type system gives a positive result. By repeating the process for increasing degrees, the sized type for a function definition will eventually be found, if the function is typable. In case it does not exist, or the function does not terminate, the procedure does not terminate. Thus, the sized-type inference problem is *semi-decidable* for terminating functions. Complete shape-checking and inference procedures, even for the expressions subject to the syntactic condition, cannot exist. So, the type system is incomplete; non-termination due to absence of a type means either that the function is not shapely, or shapely, but not typable. However, a large non-trivial class of shapely functions is typable in the system.

A further development of this system would, amongst others, include an adaptation to upper and lower bounds and support for other data structures.

3.6   RELATED WORK

The presented combination of amortization and types generalizes the approach from [10] which forms the foundational basis of the EU funded project *Mobile Resource Guarantees* [16]. The project "has developed the infrastructure needed to endow mobile code with independently verifiable certificates describing its resource behavior (space, time)." Its functional language *Camelot* is an implementation of the underlying language from [10]. A Camelot program is compiled into *Grail*, which a structured version of the Java Byte Code. The high-level type system is mirrored in a specialized heap-aware Hoare logic for the byte-code.

The **AHA** project can be considered as one of the successors of MRG. Firstly, it is aimed to extend the high-level type system of MRG to type-systems for non-linear heap consumption bounds. Secondly, applications of the methodology to object-oriented programming will involve MRG experience with the byte-code: one considers imperative object-oriented structures that have counterparts in functional programming. Finally, soundness of the type systems, type-checking and inferences procedures, object-oriented extensions will be implemented in an environment similar to the program-logic environment designed for MRG.

MRG has a few other successors. First, one should mention a large consortium *Mobius* [4], which, as well as MRG, runs under EU framework *Global Computing*. Its aim is to design a byte-code verification tool that allows to employ a large variety of formal methods. The byte-code properties of interest include information flows and resource consumption.

The aims of the *EmBounded* project [9] are "to identify, to quantify and to certify resource-bounded code in Hume, a domain-specific high-level programming language for real-time embedded systems." The project develops static analyzes for time and space consumption, involving size and effect type systems. The foundational results have realistic applications for embedded systems.

The *ReQueSt* project [2], funded by UK government's agency EPSRC, aims to prevent abrupt lack-of-memory termination of an expensive user's request in a GRID application.

Together, these projects seem to constitute an upcoming resource consumption trend in functional programming research.

3.7 CONCLUSION

The **AHA** project aims to contribute to the analysis of the resource consumption by improving the state of the art in inferring upper bounds for heap-space usage. Improvements lie in the complexity of the bounds and the applicability to widely used languages. Ultimately, we want to implement both a type checking and a type inference system for heap space usage bounds of lazy functional and imperative programs.

3.8 ACKNOWLEDGEMENTS

We would like to thank Martin Hofmann for the foundational results that inspired this project and the anonymous reviewers for their helpful comments and suggestions.

REFERENCES

[1] D. Aspinalll and M. Hofmann. Another type system for in-place update. In *ESOP'2002*, volume 2305 of *LNCS*, pages 36 – 52, 2002.

[2] R. Atkey and K. MacKenzie. Request: Resource quantification for e-science technologies. In *International Workshop on Proof-Carrying Code*, 2006.

[3] E. Barendsen and S. Smetsers. Uniqueness typing for functional languages with graph rewriting semantics. *Mathematical Structures in Computer Science*, 6:579–612, 1996.

[4] G. Barthe, L. Beringer, P. Crégut, B. Grégoire, M. Hofmann, P. Müller, E. Poll, G. Puebla, I. Stark, and E. Vétillard. Mobius: Mobility, ubiquity, security. Objectives and progress report. In *TGC 2006: Proceedings of the second symposium on Trustworthy Global Computing*, LNCS. Springer-Verlag, 2007. To appear.

[5] J. van den Berg, M. Huisman, B. Jacobs, and E. Poll. A type-theoretic memory model for verification of sequential Java programs. In D. Bert and C. Choppy, editors, *Recent Trends in Algebraic Development Techniques (WADT'99)*, volume 1827 of *LNCS*. Springer, 2000.

[6] V. Braberman, D. Garbervetsky, and S. Yovine. A static analysis for synthesizing parametric specifications of dynamic memory consumption. *Journal of Object Technology*, 5(5):31–58, June 2006.

[7] W.-N. Chin, H. H. Nguen, S. Qin, and M. Rinard. Predictable memory usage for object-oriented programs. Technical report, National University of Singapore, Massachusetts Institute of Technology, 2004.

[8] T. H. Cormen, C. E. Leiserson, R. L. Rivest, and Cliff Steinet. *Introduction to algorithms*. MIT press, 2001.

[9] K. Hammond, R. Dyckhoff, Ch. Ferdinand, R. Heckmann, M. Hofmann, S. Jost, H.-W. Loidl, G. Michaelson, R. Pointon, N. Scaife, J.Sérot, and A. Wallace. Project start paper: The embounded project. In Marko van Eekelen, editor, *Trends in Functional Programming*, volume 6, pages 195–210. Intellect.

[10] M. Hofmann and S. Jost. Static prediction of heap space usage for first-order functional programs. In *Proceedings of the 30th ACM Symposium on Principles of Programming Languages*, volume 38-1, pages 185–197. ACM Press, 2003.

[11] B. Jacobs and E. Poll. Java program verification at Nijmegen: Developments and perspective. In *International Symposium on Software Security (ISSS'2003), Tokyo, Japan*, LNCS, pages 134–153. Springer, 2004.

[12] M. Konechny. Typing with conditions and guarantees for functional in-place update. In *TYPES 2002 Workshop, Nijmegen*, volume 2646 of *LNCS*, pages 182 – 199. Springer, 2003.

[13] H.-W. Loidl and K. MacKenzie. *A Gentle Introduction to Camelot*, September 2004. http://groups.inf.ed.ac.uk/mrg/camelot/Gentle-Camelot/.

[14] Yu. Matiyasevich and J. P. Jones. Proof of recursive unsolvability of Hilbert's tenth problem. *American Mathematical Monthly*, 98(10):689–709, October 1991.

[15] Ch. Okasaki. *Purely Functional Data Structures*. Cambridge University Press, 1998.

[16] D. Sanella, M. Hofmann, D. Aspinall, S. Gilmore, I. Stark, L. Beringer, H.-W. Loidl, K. MacKenzie, A. Momigliano, and O. Shkaravska. Project evaluation paper: Mobile resource guarantees. In Marko van Eekelen, editor, *Trends in Functional Programming*, volume 6, pages 211–226. Intellect.

[17] B. Schoenmakers. *Data Structures and Amortized Complexity in a Functional Setting*. PhD thesis, Eindhoven University of Technology, September 1992.

[18] O. Shkaravska, R. van Kesteren, and M. van Eekelen. Polynomial size analysis for first-order functions. In S. Ronchi Della Rocca, editor, *Typed Lambda Calculi and Applications (TLCA'2007), Paris, France*, volume 4583 of *LNCS*, pages 351 – 366. Springer, 2007.

Chapter 4

Unifying Hybrid Types and Contracts

Jessica Gronski[1], Cormac Flanagan[1]

Abstract: Contract systems and hybrid type systems provide alternative approaches for enforcing precisely defined interface specifications, with complementary advantages: contract systems excel at blame assignment, whereas hybrid type systems support type-based static analysis.

We unify these two approaches by demonstrating that hybrid type checking is sufficiently expressive to encode higher-order contracts with proper blame assignment. In particular, a contract obligation that enforces both sides of a contract is decomposed into *two* type casts that each enforce one side of the contract. This expressiveness result provides several benefits, including allowing one of these casts to be lifted from variable references to variable definitions, resulting in improved contract coverage and removing the need for privileged contract obligations.

4.1 INTRODUCTION

The development of large software systems requires a modular development strategy where software modules communicate via well-understood interfaces. Ideally, these interfaces should be formally specified and mechanically enforced in order to detect, isolate, and localize software errors. Static type systems and dynamic contract systems [6] are two complementary approaches for enforcing software interfaces. Recent work on hybrid type checking [7] combines these two approaches, providing both the expressiveness benefits of contract systems while still verifying or refuting many properties at compile time, much like traditional type systems.

A key feature of modern contract systems is that they excel at *blame assignment*. Each contract obligation contains the labels of both modules that are party to that contract, so that the appropriate module can be blamed for any contract vio-

---

[1]University of California Santa Cruz, 1156 High Street, Santa Cruz, CA 95064, USA

lation. Blame assignment works correctly even in the presence of complex control and data-flow operations involving higher-order functions, callbacks, etc. In large software systems, this ability to not only detect but also to localize software errors is extremely important.

For hybrid type systems, however, the analogous *type cast* operation contains only one module label (instead of two). This difference suggests that hybrid type systems are weaker at blame assignment, and, in this sense, fundamentally less expressive than contract systems [4].

This paper investigates the relationship between contract systems and hybrid type systems. We work in the context of two idealized languages: a contract language λ^C (based on λ^{Con} [6]) and the hybrid-typed language λ^H [7]. Surprisingly, we show that λ^H is sufficiently powerful to express all λ^C programs. In particular, the doubly labeled contract obligation of λ^C (which enforces both sides of a contract) is equivalent to *two* singly labeled type casts in λ^H (each of which enforces only one side of the contract). Prior work showed that contracts can naturally be implemented as pairs of projections, each with a single blame label [5]. This paper carries that development one step further, by showing that the type casts of λ^H exactly provide this projection functionality. Moreover, we believe that reifying these projections as a syntactic construct in the language provides additional flexibility and clarity.

In addition to our main expressiveness result, this connection between contract systems and hybrid type systems provides a formal foundation for understanding the relationship between these two approaches, which we hope will facilitate further cross-pollination between these domains. In particular, our result suggests that the static-analysis machinery of hybrid type systems (including recent results on the decidability of type inference [11]) could be applicable to λ^C contracts and programs, perhaps strengthening existing contract-based analysis [16].

An immediate benefit of expressing a λ^C contract as two λ^H casts is that it allows one of these casts to be lifted or *refactored* from the reference to an exported variable to the definition of that variable, which provides earlier error detection and improved contract coverage over λ^C.[2] This refactoring means that the type of each exported variable explicates the contract on that variable. In addition, this refactoring allows *privileged* contract obligations to be replaced by unprivileged type casts. That is, contract obligations are privileged in that a contract obligation in one module may need to assign blame to a different module, and so contract obligations should be inserted only by a trusted pre-processor or *elaborator*, and should not be present in source programs. A type cast is unprivileged if it only blames its containing module. In the refactored λ^H program, each module only contains unprivileged type casts that dynamically enforce that module's side of each contract. The λ^H type system then ensures, via assume-guarantee reasoning, that any assumption one module makes about a second module is guaranteed via dynamic type casts in that second module.

---

[2]DrScheme's projection-based implementation of contracts includes a similar optimization [5].

Figure 4.1: λ^C Syntax and Evaluation Rules

$$
\begin{array}{lll}
B & ::= Int \mid Bool & \textit{Base Types} \\
T & ::= B \mid T \to T & \textit{Types} \\
c & ::= \texttt{contract } B\ v \mid c \mapsto c & \textit{Contracts} \\
t & ::= v \mid t\ t \mid \texttt{let}^l\ x : T : c = t \texttt{ in } t \mid \texttt{blame}(l) \mid t^{c,l,l'} & \textit{Expressions} \\
v & ::= x \mid k \mid \lambda x : T.t \mid v^{c \to c,l,l'} & \textit{Values} \\
k & ::= + \mid - \mid < \mid > \mid = \mid 0 \mid 1 \mid \ldots & \textit{Constants}
\end{array}
$$

Evaluation Contexts $\qquad\qquad\qquad\qquad\qquad\qquad\qquad\boxed{E}$

$$
E = \bullet\ t \mid v\ \bullet \mid \texttt{let}^l\ x : T : c = \bullet \texttt{ in } t \mid \bullet^{c,l,l'}
$$

Evaluation Rules $\qquad\qquad\qquad\qquad\qquad\qquad\qquad\boxed{t \to_c t'}$

$$
\begin{array}{lll}
k\ v \to_c [\![k]\!]\ (v) & & [\text{E-Const}] \\
(\lambda x : T.t)\ v \to_c t[x := v] & & [\text{E-Beta}] \\
\texttt{let}^l\ x : T : c = v \texttt{ in } t \to_c t[x := v] & & [\text{E-Let}] \\
v^{\texttt{contract } B\ v',l,l'} \to_c v & \text{if } v'\ v \to_c^* \texttt{true} & [\text{E-Ok}] \\
v^{\texttt{contract } B\ v',l,l'} \to_c \texttt{blame}(l) & \text{if } v'\ v \to_c^* \texttt{false} & [\text{E-Fail}] \\
v^{c \to c',l,l'}\ v' \to_c [v\ (v'^{c,l',l})]^{c',l,l'} & & [\text{E-Fun}] \\
E[t_1] \to_c E[t_2] & \text{if } t_1 \to_c t_2 & [\text{E-Compat}] \\
E[\texttt{blame}(l)] \to_c \texttt{blame}(l) & & [\text{E-Blame}]
\end{array}
$$

In the remainder of the paper, we first briefly review the two languages being compared, λ^C and λ^H, in Sections 4.2 and 4.3, respectively. Section 4.4 describes our translation from contracts to types. Section 4.5 shows how λ^H enables a notion of lifting that improves contract coverage. Section 4.6 proves the correctness of our translation. We conclude with a discussion of related work.

4.2   THE CONTRACT LANGUAGE λ^C

We begin by reviewing λ^C (see Figure 4.1), which extends the simply typed lambda calculus with contracts along the lines of Findler and Felleisen [6]. The language is typed and includes both base types B (*Int* and *Bool*) and function types $T \to T$. In addition to these simple types, the language includes contracts that more precisely define module interfaces[3]. A base contract (`contract` $B\ v$) describes the set of values of base type B that also satisfy the predicate v of type $B \to Bool$. A function contract $c \mapsto c'$ describes functions that take an argument satisfying contract c and return values satisfying contract c'.

A key goal of the contract system is to attribute blame for contract violations to particular program modules. To avoid complicating the language with a module system, λ^C modules are defined via let expressions. That is,

$$
\texttt{let}^l\ x : T : c = t_1 \texttt{ in } t_2
$$

---

[3]Other languages, such as Eiffel [18], also include both types and contracts.

defines a module t_1 identified by label l, that exports a variable x of type T and contract c. Code outside a let-bound expression is part of the *main* module.

Before execution, a λ^C program is first pre-processed (or *elaborated*) so that each reference to the above let-bound variable x from a different module l' is replaced by the *contract obligation* $x^{c,l,l'}$. A contract obligation enforces the contract c, and blames any contract violation on either the *server* module l that exports x or the *client* module l' that imports x.

The evaluation rules of λ^C programs are mostly straightforward: see Figure 4.1. The rule [E-CONST] relies on the auxiliary partial function $[\![k]\!] : Expression \rightarrow Expression$ to define the semantics of constant functions. For example, $[\![+]\!](3) = +_3$ and $[\![+_3]\!](4) = 7$. The rules [E-BETA] and [E-LET] perform by-value evaluation of function applications and let expressions. The rule [E-COMPAT] compatibly closes the evaluation relation $\rightarrow_c$ over the evaluation context E.

The more interesting rules are those for evaluating a contract obligation $v^{c,l,l'}$. If c is a base contract $(\texttt{contract } B \; v')$ and $(v' \; v)$ evaluates to $\texttt{false}$, then the contract obligation reduces, via [E-FAIL], to $\texttt{blame}(l)$, which blames the server l for providing an inappropriate value v for x. Otherwise, if $(v' \; v)$ evaluates to $\texttt{true}$, then the contract is fulfilled and the rule [E-OK] removes the contract obligation from v. If c is a function contract $c \mapsto c'$, then $v^{c \mapsto c',l,l'}$ is considered a value. Once this value is applied to an argument, the obligation decomposes into two smaller obligations on the argument and the result of v, via [E-FUN].

The λ^C type system is defined via the usual judgement $\Gamma \vdash t : T$, which states that the expression t has type T in environment Γ. The auxiliary judgement $\Gamma \vdash_c c : T$ checks that the contract c is applicable to values of type T. The rules defining these two judgements are mostly straightforward: see Figure 4.2.

To illustrate the operational semantics of contracts, consider the following elaborated program P:

$$\texttt{let}^f \; f : (Int \rightarrow Int) : (cNeg \mapsto cPos) = \lambda x : Int.x \; \texttt{in}$$
$$\texttt{let}^m \; m : Int : cPos = f^{cNeg \mapsto cPos,f,m} \; 4 \; \texttt{in} \; m^{cPos,m,main}$$

where

$$cPos = (\texttt{contract } Int \; (\lambda x : Int.x > 0))$$
$$cNeg = (\texttt{contract } Int \; (\lambda x : Int.x < 0))$$

This example includes two modules, f and m, where we label each module according to its exported variable. This program is evaluated as follows, where, for clarity, we shade each contract obligation grey or white, according to whether the obligation occurs on an expression produced by the module f or m, respectively.

$$P \rightarrow_c \texttt{let}^m \; m : Int : cPos = (\lambda x : Int.x)^{cNeg \mapsto cPos,f,m} \; 4 \; \texttt{in} \; m^{cPos,m,main}$$
$$\rightarrow_c \texttt{let}^m \; m : Int : cPos = [(\lambda x : Int.x) \; 4^{cNeg,m,f}]^{cPos,f,m} \; \texttt{in} \; m^{cPos,m,main}$$
$$\rightarrow_c \texttt{let}^m \; m : Int : cPos = [(\lambda x : Int.x) \; \texttt{blame}(m)]^{cPos,f,m} \; \texttt{in} \; m^{cPos,m,main}$$
$$\rightarrow_c \texttt{blame}(m)$$

In this case, the contract obligation $4^{cNeg,m,f}$ fails and the contract labels indicate that the error originated in module m, which violated the contract $cNeg \mapsto cPos$ of module f. Alternatively, if the literal 4 is replaced with -4, the first contract

Figure 4.2: λ^C **Type Rules**

Type Environment $\boxed{\Gamma}$

$$\Gamma ::= \emptyset \mid \Gamma, x : T$$

Type rules $\boxed{\Gamma \vdash t : T}$

$$\frac{[\text{T-VAR}]}{x : T \in \Gamma} \qquad \frac{[\text{T-CONST}]}{\Gamma \vdash x : T} \qquad \frac{[\text{T-LAM}]}{\Gamma, x : T_1 \vdash t : T_2}$$
$$\frac{x : T \in \Gamma}{\Gamma \vdash x : T} \qquad \frac{}{\Gamma \vdash k : ty(k)} \qquad \frac{\Gamma, x : T_1 \vdash t : T_2}{\Gamma \vdash (\lambda x : T_1 . t) : (T_1 \rightarrow T_2)}$$

$$\frac{[\text{T-APP}]}{\Gamma \vdash t_1 : (T_1 \rightarrow T_2) \quad \Gamma \vdash t_2 : T_1} \qquad \frac{[\text{T-LET}]}{\Gamma \vdash t_1 : T_1 \quad \Gamma \vdash_c c : T_1 \quad \Gamma, x : T_1 \vdash t_2 : T_2}$$
$$\frac{\Gamma \vdash t_1 : (T_1 \rightarrow T_2) \quad \Gamma \vdash t_2 : T_1}{\Gamma \vdash t_1 \, t_2 : T_2} \qquad \frac{\Gamma \vdash t_1 : T_1 \quad \Gamma \vdash_c c : T_1 \quad \Gamma, x : T_1 \vdash t_2 : T_2}{\Gamma \vdash \text{let}^l \, x : T_1 : c = t_1 \text{ in } t_2 : T_2}$$

$$\frac{[\text{T-BLAME}]}{\Gamma \vdash \text{blame}(l) : T} \qquad \frac{[\text{T-OBLIG}]}{\Gamma \vdash t : T \quad \Gamma \vdash_c c : T}$$
$$\frac{}{\Gamma \vdash \text{blame}(l) : T} \qquad \frac{\Gamma \vdash t : T \quad \Gamma \vdash_c c : T}{\Gamma \vdash t^{c,l,l'} : T}$$

Contract Type Rules $\boxed{\Gamma \vdash_c c : T}$

$$\frac{[\text{T-BASEC}]}{\Gamma \vdash v : (B \rightarrow Bool)} \qquad \frac{[\text{T-FUNC}]}{\Gamma \vdash_c c : T_1 \quad \Gamma \vdash_c c' : T_2}$$
$$\frac{\Gamma \vdash v : (B \rightarrow Bool)}{\Gamma \vdash_c \text{contract } B \, v : B} \qquad \frac{\Gamma \vdash_c c : T_1 \quad \Gamma \vdash_c c' : T_2}{\Gamma \vdash_c c \mapsto c' : (T_1 \rightarrow T_2)}$$

obligation would succeed and P would evaluate to:

$$\text{let}^m \, m : Int : cPos = \boxed{-4^{cPos,f,m}} \text{ in } m^{cPos,m,main}$$

in this case blaming f for the violation. Although P includes only first-order functions, blame assignment also works in more complicated, higher-order situations where functions are passed as arguments to other functions, etc.

4.3 THE HYBRID-TYPED λ^H CALCULUS

Whereas λ^C incorporates both a static type system and a dynamic contract system, λ^H [7] unifies these two interface specification systems into a single expressive type system.

The syntax of λ^H is shown in Figure 4.3 and includes types (S), expressions (s) and values (w). Types include refinement types of the form $\{x : B \mid s\}$, which describe the set of values of base type B that satisfy the predicate s. For example, $\{x : Int \mid x \geq 0\}$ describes the set of positive numbers. We sometimes use a base type B to abbreviate the trivial refinement type $\{x : B \mid \texttt{true}\}$. In λ^H, types can be enforced dynamically, via a type cast $\langle S_2 \Leftarrow S_1 \rangle^l \, s$. Here the expression s

Figure 4.3: λ^H Syntax

$$
\begin{aligned}
S &::= \{x{:}B\,|\,s\} \mid S \to S & \textit{Types}\\
s &::= w \mid s\,s \mid \mathtt{let}^l\,x:S = s\ \mathtt{in}\ s \mid \mathtt{blame}(l) \mid \langle S \Leftarrow S\rangle^l\,s & \textit{Expressions}\\
w &::= x \mid k \mid \lambda x:S.s \mid \langle S \to S \Leftarrow S \to S\rangle^l\,w & \textit{Values}
\end{aligned}
$$

Evaluation Contexts $\boxed{F}$

$$F ::= \bullet\,s \mid w\,\bullet \mid \mathtt{let}^l\,x:S = \bullet\ \mathtt{in}\ s \mid \langle S_2 \Leftarrow S_1\rangle^l\,\bullet$$

Evaluation Rules $\boxed{s \to_h s'}$

$$
\begin{array}{llr}
k\,w \to_h [\![k]\!]\,(w) & & [\text{F-CONST}]\\[2pt]
(\lambda x:S.\,s)\,w \to_h s[x := w] & & [\text{F-BETA}]\\[2pt]
\mathtt{let}^l\,x:S = w\ \mathtt{in}\ s \to_h s[x := w] & & [\text{F-LET}]\\[2pt]
\langle\{x{:}B\,|\,s_2\} \Leftarrow \{x{:}B\,|\,s_1\}\rangle^l\,w \to_h w & \text{if } s_2[x := w] \to_h^* \mathtt{true} & [\text{F-OK}]\\[2pt]
\langle\{x{:}B\,|\,s_2\} \Leftarrow \{x{:}B\,|\,s_1\}\rangle^l\,w \to_h \mathtt{blame}(l) & \text{if } s_2[x := w] \to_h^* \mathtt{false} & [\text{F-FAIL}]\\[2pt]
(\langle(S_3 \to S_4) \Leftarrow (S_1 \to S_2)\rangle^l\,w)\,w' \to_h \langle S_4 \Leftarrow S_2\rangle^l\,[w\,(\langle S_1 \Leftarrow S_3\rangle^l\,w')] & & [\text{F-FUN}]\\[2pt]
\langle(S_1 \to S_2) \Leftarrow \{x{:}B\,|\,s_1\}\rangle^l\,w \to_h \mathtt{blame}(l) & & [\text{F-BAD1}]\\[2pt]
\langle\{x{:}B\,|\,s_1\} \Leftarrow (S_1 \to S_2)\rangle^l\,w \to_h \mathtt{blame}(l) & & [\text{F-BAD2}]\\[2pt]
F[s_1] \to_h F[s_2] & \text{if } s_1 \to_h s_2 & [\text{F-CTX}]\\[2pt]
F[\mathtt{blame}(l)] \to_h \mathtt{blame}(l) & & [\text{F-BLAME}]
\end{array}
$$

is statically typed as S_1 and the type cast dynamically enforces that the value produced by s also has type S_2; if not, the module labeled l is blamed.

Figure 4.3 defines the evaluation rules for λ^H; of particular interest are the rules for type casts. Casting a value w to a base refinement type $\{x{:}B\,|\,s\}$ involves checking if the predicate $s[x := w]$ evaluates to $\mathtt{true}$.

A function cast $\langle(S_3 \to S_4) \Leftarrow (S_1 \to S_2)\rangle^l\,w$ is considered a value; once an argument w' is supplied, that cast is decomposed into two smaller casts on the function argument and result, via [F-FUN]:

$$(\langle(S_3 \to S_4) \Leftarrow (S_1 \to S_2)\rangle^l\,w)\,w' \to_h \langle S_4 \Leftarrow S_2\rangle^l\,[w\,(\langle S_1 \Leftarrow S_3\rangle^l\,w')]$$

Function casts involve a subtle mix of static and dynamic reasoning. Since the original function w has type $S_1 \to S_2$, the evaluation rules must ensure that w is only applied to values of type S_1. The argument cast generated by [F-FUN], $\langle S_1 \Leftarrow S_3\rangle^l\,w'$, relies on the type system to ensure that w' has type S_3, and then dynamically casts w' to a value of type S_1. Thus, in the function cast $\langle(S_3 \to S_4) \Leftarrow (S_1 \to S_2)\rangle^l\,w$, the types S_1 and S_4 are enforced dynamically, whereas the type system is responsible for enforcing S_2 and S_3.

The λ^H type system is defined via the judgement $\Delta \vdash s : S$, which states that the expression s has type S in environment Δ: see Figure 4.4. The auxiliary judgement $\Delta \vdash S$ checks that S is a well-formed type. Subtyping between function types is straightforward, via [SUB-FUN]. Subtyping between refinement types is defined via [SUB-BASE]. This rule uses the auxiliary judgement $\Delta \vdash s_1 \Rightarrow s_2$, which states that s_2 is true whenever s_1 is, in any variable substitution that is consistent with the type environment Δ. This notion of consistency between a substitution σ (from variables to values) with an environment Δ is formalized via the final judgement $\Delta \models \sigma$, and we refer the interested reader to [7] for more details.

Type checking for λ^H is in general undecidable. In this paper, however, since we start with well-typed λ^C programs and translate expressions in a manner that is type-preserving, our generated λ^H programs are well-typed by construction.

4.4 EXPRESSING CONTRACTS AS TYPES

We now show that λ^H is sufficiently powerful to express all λ^C programs, including proper attribution of contract violations to appropriate modules.

We begin by translating λ^C types (T) into more expressive λ^H types (S) via the translation $\phi_t : T \rightarrow S$, which adds the trivial refinement predicate $\texttt{true}$ to base types.

$$\phi_t(B) = \{x : B \mid \texttt{true}\}$$
$$\phi_t(T_1 \rightarrow T_2) = \phi_t(T_1) \rightarrow \phi_t(T_2)$$

We also translate λ^C contracts (c) into λ^H types (S) via the translation $\phi_c : c \rightarrow S$, which uses refinement types to emulate contracts.

$$\phi_c(\texttt{contract } B\ v) = \{x : B \mid \phi(v)\,x\} \qquad \text{if } x \notin FV(v)$$
$$\phi_c(c \mapsto c') = \phi_c(c) \rightarrow \phi_c(c')$$

These two translations already shed some light on the relationship between λ^C types and contracts. Suppose that c is a contract over some type T (i.e. $\Gamma \vdash_c c : T$). Since the contract c is a "restriction" of T, we might expect that $\phi_c(c)$ would be a subtype of $\phi_t(T)$. This property holds for base contracts, but not for function contracts, because of the contravariance of function domains. Thus $\phi_c(c)$ and $\phi_t(T)$ may be incomparable under the subtyping relation. The two λ^H types $\phi_c(c)$ and $\phi_t(T)$ are, however, identical in structure, except that $\phi_c(c)$ has more precise refinement predicates. That is, $base(\phi_c(c)) = \phi_t(T)$, where $base : S \rightarrow S$ is a function that strips refinement predicates from λ^H types.

$$base(\{x : B \mid s\}) = \{x : B \mid \texttt{true}\}$$
$$base(S_1 \rightarrow S_2) = base(S_1) \rightarrow base(S_2)$$

Finally, we consider how to translate λ^C expressions into behaviorally equivalent λ^H expressions, and in particular, how to translate the contract obligation in our earlier example P:

$$f^{cNeg \mapsto cPos, f, m}\ 4$$

Recall that f has type $Int \rightarrow Int$. The translated expression $\phi(f)$ should then have type $sInt \rightarrow sInt$, where $sInt$ is the trivial refinement type $\{x : Int \mid \texttt{true}\}$.

As a first attempt we could translate the above contract obligation into a corresponding type cast, yielding the λ^H expression

$$[\langle S \Leftarrow base(S) \rangle^f\ f]\ 4$$

Figure 4.4: λ^H Type Rules

Type Environment $\boxed{\Delta}$

$$\Delta ::= \emptyset \mid \Delta, x : S$$

Type Rules $\boxed{\Delta \vdash s : S}$

[S-VAR]
$$\frac{x : S \in \Delta}{\Delta \vdash x : S}$$

[S-CONST]
$$\frac{}{\Delta \vdash k : ty(k)}$$

[S-LAM]
$$\frac{\Delta \vdash S_1 \quad \Delta, x : S_1 \vdash s : S_2}{\Delta \vdash (\lambda x : S_1 . s) : (S_1 \to S_2)}$$

[S-APP]
$$\frac{\Delta \vdash s_1 : (S_1 \to S_2) \quad \Delta \vdash s_2 : S_1}{\Delta \vdash s_1\, s_2 : S_2}$$

[S-LET]
$$\frac{\Delta \vdash s_1 : S_1 \quad \Delta, x : S_1 \vdash s_2 : S_2[x := s_1]}{\Delta \vdash \texttt{let}^l\, x : S_1 = s_1 \texttt{ in } s_2 : S_2[x := s_1]}$$

[S-BLAME]
$$\frac{\Delta \vdash S}{\Delta \vdash \texttt{blame}(l) : S}$$

[S-CAST]
$$\frac{\Delta \vdash S_2 \quad \Delta \vdash s : S_1}{\Delta \vdash \langle S_2 \Leftarrow S_1 \rangle^l\, s : S_2}$$

[S-SUB]
$$\frac{\Delta \vdash s : S_1 \quad \Delta \vdash S_2 \quad \Delta \vdash S_1 <: S_2}{\Delta \vdash s : S_2}$$

Well-Formed Types $\boxed{\Delta \vdash S}$

[WF-FUN]
$$\frac{\Delta \vdash S_1 \quad \Delta \vdash S_2}{\Delta \vdash (S_1 \to S_2)}$$

[WF-BASE]
$$\frac{\Delta, x : B \vdash s : Bool}{\Delta \vdash \{x : B \mid s\}}$$

Subtyping $\boxed{\Delta \vdash S_1 <: S_2}$

[SUB-FUN]
$$\frac{\Delta \vdash S_3 <: S_1 \quad \Delta \vdash S_2 <: S_4}{\Delta \vdash (S_1 \to S_2) <: (S_3 \to S_4)}$$

[SUB-BASE]
$$\frac{\Delta, x : B \vdash s_1 \Rightarrow s_2}{\Delta \vdash \{x : B \mid s_1\} <: \{x : B \mid s_2\}}$$

Implication Rule $\boxed{\Delta \vdash s_1 \Rightarrow s_2}$

[IMP]
$$\frac{\forall \sigma.\, (\Delta \models \sigma \text{ and } \sigma(s_1) \to_h^* \texttt{true implies } \sigma(s_2) \to_h^* \texttt{true})}{\Delta \vdash s_1 \Rightarrow s_2}$$

Consistent Substitutions $\boxed{\Delta \models \sigma}$

[CS-EMPTY]
$$\frac{}{\emptyset \models \emptyset}$$

[CS-EXT]
$$\frac{\emptyset \vdash s : S \quad (x := s)\Delta \models \sigma}{x : S, \Delta \models (x := s)\sigma}$$

where

$$S = (sNeg \rightarrow sPos) \qquad\qquad sNeg = \phi_c(cNeg)$$
$$base(S) = (sInt \rightarrow sInt) \qquad\qquad sPos = \phi_c(cPos)$$

This translation has two problems, however. First, it retains only one blame label, resulting in incorrect blame assignment. Second, and more importantly, the translated program is ill-typed, since the casted function has type $S = sNeg \rightarrow sPos$, and so should not be applied to 4, an expression of type $sInt$. Thus, this program is both ill-typed and also no longer enforces the original $cNeg$ domain contract.

To solve both these problems, we introduce a second type cast to dynamically enforce the domain part of function contracts, yielding the translated λ^H program:

$$[\langle base(S) \Leftarrow S \rangle^m \, (\langle S \Leftarrow base(S) \rangle^f \, f)] \, 4$$

Thus, given f of type $base(S) = (sInt \rightarrow sInt)$, the first type cast $\langle S \Leftarrow base(S) \rangle^f$ dynamically ensures the covariant property, that the function only returns positive integers, but relies on the type system to ensure the contravariant property, that the casted function is only applied to negative integers. The second type cast $\langle base(S) \Leftarrow S \rangle^m$ dynamically fulfills this second obligation, producing a function of type $(sInt \rightarrow sInt)$ that statically may be applied to any integer, but dynamically fails and blames module m if ever given non-negative arguments. Together, these two type casts exactly enforce the semantics of the original λ^C contract obligation, with correct blame assignment.

The complete translation $\phi : t \rightarrow s$ from λ^C expressions to λ^H expressions is then the compatible closure of this rule for translating contract obligations:

$$\phi(t^{c,l,l'}) = \langle base(S) \Leftarrow S \rangle^{l'} \langle S \Leftarrow base(S) \rangle^l \phi(t) \quad \text{where } S = \phi_c(c)$$
$$\phi(x) = x$$
$$\phi(k) = k$$
$$\phi(\lambda x : T.t) = \lambda x : \phi_t(T).\phi(t)$$
$$\phi(t_1 \, t_2) = \phi(t_1) \, \phi(t_2)$$
$$\phi(\texttt{let}^l \, x : T : c = t_1 \texttt{ in } t_2) = \texttt{let}^l \, x : \phi_t(T) = \phi(t_1) \texttt{ in } \phi(t_2)$$
$$\phi(\texttt{blame}(l)) = \texttt{blame}(l)$$

4.4.1   Example

To illustrate this translation, consider the translation of the earlier example $\phi(P)$:

$$\texttt{let}^f \, f : (sInt \rightarrow sInt) = \lambda x : sInt.x \texttt{ in}$$
$$\texttt{let}^m \, m : sInt = [\langle base(S) \Leftarrow S \rangle^m \langle S \Leftarrow base(S) \rangle^f \, f] \, 4 \texttt{ in}$$
$$\langle sInt \Leftarrow sPos \rangle^{main} \langle sPos \Leftarrow sInt \rangle^m \, m$$

where the λ^H type $S = sNeg \rightarrow sPos$ encodes the original contract. Note that $\phi(P)$ mostly includes only simple types; precise refinement types are only used in casts to implement contract obligations in the original program. These precise refinement types occur in matched pairs such as $\langle sInt \Leftarrow sPos \rangle^{main} \langle sPos \Leftarrow sInt \rangle^m \, m$, where the precise type $sPos$ is first dynamically enforced and then statically assumed. Note that the base contract $cPos$ on module m has no contravariant component, and so the second resulting type cast $\langle sInt \Leftarrow sPos \rangle^{main}$ is actually an up-cast, and could be optimized away. That is, the second cast is only necessary for function contracts that involve bidirectional communication between modules.

The program $\phi(P)$ evaluates as follows, correctly blaming m:

$$\rightarrow_h \texttt{let}^m \; m : sInt = [\langle base(S) \Leftarrow S \rangle^m \langle S \Leftarrow base(S) \rangle^f (\lambda x : sInt . x)] \; 4 \; \texttt{in} \; \ldots$$
$$\rightarrow_h \texttt{let}^m \; m : sInt =$$
$$\quad \langle sInt \Leftarrow sPos \rangle^m ([\langle S \Leftarrow base(S) \rangle^f (\lambda x : sInt . x)] \; \langle sNeg \Leftarrow sInt \rangle^m 4) \; \texttt{in} \; \ldots$$
$$\rightarrow_h \texttt{let}^m \; m : sInt = \langle sInt \Leftarrow sPos \rangle^m ([\langle S \Leftarrow base(S) \rangle^f (\lambda x : sInt . x)] \; \texttt{blame}(m)) \; \ldots$$
$$\rightarrow_h \texttt{blame}(m)$$

Conversely, if the literal 4 were replaced with -4, then $\phi(P)$ would evaluate as follows, blaming f:

$$\texttt{let}^m \; m : sInt = \langle sInt \Leftarrow sPos \rangle^m \langle sPos \Leftarrow sInt \rangle^f (-4) \; \texttt{in} \; \ldots$$

4.5   IMPROVING CONTRACT COVERAGE

In the above program $\phi(P)$, every reference to an exported variable, such as f, is enclosed in a cast, such as $\langle S \Leftarrow base(S) \rangle^f \; f$, which does not mention the client module. Hence, we could refactor this program to avoid repeatedly re-checking these casts at each reference of an exported variable, and instead check those casts only once, as variables are exported.

$$\texttt{let}^f \; f : S = \langle S \Leftarrow base(S) \rangle^f \; (\lambda x : sInt . x) \; \texttt{in}$$
$$\texttt{let}^m \; m : sPos = \langle sPos \Leftarrow sInt \rangle^m [(\langle base(S) \Leftarrow S \rangle^m \; f) \; 4] \; \texttt{in} \; m$$

In this refactored program (with up-casts optimized away), the "contract" on the exported variable f is explicated via the precise type $S = sNeg \rightarrow sPos$; this precise type is enforced via the dynamic type cast $\langle S \Leftarrow base(S) \rangle^f$ inside module f. The second cast $\langle base(S) \Leftarrow S \rangle^m \; f$ remains in the client module m to detect attempts by m to pass incorrect arguments to f.

This refactoring yields two main advantages. First, evaluating the cast $\langle S \Leftarrow base(S) \rangle^f$ only once instead of multiple times may result in better performance. Second, the refactoring provides earlier, and hence better, error detection.

To illustrate this idea, consider the following λ^C program, where the module f exports the literal 4, in clear violation of its $cNeg$ contract:

$$P' = \texttt{let}^f \; f : Int : cNeg = 4 \; \texttt{in} \; \ldots \; (f^{cNeg, f, main}) \; \ldots$$

In both this program and the corresponding λ^H program $\phi(P')$, the contract violation is not actually detected unless the contract obligation $f^{cNeg, f, main}$ is evaluated, which may of course only happen when certain code paths are exercised. In contrast, the refactored λ^H version of this program:

$$\texttt{let}^f \; f : sNeg = \langle sNeg \Leftarrow sInt \rangle^f \; 4 \; \texttt{in} \; \ldots \; \langle sInt \Leftarrow sNeg \rangle^{main} \; f \; \ldots$$

would detect this error immediately. Thus, the refactoring enabled by the translation to λ^H permits somewhat increased *contract coverage* over λ^C.

4.6   CORRECTNESS OF THE TRANSLATION

We now prove that ϕ is a semantics preserving translation. First, ϕ is type-preserving in that it maps well-typed λ^C expressions to well-typed λ^H expressions. The formal statement and proof of this property relies on an auxiliary function ϕ_Γ that maps λ^C type environments to λ^H type environments by translating the types in the bindings.

$$\phi_\Gamma(\emptyset) = \emptyset$$
$$\phi_\Gamma(\Gamma, x : T) = \phi_\Gamma(\Gamma), x : \phi_t(T)$$

Theorem 4.1 (Type Preservation).

1. If $\Gamma \vdash t : T$ then $\phi_\Gamma(\Gamma) \vdash \phi(t) : \phi_t(T)$

2. If $\Gamma \vdash_c c : T$ then $\phi_\Gamma(\Gamma) \vdash \phi_c(c)$

Second, the translation ϕ also preserves the operational semantics in that if a λ^C expression t evaluates to t', then the translation $\phi(t)$ evaluates in λ^H to some expression s that is also reachable from $\phi(t')$.

Theorem 4.2 (Behavioral Equivalence). *If $t \rightarrow_c^* t'$ then $\exists s$ such that $\phi(t) \rightarrow_h^* s$ and $\phi(t') \rightarrow_h^* s$.*

4.7   RELATED AND FUTURE WORK

The enforcement of complex program specifications, or *contracts*, is the subject of a large body of prior work [1, 5, 6, 9, 10, 12, 13, 14, 17, 20]. Since these contracts are typically not expressible in classical type systems, they have previously been relegated to dynamic checking, as in, for example, Eiffel [17]. Eiffel's expressive contract language is strictly separated from its type system. The Bigloo Scheme compiler [21] introduced higher-order contracts. Findler and Felleisen [6] describe λ^{Con}, a language with a higher-order contract system that provides an elegant way to introduce, propagate, and enforce contracts, and to assign blame appropriately. Blume and McAllester [2] model λ^{Con} in order to prove the soundness of the contract checker and extend the system with recursive contracts. Recently, Mathews and Findler [15] have employed higher order contracts, there called *cross-language casts*, to protect type invariants in multi-language systems. Their work also employs a hybrid approach by using the guarantees of the ML type system to eliminate some cross-language casts.

   Work on advanced type systems influenced our choice of how to express program invariants in λ^H. In particular, Freeman and Pfenning [8] extended ML with another form of refinement types. Their work focuses on providing both decidable type checking and type inference, instead of on supporting arbitrary refinement predicates. Xi and Pfenning have explored applications of dependent types in Dependent ML [22, 23]. In a complementary approach, Chen and Xi [3] address decidability limitations by providing a mechanism through which the programmer can provide proofs of subtle properties in the source code. Recently, Ou et al. [19] developed a dependent type system that leverages dynamic checks. In comparison to λ^H, their system is less expressive but decidable, and they leverage dynamic checks to reduce the need for precise type annotations in explicitly labeled regions of programs. Finally, unlike λ^H, Ou et al.'s system considers mutable data.

This paper attempts to connect these two fields of study by developing a formal connection between type systems and contract systems, and by showing how hybrid type system can express higher-order contracts obligations with precise blame assignment.

Recently, Meunier et al. investigated statically verifying contracts via set-based analysis [16], and Findler and Blume [5] defined a partial-order for higher-order contracts that is contravariant in the domain. These ideas appear closely related to the corresponding notions of type inference and subtyping in type theory. We plan to use the framework of this paper to formally explore these kinds of deep connections between contract theory and type theory. Further cross-pollination between these two fields may yield additional contributions to type theory, and may also help apply existing type theory to contract-based programs.

Acknowledgements   We would like to thank Robby Findler and Matthias Felleisen for valuable feedback on this paper. This work was supported by a Sloan Fellowship and by NSF grant CCR-0341179.

A   PROOF OF TYPE PRESERVATION

The proof of type preservation relies on following two simple lemmas:

Lemma 4.3 (Well-Formed Translations). $\forall \Delta, T.\ \Delta \vdash \phi_t(T)$

Lemma 4.4. *If* $\Gamma \vdash_c c : T$ *then* $base(\phi_c(c)) = \phi_t(T)$

Assumption 1 *Let* ty^C *and* ty^H *be the constant typing functions for* λ^C *and* λ^H *respectively. We assume that* $\forall k.\ ty^H(k) <: \phi_t(ty^C(k))$. *Also, following [7], we assume that each basic constant is assigned a singleton type that denotes exactly that constant. For example,* $ty^H(3) = \{x : Int \mid x = 3\}$.

Restatement of Theorem 4.1 (Type Preservation)

1. If $\Gamma \vdash t : T$ *then* $\phi_\Gamma(\Gamma) \vdash \phi(t) : \phi_t(T)$

2. If $\Gamma \vdash_c c : T$ *then* $\phi_\Gamma(\Gamma) \vdash \phi_c(c)$

Proof. The proof is an induction on the type derivation for $\Gamma \vdash t : T$ and $\Gamma \vdash_c c : T$.

1. [T-LAM] Suppose $\Gamma \vdash (\lambda x : T_1.t) : (T_1 \to T_2)$. Then $\Gamma, x : T_1 \vdash t : T_2$.
   By induction, $\phi_\Gamma(\Gamma), x : \phi_t(T_1) \vdash \phi(t) : \phi_t(T_2)$.
   By Lemma 4.3, $\phi_\Gamma(\Gamma) \vdash \phi_t(T_1)$.
   Hence, $\phi_\Gamma(\Gamma) \vdash \phi(\lambda x : T_1.t) : (\phi_t(T_1) \to \phi_t(T_2))$ via [S-LAM].

   [T-CONST] Suppose $\Gamma \vdash k : ty^C(k)$.
   By Assumption 1, $\phi_\Gamma(\Gamma) \vdash k : ty^H(k)$, via [S-CONST].

   [T-VAR] Suppose $\Gamma \vdash x : T$. Then $x : T \in \Gamma$.
   By construction, $x : \phi_t(T) \in \phi_\Gamma(\Gamma)$.
   Hence, $\phi_\Gamma(\Gamma) \vdash x : \phi_t(T)$ via [S-VAR].

   [T-APP] Suppose $\Gamma \vdash t_1\, t_2 : T_2$. Then $\Gamma \vdash t_1 : (T_1 \to T_2)$ and $\Gamma \vdash t_2 : T_1$.
   By induction, $\phi_\Gamma(\Gamma) \vdash \phi(t_1) : (\phi_t(T_1) \to \phi_t(T_2))$ and $\phi_\Gamma(\Gamma) \vdash \phi(t_2) : \phi_t(T_1)$.
   Hence, $\phi_\Gamma(\Gamma) \vdash \phi(t_1\, t_2) : \phi_t(T_2)$ via [S-APP].

   [T-LET] Suppose $\Gamma \vdash \mathtt{let}^l\ x : T_1 : c = t_1\ \mathtt{in}\ t_2 : T_2$. Then $\Gamma \vdash t_1 : T_1$ and $\Gamma, x : T_1 \vdash t_2 : T_2$.
   By induction, $\phi_\Gamma(\Gamma) \vdash \phi(t_1) : \phi_t(T_1)$ and $\phi_\Gamma(\Gamma), x : \phi_t(T_1) \vdash \phi(t_2) : \phi_t(T_2)$.
   Hence, $\phi_\Gamma(\Gamma) \vdash \phi(\mathtt{let}^l\ x : T_1 : c = t_1\ \mathtt{in}\ t_2) : \phi_t(T_2)$, via [S-LET] since $x \notin FV(\phi_t(T_2))$.

   [T-BLAME] Suppose $\Gamma \vdash \mathtt{blame}(l) : T$. Then $\phi_\Gamma(\Gamma) \vdash \mathtt{blame}(l) : \phi_t(T)$ via [S-BLAME] and Lemma 4.3.

   [T-OBLIG] Suppose $\Gamma \vdash t^{c,l_1,l_2} : T$. Then $\Gamma \vdash t : T$ and $\Gamma \vdash_c c : T$.
   Let $S = \phi_c(c)$. By Lemma 4.4, $base(S) = \phi_t(T)$.
   Hence, $\phi_\Gamma(\Gamma) \vdash \phi(t) : base(S)$ and $\phi_\Gamma(\Gamma) \vdash S$ by induction.
   By Lemma 4.3, $\phi_\Gamma(\Gamma) \vdash base(S)$.
   Hence via two applications of [S-CAST],
   $\phi_\Gamma(\Gamma) \vdash [\langle base(S) \Leftarrow S \rangle^{l_2} \langle S \Leftarrow base(S) \rangle^{l_1} \phi(t)] : base(S)$
   Or equivalently $\phi_\Gamma(\Gamma) \vdash \phi(t^{c,l_1,l_2}) : \phi_t(T)$.

2. [T-BASEC] Suppose $\Gamma \vdash_c \mathtt{contract}\ B\ v : B$. Then $\Gamma \vdash v : (B \to Bool)$.
   By induction $\phi_\Gamma(\Gamma) \vdash \phi(v) : (B \to Bool)$.
   Let $x \notin FV(\phi(v))$. Then $\phi_\Gamma(\Gamma), x : B \vdash \phi(v) : (B \to Bool)$.
   By [S-FUN], $\phi_\Gamma(\Gamma), x : B \vdash \phi(v)\, x : Bool$.
   By [WF-BASE], $\phi_\Gamma(\Gamma) \vdash \{x : B \,|\, \phi(v)\, x\}$ or $\phi_\Gamma(\Gamma) \vdash \phi_c(\mathtt{contract}\ B\ v)$.

   [T-FUNC] Suppose $\Gamma \vdash_c c \mapsto c' : (T_1 \to T_2)$. Then $\Gamma \vdash_c c : T_1$ and $\Gamma \vdash_c c' : T_2$.
   By induction $\phi_\Gamma(\Gamma) \vdash \phi_c(c)$ and $\phi_\Gamma(\Gamma) \vdash \phi_c(c')$.
   By [WF-FUN] $\phi_\Gamma(\Gamma) \vdash \phi_c(c) \to \phi_c(c')$ or $\phi_\Gamma(\Gamma) \vdash \phi_c(c \mapsto c')$.

B   PROOF OF BEHAVIORAL EQUIVALENCE

The proof of behavioral equivalence relies on the following lemmas:

Lemma 4.5. $\phi(t_1[x := t_2]) = \phi(t_1)[x := \phi(t_2)]$

Lemma 4.6. *The translation ϕ maps λ^C values to λ^H values.*

Assumption 2 *Let* $[\![\cdot]\!]^C$ *and* $[\![\cdot]\!]^H$ *define the semantics of primitive functions k for* λ^C *and* λ^H *respectively. We assume each primitive function k behaves equivalently on any* λ^C *value v and on the corresponding* λ^H *value* $\phi(v)$*, i.e.* $\phi([\![k]\!]^C \ v) = [\![k]\!]^H \ \phi(v)$*.*

Lemma 4.7 (Single Step Behavioral Equivalence). *If* $t \to_c t'$ *then* $\exists s. \phi(t) \to_h^* s$ *and* $\phi(t') \to_h^* s$*.*

Proof. The proof is by induction on the derivation of $t \to_c t'$. For all cases except the [E-FUN] case, $s = \phi(t')$.

[E-CONST] Suppose $k \ v \to_c [\![k]\!] \ (v)$.
$$\phi(k \ v) = k \ \phi(v)$$
$$\to_h [\![k]\!]^H \ \phi(v) \text{ by Lemma 4.6 and [F-CONST]}.$$
$$= \phi([\![k]\!]^C \ v) \text{ by Assumption 2.}$$

[E-BETA] Suppose $(\lambda x : T. t) \ v \to_c t[x := v]$.
$$\phi((\lambda x : T. t) \ v) = (\lambda x : \phi_t(T). \phi(t)) \ \phi(v)$$
$$\to_h \phi(t)[x := \phi(v)] \text{ by Lemma 4.6 and [F-BETA]}.$$
$$= \phi(t[x := v]) \text{ by Lemma 4.5.}$$

[E-LET] Suppose $\text{let}^l \ x : T : c = v \ \text{in} \ t' \to_c t'[x := v]$.
$$\phi(\text{let}^l \ x : T : c = v \ \text{in} \ t') = \text{let}^l \ x : \phi_t(T) = \phi(v) \ \text{in} \ \phi(t')$$
$$\to_h \phi(t')[x := \phi(v)] \text{ by Lemma 4.6 and [F-LET]}.$$
$$= \phi(t'[x := v]) \text{ by Lemma 4.5.}$$

[E-BLAME] Suppose $E[\text{blame}(l)] \to_c \text{blame}(l)$.
For some F, $\phi(E[\text{blame}(l)]) = F[\text{blame}(l)]$
$$\to_h \text{blame}(l) \text{ by [F-BLAME]}.$$
$$= \phi(\text{blame}(l)) \text{ by definition.}$$

[E-OK] Suppose $v^{\text{contract} \ B \ v', l_1, l_2} \to_c v$ and $v' \ v \to_c^* \text{true}$.
$$\phi([v^{\text{contract} \ B \ v', l_1, l_2}])$$
$$= \langle \phi_t(B) \Leftarrow \{x : \phi_t(B) \mid \phi(v') \ x\} \rangle^{l_2} \langle \{x : \phi_t(B) \mid \phi(v') \ x\} \Leftarrow \phi_t(B) \rangle^{l_1} \phi(v)$$
$$\to_h \langle \phi_t(B) \Leftarrow \{x : \phi_t(B) \mid \phi(v') \ x\} \rangle^{l_2} \phi(v) \text{ by [F-OK]}$$
$$\text{because of Lemma 4.6 and } \phi(v' \ v) \to_c^* \text{true by induction.}$$
$$\to_h \phi(v)$$

[E-FAIL] Suppose $v^{\text{contract} \ B \ v', l_1, l_2} \to_c \text{blame}(l)$ and $v' \ v \to_c^* \text{false}$.
$$\phi([v^{\text{contract} \ B \ v', l_1, l_2}])$$
$$= \langle \phi_t(B) \Leftarrow \{x : \phi_t(B) \mid \phi(v') \ x\} \rangle^{l_2} \langle \{x : \phi_t(B) \mid \phi(v') \ x\} \Leftarrow \phi_t(B) \rangle^{l_1} \phi(v)$$
$$\to_h \langle \phi_t(B) \Leftarrow \{x : \phi_t(B) \mid \phi(v') \ x\} \rangle^{l_2} \text{blame}(l_1) \text{ by [F-FAIL]}$$
$$\text{by Lemma 4.6 and since } \phi(v' \ v) \to_c^* \text{false by induction.}$$
$$\to_h \text{blame}(l_1) \text{ by [F-BLAME]}$$
$$= \phi(\text{blame}(l_1)).$$

[E-FUN] Suppose $[v^{c \to c', p, n} \ v'] \to_c [(v \ v'^{c, n, p})^{c', p, n}]$. Let $S = \phi_c(c)$ and $S' = \phi_c(c')$. and $s_f = (\langle S \Leftarrow base(S) \rangle^n \ \phi(v'))$.

$$\phi([v^{c \to c', p, n} \; v'])$$
$$= \quad [\langle base(S \to S') \Leftarrow (S \to S')\rangle^n \langle (S \to S') \Leftarrow base(S \to S')\rangle^p \; \phi(v)] \; \phi(v')$$
$$\to_h \quad \langle base(S') \Leftarrow S'\rangle^n \; [[\langle (S \to S') \Leftarrow base(S \to S')\rangle^p \; \phi(v)] \; s_f]$$

If S is a function type, then s_f is a value, and so:

$$\langle base(S') \Leftarrow S'\rangle^n \; [[\langle (S \to S') \Leftarrow base(S \to S')\rangle^p \; \phi(v)] \; s_f]$$
$$\to_h \quad \langle base(S') \Leftarrow S'\rangle^n \langle S' \Leftarrow base(S')\rangle^p \; (\phi(v) \; [\langle base(S) \Leftarrow S\rangle^p \; s_f])$$
$$= \quad \phi([(v \; v'^{c,n,p})^{c',p,n}])$$

If S is a base refinement type and $s_f \to_h \mathtt{blame}(n)$, then:

$$\langle base(S') \Leftarrow S'\rangle^n \; [[\langle (S \to S') \Leftarrow base(S \to S')\rangle^p \; \phi(v)] \; s_f]$$
$$\to_h \quad \langle base(S') \Leftarrow S'\rangle^n \; [[\langle (S \to S') \Leftarrow base(S \to S')\rangle^p \; \phi(v)] \; \mathtt{blame}(n)]$$
$$\to_h \quad \mathtt{blame}(n)$$

$$\phi([(v \; v'^{c,n,p})^{c',p,n}])$$
$$= \quad \langle base(S') \Leftarrow S'\rangle^n [\langle S' \Leftarrow base(S')\rangle^p \; (\phi(v) \; [\langle base(S) \Leftarrow S\rangle^p \; s_f])]$$
$$\to_h \quad \langle base(S') \Leftarrow S'\rangle^n [\langle S' \Leftarrow base(S')\rangle^p \; (\phi(v) \; [\langle base(S) \Leftarrow S\rangle^p \; \mathtt{blame}(n)])]$$
$$\to_h \quad \mathtt{blame}(n)$$

Otherwise, S is a base refinement type and $s_f \to_h \phi(v')$, and:

$$\langle base(S') \Leftarrow S'\rangle^n \; [[\langle (S \to S') \Leftarrow base(S \to S')\rangle^p \; \phi(v)] \; s_f]$$
$$\to_h \quad \langle base(S') \Leftarrow S'\rangle^n \; [[\langle (S \to S') \Leftarrow base(S \to S')\rangle^p \; \phi(v)] \; \phi(v')]$$
$$\to_h \quad \langle base(S') \Leftarrow S'\rangle^n [\langle S' \Leftarrow base(S')\rangle^p \; (\phi(v) \; [\langle base(S) \Leftarrow S\rangle^p \; \phi(v')])]$$
$$\phi([(v \; v'^{c,n,p})^{c',p,n}])$$
$$= \quad \langle base(S') \Leftarrow S'\rangle^n [\langle S' \Leftarrow base(S')\rangle^p \; (\phi(v) \; [\langle base(S) \Leftarrow S\rangle^p \; s_f])]$$
$$\to_h \quad \langle base(S') \Leftarrow S'\rangle^n [\langle S' \Leftarrow base(S')\rangle^p \; (\phi(v) \; [\langle base(S) \Leftarrow S\rangle^p \; \phi(v')])]$$

[E-CTX] Suppose $E[t_1] \to_c E[t_2]$ and $t_1 \to_c t_2$. This case holds by inspection. $\forall E. \phi(E[t_1]) \to_h \phi(E[t_2])$.

Lemma 4.8. *The operational semantics for λ^C and λ^H are deterministic.*

Restatement of Theorem 4.2 (Behavioral Equivalence) *If $t \to_c^* t'$ then $\exists s$ such that $\phi(t) \to_h^* s$ and $\phi(t') \to_h^* s$.*

Proof. This proof is by induction on the length of the reduction $t \to_c^* t'$. The notation $\to_c^n$ and $\to_h^n$ indicates that n steps have occurred.

The base case where $n = 0$ is trivially true.

For the inductive case, suppose $t \to_c^n t' \to_c t''$.

By induction $\exists m_1, m_2 \in \mathbb{N}, s'$ such that $\phi(t) \to_h^{m_1} s'$ and $\phi(t') \to_h^{m_2} s'$.

By Lemma 4.7, $\exists m_3, m_4 \in \mathbb{N}, s''$ such that $\phi(t') \to_h^{m_3} s''$ and $\phi(t'') \to_h^{m_4} s''$.

Suppose $m_3 \leq m_2$. Then, since the evaluation from $\phi(t')$ is deterministic (Lemma 4.8), we have that $\phi(t) \to_h^{m_1} s'$ and $\phi(t'') \to_h^{m_4} s'' \to_h^{m_2 - m_3} s'$.

The case where $m_3 \geq m_2$ is symmetric.

REFERENCES

[1] Matthias Blume and David McAllester. A sound (and complete) model of contracts. In *Proceedings of the ACM SIGPLAN International Conference on Functional Programming (ICFP)*, pages 189–200, New York, NY, USA, 2004. ACM Press.

[2] Matthias Blume and David McAllester. Sound and complete models of contracts. *Journal of Functional Programming (JFP)*, 16(4-5):375–414, 2006.

[3] Chiyan Chen and Hongwei Xi. Combining programming with theorem proving. In *Proceedings of the ACM SIGPLAN International Conference on Functional Programming (ICFP)*, pages 66–77, New York, NY, USA, 2005. ACM Press.

[4] Robert Bruce Findler. Personal communication, October 2006.

[5] Robert Bruce Findler and Matthias Blume. Contracts as pairs of projections. In Masami Hagiya and Philip Wadler, editors, *Proceedings of the 8th International Symposium on Functional and Logic Programming (FLOPS)*, volume 3945. Springer, 2006.

[6] Robert Bruce Findler and Matthias Felleisen. Contracts for higher-order functions. In *Proceedings of the ACM SIGPLAN International Conference on Functional Programming (ICFP)*, pages 48–59, New York, NY, USA, 2002. ACM Press.

[7] Cormac Flanagan. Hybrid type checking. In *Proceedings of the 33rd ACM SIGPLAN-SIGACT Symposium on Principles of Programming Langauges (POPL)*, pages 245–256, New York, NY, USA, 2006. ACM Press.

[8] Tim Freeman and Frank Pfenning. Refinement types for ML. In *Proceedings of the ACM SIGPLAN'91 Conference on Programming Language Design and Implementation (PLDI)*, pages 268–277, New York, NY, USA, 1991. ACM Press.

[9] B. Gomes, D. Stoutamire, B. Vaysman, and H. Klawitter. A language manual for Sather 1.1, 1996.

[10] R. C. Holt and J. R. Cordy. The Turing programming language. *Communications of the ACM*, 31:1310–1424, 1988.

[11] Kenneth Knowles and Cormac Flanagan. Type reconstruction for general refinement types. In *European Symposium on Programming (ESOP)*. Springer, 2007.

[12] M Kölling and J. Rosenberg. Blue: Language specification, version 0.94, 1997.

[13] Gary T. Leavens and Yoonsik Cheon. Design by contract with JML, 2005. available at `http://www.cs.iastate.edu/˜leavens/JML/`.

[14] David Luckham. Programming with specifications. *Texts and Monographs in Computer Science*, 1990.

[15] Jacob Matthews and Robert Bruce Findler. Operational semantics for multi-language programs. In *Proceedings of the 34rd ACM SIGPLAN-SIGACT Symposium on Principles of Programming Langauges (POPL)*, pages 3–10, New York, NY, USA, 2007. ACM Press.

[16] Philippe Meunier, Robert Bruce Findler, and Matthias Felleisen. Modular set-based analysis from contracts. In *Proceedings of the 33rd ACM SIGPLAN-SIGACT Symposium on Principles of Programming Langauges (POPL)*, pages 218–231, New York, NY, USA, 2006. ACM Press.

[17] Bertrand Meyer. *Object-oriented Software Construction*. Prentice Hall, 1988.

[18] Bertrand Meyer. *Eiffel: the language*. Prentice-Hall, Inc., Upper Saddle River, NJ, USA, 1992.

[19] Xinming Ou, Gang Tan, Yitzhak Mandelbaum, and David Walker. Dynamic typing with dependent types. In *IFIP International Conference on Theoretical Computer Science*, pages 437–450, 2004.

[20] D. L. Parnas. A technique for software module specification with examples. *Communications of the ACM*, 15(5):330–336, 1972.

[21] Micheal Serrano. *Bigloo: A practical Scheme Compiler*, 1992-2002.

[22] Hongwei Xi. Imperative programming with dependent types. In *15th IEEE Symposium on Logic in Computer Science (LICS)*, pages 375–387, Washington, DC, USA, 2000. IEEE Computer Society.

[23] Hongwei Xi and Frank Pfenning. Dependent types in practical programming. In *Proceedings of the 24th ACM SIGPLAN-SIGACT Symposium on Principles of Programming Langauges (POPL)*, pages 214–227, New York, NY, USA, 1999. ACM Press.

Chapter 5

Towards a Box Calculus for Hierarchical Hume

Gudmund Grov[1] and Greg Michaelson[1]

Abstract: Reasoning about and transforming flat Hume programs is complicated by the global effects of even minor local changes, where modifications to control constructs within a box have timing, and hence coordination, implications for the wider system. Here, we present an outline of a calculus of transformations of Hume boxes, built on the Hierarchical Hume extension, which enables us to manipulate individual program components independently of the rest of a program. A base set of rules for introducing, changing, composing, separating and eliminating Hume boxes and wires within hierarchies is presented, additional strategies are derived, and the approach is illustrated through two examples.

5.1 INTRODUCTION

We have been exploring a new cost-driven, transformational approach to software construction from certified components which is highly suited to dynamic, reconfigurable embedded systems. This approach builds on the modern *layered* programming language *Hume*[10], based on autonomous *boxes* linked by *wires* and controlled by generalized transitions. A major strength of Hume lies in the explicit separation of inter-box *coordination* and intra-box *control* concerns.

Boxes and wires are defined in the finite state *coordination language* with transitions defined in the *expression language* through pattern matching and associated recursive actions. Both coordination and expression languages share a rich polymorphic type system, comparable to contemporary functional languages like Haskell and Standard ML.

Hume offers programmers different programming *levels* where expressibility is balanced against accuracy of behavioral modeling. *Full Hume* is a general pur-

---

[1]School of Mathematical and Computer Sciences,Heriot-Watt University, Riccarton, Scotland, EH14 4AS, E-mail: {gudmund, greg}@macs.hw.ac.uk

pose, Turing complete language with undecidable correctness, termination and resource bounds. *PR-Hume* restricts Full-Hume expressions to primitive recursive constructs, enabling decidable termination and bounded resource prediction. *Template-Hume* further restricts expressions to higher-order functions with precise cost models, enabling stronger resource prediction. In *FSM-Hume*, types are restricted to those of fixed size and expressions to conditions over base operations, enabling highly accurate resource bounds. Finally, *HW-Hume* is a basic finite state language over tuples of bits, offering decidable correctness and termination, and exact resource analysis.

However, rather than requiring programmers to choose a level from the outset, we have elaborated an iterative methodology based on cost-driven transformation. An initial Hume program, designed to meet its specification, is analyzed to establish resource bounds. Where established bounds are unacceptable, the offending program constructs are transformed, usually to lower levels, and the program is again analyzed, with the cycle continuing until the required analytic precision is reached.

At present, transformations are chosen on an ad-hoc basis and applied by hand. In this paper we propose a calculus to direct the transformation of an extension of Hume, called *Hierarchical Hume*. The calculus is intended to guarantee that each step of a transformation preserves the program's behavior, and therefore introduces the *correctness by construction* principle.

5.2 HIERARCHICAL HUME

In Hume, a program consists of unitary boxes connected by wires, where a box consists solely of transitions from inputs to outputs. The transitions are guided by a list of *matches* – each consisting of a *pattern* and a corresponding *expression*. A pattern match triggers the corresponding expression which produces the output. '$*$' in any pattern/expression means ignore input/output. A box is *Blocked* if an output cannot be asserted because there is already a value on one of its output wires. The box will not execute again until that output can be asserted i.e. another box consumes the old wire value.

The Hume execution model is based on cyclical execution, where on each cycle all boxes attempt to consume inputs to generate outputs once, and all input/output changes are then resolved in a unitary super-step. In this model, execution order is irrelevant: boxes are stateless and have no side effects on the external environment. However, as every box executes once on each cycle, in a naïve implementation, as the number of boxes grows so does the potential for unnecessary but nonetheless resource consuming activity, where boxes repeatedly fail to consume inputs until other boxes make them available as outputs.

Now, the main loci of transformation from an upper to a lower level is to move activity from control to coordination, i.e. from expressions inside a box to wiring between boxes, typically reducing activity within a box but increasing the number of boxes in compensation. This increases the accuracy of behavioral modeling. For example, in moving from primitive recursive forms in PR-Hume to iterative

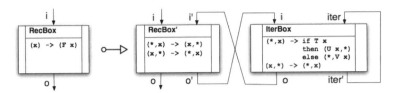

FIGURE 5.1: Recursion to Box Iteration.

forms in FSM-Hume, using a variant of the well known tail recursion optimization [16], a call to recursion within a PR-Hume box:

```
F x = if T x then U x else F (V x);
```

is replaced by wires from that box to a new FSM-Hume box using feedback wires to enable iteration:

```
while not T x do
    x := V x;
return U x;
```

See Figure 5.1. Wires, represented by labeled directed arcs, are indicative and the labels refer to the name of the output/input in the box. The original `RecBox` box would execute once for a recursion of depth N, now both `RecBox'` and `IterBox` will execute N times with the original box `RecBox'` executing needlessly. Furthermore, while box execution is order independent it is time dependent: changing the number of boxes and hence the time for each overall execution cycle may have unpredictable effects on other boxes with explicit time constraints.

In the proposed *Hierarchical Hume* extension[8], a box may contain an entire Hume program, so one box may be composed from a hierarchy of nested boxes. At the top level, the program is still scheduled by a single superstep. However, nested boxes may now be scheduled repeatedly for one cycle of the nesting box.

The introduction of nested boxes greatly mitigates the impact of transformation. If one box is replaced by a hierarchy, then timing effects are localized and may be considered independently of the rest of the program, provided the transformed box retains the same or compatible top-level timing behavior.

Figure 5.2 illustrates the effect of the transformation of a single box half adder to a hierarchical box containing the equivalent multi-box AND/XOR configuration. The original single box (a) on the left is a straight transcription of the equivalent truth table[2]. In the new hierarchy (c) on the right, the nesting box inputs and outputs are wired explicitly to the appropriate nested box inputs and outputs. In the graphical representation of the hierarchical box (b), the transition details within the box are elided.

For nested boxes, parent box inputs are immediately wired to child box inputs, and child box outputs to parent box outputs. Thus the matches in a parent box are

---

[2]as are the AND and XOR boxes within the new hierarchy (c).

```
-- Only 0 and 1
type Bit = int 1;

box half1
  in (x,y::Bit)
  out (s,c::Bit)
match
  (0,0) -> (0,0) |
  (0,1) -> (1,0) |
  (1,0) -> (1,0) |
  (1,1) -> (0,1);
```

a. Half Adder 1: Truth Table

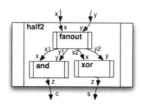

**b. Half Adder 2: (Graphic)
XOR and AND gates**

```
box half2
  in (x,y::Bit)  out (s,c::Bit)
match
  (_,_) -> (_,_)
boxes
  box fanout
    in (x,y::Bit)
    out (x1,y1,x2,y2::Bit)
  match
    (x,y) -> (x,y,x,y);
  wire fanout (half1.x,half2.y)
              (xor.x,xor.y,and.x,and.y);
  box xor
    in (x,y::Bit)  out (z::Bit)
  match
    (0,0) -> 0 |
    (0,1) -> 1 |
    (1,0) -> 1 |
    (1,1) -> 0;
  wire xor(fanout.x1,fanout.y1)
          (half1.s);
  box and
    in (x,y::Bit)  out (z::Bit)
  match
    (0,0) -> 0 |
    (0,1) -> 0 |
    (1,0) -> 0 |
    (1,1) -> 1;
  wire and (fanout.x2,fanout.y2)
           (half1.c);
end;
```

c. Half Adder 2: Source Code

FIGURE 5.2: Half Adders in Hierarchical Hume

solely indicative of the combinations of presence or absence of inputs and outputs that characterize termination. For instance, in box `half2`, ' `(_,_) -> (_,_)` '
means that it will start executing when all inputs are available and terminate when
all outputs are available.

Informally, a transformation is correct if the top level wires in the new configuration always have the same values at the same stages in execution as the
equivalent wires in the original configuration. Consequently, in a correct transformation the top level boxes observationally implement the boxes before the transformation. In the example given in Figure 5.2 this means that the transformed box
`half2` (b/c) must behave as `half1` (a). Due to the hierarchy, top level timing
can be ignored, and the focus is within the new box. Firstly, `half1` is defined for
all type correct inputs, and produces values on all outputs. As noted above, this
is achieved by the ' `(_,_) -> (_,_)` ' match of `half2`. It is easy to see that the `s`
(first) output of `half1` with the given inputs is basically an XOR gate. Further,
`c` is an AND gate. By "fanning out" the inputs to an XOR/AND pair the same
output will be produced, which is exactly the case in `half2` which therefore implements `half1`. In the example shown in Figure 5.1, if we assume functional
correctness, then the transformation is correct if `RecBox'` and `IterBox` are

nested inside a first level box, with i and o wired to the parent box.

5.3   THE RULE SYNTAX AND SEMANTICS

While the proposed box calculus should reflect the formal semantics of Hume, Hierarchical Hume does not yet have a formal semantics and many features in the Hume semantics are not relevant for this discussion. Consequently, we have simplified the Hume semantics slightly to ease presentation of the new hierarchical features.

A Hume program configuration consists of a triple $\langle \theta, \eta, bcs \rangle$: θ is the wire heap with allocated space for each wire. It also holds potential initial wire values; η is the internal heap, including internal wires for hierarchical boxes – where, for simplicity, we assume remains allocated throughout execution. bcs is a list of box configuration. Each box configuration consists of the elements $\langle id, iws, ows, rs, ii, io, ibcs \rangle$: id is the box's name; iws is a list of locations holding the input wires; ows is a list of locations holding the output wires; rs is a list of matches. The three last elements are empty (lists) if the box is not nested: ii is a list of location of internal input wires; io is a list of location of internal output wires; and $ibcs$ is a list of box configurations of internal (nested) boxes. run_{bcs} represents one execution cycle of the program including the super step. It is a predicate on two pairs of wire and internal heaps $\langle \langle \theta, \eta \rangle, \langle \theta', \eta' \rangle \rangle$ where $\langle \theta, \eta \rangle$ is a 'before heap' and $\langle \theta', \eta' \rangle$ an 'after heap'. run_{bcs} then holds if given $\langle \theta, \eta \rangle$ the result of executing bcs is $\langle \theta', \eta' \rangle$.

The box calculus consists of a set of conditional rewrite rules. A rule changes the triple $\langle \theta, \eta, bcs \rangle$ and has the syntax

$$\langle \theta, \eta, bcs \rangle \vdash \mathbf{Rule}(X_1, \cdots, X_n) \Downarrow \langle \theta', \eta', bcs' \rangle.$$

This is read as "**Rule** with parameters $X_1, \cdots, X_n$ will, under the configuration $\langle \theta, \eta, bcs \rangle$ create the configuration $\langle \theta', \eta', bcs' \rangle$". To achieve a set of rules that is expressive enough, steps that change timing behavior must be allowed. It is therefore imperative that the preconditions are strong enough to ensure that the actual behavior remains unchanged. This is mostly a coordination issue and the nature of this layer often require temporal properties. Indeed, this is the reason for using the HW-Hume level as a starting point for the calculus.

The Temporal Logic of Action (TLA) [13] allows us to separate control and coordination for reasoning, and fits well into the Hume framework [9, 8]. The TLA specification for the Hume program triple $\langle \theta, \eta, bcs \rangle$ is

$$\exists \eta : Init_\theta \wedge Init_\eta \wedge \Box(run_{bcs}).$$

$\exists \eta$ denotes that η is *hidden*. $Init_\theta \wedge Init_\eta$ holds the initial values for the two heaps. The key to proving transformations is allowing steps that do not change the state space $\langle \theta, \eta \rangle$. Such steps are internal actions and validity of formula should not depend on those. Thus, run_{bcs} will henceforth denote that if bcs does not hold between a before and an after state of an action, then $\langle \theta, \eta \rangle$ is left unchanged.

run_{bcs} must holds throughout execution and has therefore been prefixed by the temporal 'always' operator '□'.

The proof of a transformation into $\langle \theta', \eta', bcs' \rangle$ is a normal logical implication:

$$\left(\exists\, \eta' : Init_{\theta'} \wedge Init_{\eta'} \wedge \Box(run_{bcs'})\right) \;\Rightarrow\; \left(\exists\, \eta : Init_{\theta} \wedge Init_{\eta} \wedge \Box(run_{bcs})\right). \quad (5.1)$$

The introduction/elimination rules for $\exists$ is similar to those of $\exists$ in standard predicate logic, hence we must find a witness for η (η') in (5.1). We let $\overline{\eta}$ ($\overline{\eta'}$) be this witness, while $run_{\overline{bcs}}$ ($run_{\overline{bcs'}}$) represents running bcs (bcs') with $\overline{\eta}$ ($\overline{\eta'}$) replacing η (η').

The proof rules below have a complex underlying TLA machinery but full details are beyond the scope of this paper. In particular, hierarchies must be flattened for us to prove that a transformation is in fact correct, i.e. global and local steps are no longer separated at this level.

We then use an induction principle to prove (5.1) above: initially, the new heaps must be strictly stronger than before the transformation – and all actions updating the heaps must be strictly stronger than the actions before the transformation:

$$\frac{\langle \theta', \overline{\eta}' \rangle \Rightarrow \langle \theta, \overline{\eta} \rangle \qquad run_{\overline{bcs'}} \Rightarrow run_{\overline{bcs}}}{\langle \theta', \eta', bcs' \rangle \Rightarrow_T \langle \theta, \eta, bcs \rangle}.$$

Note that the primed components are the translated ones. Further, $\Rightarrow_T$ is a specialization of TLA rules for Hume, and its soundness therefore follows the soundness of TLA. An important feature, which underpins the calculus, is the transitivity of $\Rightarrow_T$:

Theorem 5.1. $\langle \theta, \eta, bcs \rangle \Rightarrow_T \langle \theta', \eta', bcs' \rangle$ *and* $\langle \theta', \eta', bcs' \rangle \Rightarrow_T \langle \theta'', \eta'', bcs'' \rangle$ *implies* $\langle \theta, \eta, bcs \rangle \Rightarrow_T \langle \theta'', \eta'', bcs'' \rangle$.

Proof. The proof reduces to transitivity of $\Rightarrow$ which is trivial. ∴.

5.4 RULES

The general categories of transformation rules in the box calculus will be familiar from many comparable calculi. Thus, there are rules to: introduce/eliminate identity boxes; introduce/eliminate nesting boxes; introduce/eliminate wires; combine/separate boxes horizontally and vertically; expand/contract match patterns and results; reorder patterns and results. Special to Hume are rules for moving activity between result expressions within boxes and coordination between boxes. Indeed, in Hume, coordination and expression level transformation are tightly coupled, and there are necessarily strong links between the apparently distinct categories above.

A full formal definition of all the rules will require much more space than available here. We will therefore limit this discussion to two rule derivations and sketch their correctness proofs. The remaining rules are listed in Appendix A. The listing also includes some auxiliary functions, which do not have any side effects on the program configuration. Details, such as preconditions, have been omitted in the listings. We use standard logical terminology in the rules: a rule postfixed by 'I' is a rule that "introduces something", and its dual, the elimination rule, is postfixed by 'E'. In the rule derivation we give an informal graphical representation of the impact of the rule. In the graphical representation we do not show any potential siblings or parents of relevant boxes. Henceforth these, together with the box itself, will be known as the *context* of the box. It is important to note timing constraints only relate to the context of a box. Everything outside the context is independent of this.

The first rule nests one box B inside another box A with name N. This rule introduces a *bounded context* for B, only consisting of A and B. By applying this rule we can ignore the top level timing dependencies when transforming B, and many (temporal) preconditions of rules require a bounded context. The rule copies input and output wires to the internal heap, by using **HeapLocs_Copy**. These are the new wires of the newly created nested box B', and the internal wires of the nesting box A. Further, A consists of one nested box B' and *generalizes* B's rule set into the more restricted hierarchical form, by **Gen_Rules**:

$$\frac{\begin{array}{c} \langle B, iws, ows, rs, iw, ow, ibcs \rangle = \textbf{get\_box}(B, bcs) \\ \langle niw, \eta'' \rangle = \textbf{HeapLocs\_Copy}(iws, \theta, \eta) \\ \langle now, \eta' \rangle = \textbf{HeapLocs\_Copy}(ows, \theta, \eta'') \\ B' = \langle B, niw, now, rs, iw, ow, ibcs \rangle \qquad irs = \textbf{Gen\_Rules}(rs) \\ A = \langle N, iws, ows, irs, niw, now, [B'] \rangle \\ \langle \theta, \eta, bcs \rangle \vdash \textbf{Replace}([A], [B]) \Downarrow \langle \theta, \eta', bcs' \rangle \end{array}}{\langle \theta, \eta, bcs \rangle \vdash \textbf{HieI}(B, N) \Downarrow \langle \theta, \eta', bcs' \rangle}$$

Next we sketch the proof that shows that the transformation is indeed correct.

Theorem 5.2.

$$\begin{array}{ll} \textit{If} & \langle \theta, \eta, bcs \rangle \vdash \textbf{HieI}(A, N) \Downarrow \langle \theta', \eta', bcs' \rangle \\ \textit{then} & \langle \theta', \eta', bcs' \rangle \Rightarrow_T \langle \theta, \eta, bcs \rangle \end{array}$$

Proof. Since we only extend $\overline{\eta}$ and do not change θ, $\langle \theta', \overline{\eta}' \rangle \Rightarrow \langle \theta, \overline{\eta} \rangle$ holds. In bcs, B is replaced by A. Since A's rule set generalizes B's the matching will be the same. Further, with this and since A only contains B, the computation and termination will be the same, and therefore also the result. Therefore $run_{\overline{bcs'}} \Rightarrow run_{\overline{bcs}}$ holds. ∴.

In the second derivation two non-nested boxes, A and B, are horizontally composed into a new box called N. However, A and B must always have the same *Blocked* status, since N will be *Blocked* if either of them is. If one, but not the other, is *Blocked* the behavior of the composed box N will not capture the sum of A and B. The inputs and outputs of A prefixes B's inputs and outputs. For all

matches, the patterns and expression of the A and B are pairwise composed by
project. This projection might introduce non-determinacy, so the patterns must
be mutually exclusive. Finally, A might execute while B fails to pattern match the
inputs, and vice verse. This is captured by postfixing the composed rule set below
with a rule set where A's rule set is composed with only '$*$'s, and the same for B.
The box N', capturing all the above, replaces A and B:

$$
\cfrac{
\begin{array}{c}
\langle A, iws_A, ows_A, rs_A, [], [], [] \rangle = \textbf{get\_box}(A, bcs) \\
\langle B, iws_B, ows_B, rs_B, [], [], [] \rangle = \textbf{get\_box}(B, bcs) \\
\Box\big(\textbf{is\_Blocked}(A) \equiv \textbf{is\_Blocked}(B)\big) \\
\textbf{mutually\_exclusive}(rs_A) \qquad \textbf{mutually\_exclusive}(rs_B) \\
iws = iws_A @ iws_B \qquad ows = ows_A @ ows_B \\
n_A = \textbf{len}(iws_A) \quad m_A = \textbf{len}(ows_A) \\
n_B = \textbf{len}(iws_B) \quad m_B = \textbf{len}(ows_B) \\
_A = [\langle \underbrace{, \cdots, *}_{n_A} \rangle \rightarrow \langle \underbrace{*, \cdots, *}_{m_A} \rangle] \quad *_B = [\langle \underbrace{*, \cdots, *}_{n_B} \rangle \rightarrow \langle \underbrace{*, \cdots, *}_{m_B} \rangle] \\
rs = \textbf{project}(rs_A, rs_B) @ \textbf{project}(rs_A, *_B) @ \textbf{project}(*_A, rs_B) \\
N' = \langle N, iws, ows, rs, [], [], [] \rangle \\
\langle \theta, \eta, bcs \rangle \vdash \textbf{Replace}([N'], [A, B]) \Downarrow \langle \theta, \eta, bcs' \rangle
\end{array}
}{
\langle \theta, \eta, bcs \rangle \vdash \textbf{HComplI}(A, B, N) \Downarrow \langle \theta, \eta, bcs' \rangle
}
$$

The unification with the empty lists ensures that the boxes are not nested when
calling **get_box**. The mutual exclusiveness test is straightforward, and the estab-
lishment of the *Blocked* status requires a temporal invariance proof. Therefore,
this has to be prefixed by the temporal 'always' operator '$\Box$' – denoting that this
must hold throughout execution.

Theorem 5.3.

$$
\begin{array}{ll}
\textit{If} & \langle \theta, \eta, bcs \rangle \vdash \textbf{HComplI}(A, B, N) \Downarrow \langle \theta, \eta, bcs' \rangle \\
\textit{then} & \langle \theta', \eta', bcs' \rangle \Rightarrow_T \langle \theta, \eta, bcs \rangle
\end{array}
$$

Proof. There is no nesting, hence $\overline{\eta} = \eta$. Further, it is obvious that $\theta' = \theta$ and
$\eta' = \eta$, thus $\langle \theta', \overline{\eta'} \rangle \Rightarrow \langle \theta, \overline{\eta} \rangle$. The proof of $run_{\overline{bcs'}} \Rightarrow run_{\overline{bcs}}$ is by case-analysis on
the "execution state" of A and B: Since $\Box\big(\textbf{is\_Blocked}(A) \equiv \textbf{is\_Blocked}(B)\big)$ we
know that A and B are always *Blocked* at the same time. Hence, if one is *Blocked*
then so is the other, and since N will be *Blocked* if either of them are, then so is
N. If both A and B succeeds then, since all possible matches are composed, so
will N. Since the patterns are mutually exclusive only one pattern can succeed,
and the result is obviously the same. If both boxes fail to execute, then so will N
since it only composes A and B. Finally, the case where only one box succeeds is
captured by the case where each match is composed with only '$*$'s. Thus the goal
holds. $\therefore$

5.5 STRATEGIES

The rules will often be too low-level to work with. Instead a user will work with higher-level *strategies*, which are derived from rules and other strategies. An example of a strategy, although still rather low-level, is the elimination of *threading*. A wire is threaded through a box if there is a one-to-one correspondence between a pattern x and an expression y in all matches. x cannot be used in other expressions $(\neq y)$. Further, x and y must form an identity box. When eliminated, the threaded value will arrive earlier at the destination. This must not have any effect on the context. Finally, a *Blocked* state on B will prevent the threaded value leaving B, which is not the case when the thread is eliminated. This must again not have any impact on the context. Since the rule is derived from other rules these preconditions can be ignored as they are implicitly captured by the precondition of the rules in the derivation. Threading elimination, **ThreadE**, is derived as follows. x and y are horizontally de-composed into a new box *Id* by **HCompE**. *Id* is then an identity box eliminated by **IdE**:

$$\frac{\langle \theta, \eta, bcs \rangle \vdash \textbf{HCompE}(B, [x], [y], Id, B) \Downarrow \langle \theta_1, \eta_1, bcs_1 \rangle \qquad \langle \theta_1, \eta_1, bcs_1 \rangle \vdash \textbf{IdE}(Id) \Downarrow \langle \theta', \eta', bcs' \rangle}{\langle \theta, \eta, bcs \rangle \vdash \textbf{ThreadE}(B, x, y) \Downarrow \langle \theta', \eta', bcs' \rangle}$$

The correctness proof for strategies are trivial since they only rely on Theorem 5.1:

Theorem 5.4.

$$\begin{aligned} &\textit{If} \qquad \langle \theta, \eta, bcs \rangle \vdash \textbf{ThreadE}(B, x, y) \Downarrow \langle \theta', \eta', bcs' \rangle \\ &\textit{then} \qquad \langle \theta', \eta', bcs' \rangle \Rightarrow_T \langle \theta, \eta, bcs \rangle \end{aligned}$$

Proof. Since the two given are applied sequentially the proof reduces to the transitivity of $\Rightarrow_T$. This is proved by Theorem 5.1. $\therefore$

5.6 EXAMPLES

We now illustrate the calculus by applying it to two simple examples based on single bit adder circuits. The first example shows the decomposition of a half adder box into a simple binary tree of three elementary logic gate boxes. The second example shows the decomposition of a full adder box into two half adders and an elementary logic gate, but with staged mutual dependencies. The examples are chosen to illustrate both the deployment of a characteristic range of base rules, and the use of derived rules.

5.6.1 Example 1: Half-Adder

First we apply the box calculus to the half adder example above. We will do so stepwise, and a graphical representation of each of these steps is shown in Figure

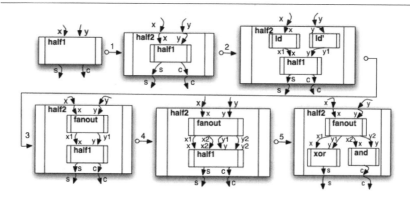

FIGURE 5.3: Transformation of Half Adder

5.3. We use a dot '.' notation to refer to nested boxes, starting from the first level. If a rule has more than one parameter, it is sufficient to give the full path to one of the boxes, since we can only work in one context at a time. We omit the configuration triple to make the text easier to read. The rules are sequentially applied.

1. Since the transformation has a forward direction we start with the box shown in Figure 5.2a. First rule **HieI**(half1,half2) which replaces box half1 with a box half2 that simply nests it.

2. Since there is no '*' in the context nested by half2 there are no dependencies. We can therefore introduce identity boxes for both input wires of half1: **IdI**(half2.half1,x,Id) followed by **IdI**(half2.half1,y,Id'). The input/output variables of the identity boxes are v/v' by default. These are renamed to x/x1 and y/y1 respectively: **VRename**(half2.Id,v,x), **VRename**(half2.Id,v',x1), **VRename**(half2.Id',v,y) and **VRename** (half2.Id',v',y1).

3. The two identity boxes are then horizontally composed into one box called fanout: **HCompI**(half2.Id,Id',fanout):
   ```
   box fanout
      in (x,y::Bit)   out (x1,y1::Bit)
   match
         (x,y)->(x,y)  |  (x,*)->(x,*)  |  (*,y)->(*,y) ;
   ```
   A simple invariant of the internal behavior of half2 shows that it will never be the case that only one of fanout's inputs is empty. The last two matches of fanout will therefore never succeed. This is the only precondition in the match elimination rule which can therefore be applied: **MatchE**(half2.fanout,3) and **MatchE**(half2.fanout,2).

4. We then duplicate the two wires connecting fanout and half1. We name them x2 and y2: **DupI**(half2.fanout,x1,x2,half1,x,x2) followed by **DupI**(half2.fanout,y1,y2,half1,y,y2).

```
box adder1
in (x,y,c::Bit)
out (s,c'::Bit)
match
  (0,0,0) -> (0,0) |
  (0,1,0) -> (1,0) |
  (1,0,0) -> (1,0) |
  (1,1,0) -> (0,1) |
  (0,0,1) -> (1,0) |
  (0,1,1) -> (0,1) |
  (1,0,1) -> (0,1) |
  (1,1,1) -> (1,1) ;
```
a. Adder 2: Truth Table

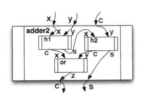

b. Adder 2: (Graphic) Half Adder and OR gate

```
box adder2
   in (x,y,c::Bit)  out (s,c'::Bit)
match
  (_,_,_) -> (_,_)
boxes
  box h1
     in (x,y::Bit) out (s,c::Bit)
  match
     (0,0) -> (0,0) |
     (0,1) -> (1,0) |
     (1,0) -> (1,0) |
     (1,1) -> (0,1);
  wire h1(adder2.x,adder2.y)(h2.x,or.x);

  box h2
     in (x,y::Bit) out (s,c::Bit)
  match ... -- same as h1
  wire h2(h1.c,adder2.c)(adder2.s,or.y);

  box or
     in (x,y::Bit)  out (z::Bit)
  match
     (0,0) -> 0 |
     (0,1) -> 1 |
     (1,0) -> 1 |
     (1,1) -> 1;
  wire or(h1.c,h2.c)(adder2.c);
end;
```
c. Adder 2: Source Code

FIGURE 5.4: Full Adders in Hierarchical Hume

5. In $\mathtt{half1}$ we now have two sets of identical inputs: $\{x,y\}$ and $\{x2,y2\}$. We can then state that output s depends on the first set and c on the second, and decompose the box. The first of these boxes is exactly the same as the $\mathtt{xor}$ while the second is the same as the $\mathtt{and}$ box of Figure 5.2(b/c): **HCompE**($\mathtt{half2.half1}, [x,y], [s], \mathtt{xor}, \mathtt{and}$). Finally, we rename the inputs of the $\mathtt{and}$ box: **VRename**($\mathtt{half2.and}, x2, x$) and **VRename** ($\mathtt{half2.and}, y2, y$). This concludes the transformation.

5.6.2   Example 2: A Full Adder

The second example is more complex: A full adder represented as a truth table (Figure 5.4a) is transformed into a representation using two half adders and an OR gate (Figure 5.4b/c). Again, the transformation is step-by-step and each step is graphically illustrated in Figure 5.5:

1. The transformation starts with $\mathtt{adder1}$ from Figure 5.4a. First we move all the matches inside a case expression. Since the patterns are total with respect to the $\mathtt{Bit}$ type this is allowed: **CaseI**($\mathtt{adder1}, 1, 8$):
```
box adder1
   in (x,y,c::Bit) out (s,c'::Bit)
match
   (a,b,c) -> case (a,b,c) of  ...;
```

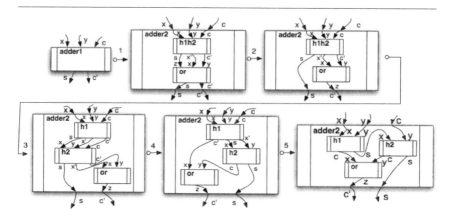

FIGURE 5.5: Transformation of Full Adder

```
f(a,b,c) = case (a,b,c) of          g(a,b,c) = case (a,b,c) of
           (0,0,0) -> (0,0,0) |                (0,0,0) -> (0,0) |
           (0,0,1) -> (1,0,0) |                (1,0,0) -> (1,0) |
           (0,1,0) -> (1,0,0) |                (0,0,1) -> (0,1) |
           (0,1,1) -> (0,0,1) ...;             (1,0,1) -> (1,1) ...;


ff(a,b,c) = case (a,b,c) of         gg(a,b,c) = case (a,b,c) of
            (0,0,0) -> (0,0,0) |                (0,0,0) -> (0,0,0) |
            (0,0,1) -> (1,0,0) |                (0,0,1) -> (0,1,0) |
            (0,1,0) -> (0,1,0) |                (0,1,0) -> (1,0,0) |
            (0,1,1) -> (1,1,0) ...;             (0,1,1) -> (1,1,0) ...;
```

FIGURE 5.6: Auxiliary Functions Used in Full Adder Transformation

The case expression is then replaced by the function composition $g \cdot f(a, b, c)$: **ReplaceExpr**(adder1,1,$g \cdot f(a,b,c)$)) where f and g are shown in Figure 5.6. The next step is to vertically de-compose this box – where *f* is the expression of the first and *g* the expression of the second box. However, this will introduce an extra step, and we do not know anything about the context, so we need to nest the boxes first: **HieI**(adder1,adder2). The boxes can then safely be de-composed: **VCompE**(adder2.adder1,h1h2,[s,x', c'],or,[z,x,y]).

2. The newly created or box has one match with the expression g, where g consists of a (total) case expression. We unfold g and move the case-expression into the match: **Unfold**(adder2.or,g) followed by **CaseE** (adder2.or,1). The result is illustrated on the left side below. The first pattern and expression are identical (and total). We therefore replace them by a variable: **MatchVarI**(adder2.or,x,s). We now have a threading of a variable which we can eliminate (since there are no '*' in the context): **ThreadE**(adder2.or,x,s). The result is illustrated on the right side:

```
box or                          box or
  in (z,x,y::Bit)                 in (x,y::Bit)
  out (s,c'::Bit)                 out (c'::Bit)
match                           match
    (0,0,0) -> (0,0) |              (0,0) -> 0 |
    (1,0,0) -> (1,0) |              (0,0) -> 0 |
    (0,0,1) -> (0,1) |              (0,1) -> 1 |
    (1,0,1) -> (1,1) ...;          (0,1) -> 1 ...;
```

Matches $2, 4, 6$ and 8 are now duplicates of their previous matches, and can therefore be removed: **MatchE**(adder2.or, 8),**MatchE**(adder2.or, 6), **MatchE**(adder2.or, 4) and **MatchE**(adder2.or, 2). Finally, the output wire is renamed to z: **VRename**(adder2.or, c', z). The or box is now the same as in Figure 5.4c.

3. Box h1h2 consists of one match with expression f. This function can be replaced by function composition gg·ff(a, b, c) where ff and gg are shown in Figure 5.6: **ReplaceExpr**(adder2.h1h2, 1, gg·ff(a, b, c)). Since the context does not contain any '$*$'s we can apply vertical function de-composition **VCompE**(adder2.h1h2, h1, [s, x', c'], h2, [x, y, c]):

4. In box h2 the match has the expression gg which is unfolded and the (total) case-expression is moved into the body: **Unfold**(adder2.h2, gg) and **CaseE**(adder2.h2, 1) as illustrated on the left side below. The last pattern and second expression in all matches can be replaced by a variable, which creates a threading that can be eliminated: **MatchVarI**(adder2.h2, c, s) and **ThreadE**(adder2.h2, c, s) – as illustrated on the right side:

```
box h2                          box h2
  in (x,y,c::Bit)                 in (x,y::Bit)
  out (s,x',c'::Bit)              out (s,c'::Bit)
match                           match
    (0,0,0) -> (0,0,0) |            (0,0) -> (0,0) |
    (0,0,1) -> (0,1,0) |            (0,0) -> (0,0) |
    (0,1,0) -> (1,0,0) |            (0,1) -> (1,0) |
    (0,1,1) -> (1,1,0) ...;        (0,1) -> (1,0) ...;
```

Matches $2, 4, 6$ and 8 are now duplicates of previous matches and therefore removed: **MatchE**(adder2.h2, 8), **MatchE**(adder2.h2, 6), **MatchE**(adder2.h2, 4) and **MatchE**(adder2.h2, 2). After renaming the last output to c' we have created a correct implementation of a half adder: **VRename**(adder2.h2, c', c).

5. The transformation of h1 follows the same pattern as h2 (and or): First the case expression is removed, followed by a variable introduction and threading elimination: **Unfold**(adder2.h1, ff), **CaseE**(adder2.h1, 1), **MatchVarI**(adder2.h1, c, x') and **ThreadE**(adder2.h2, c, x'). Then the duplicate matches are removed, which creates a correct implementation of a *half*-adder: **MatchE**(adder2.h1, 8), **MatchE**(adder2.h1, 6),

MatchE(adder2.h1, 4) and **MatchE**(adder2.h1, 2). By renaming c' to
c we have concluded the transformation: **VRename**(adder2.h1,c',c). To
achieve an even lower level representation we can now apply the half-adder
transformation to h1 and h2, as explained above.

5.7   RELATED WORK

A Hume *transformation* is a strategy. Following Visser [19] this can either be
categorized as a *program rephrasing*, where the source and target language are
the same, or as a *program translation*, where the target language deviates from
the source language.

 We have already stated that a transformation from an upper to a lower level
is a move of activity from control to coordination, i.e. a translation from the
expression layer of a box into the coordination layer, between components of a
nested box. This has also been illustrated by our examples, where relatively rich
single-box truth-tables are dissolved into configurations of simpler boxes. A full
transformation can therefore be seen as the form of program translation termed
program synthesis from a control to a coordination representation. In particular,
our correctness proof rule is based on a form of synthesis called *program refinement*: the lower level transformed program *implements* the upper level program.
In TLA such implementation is represented as logical implication.

 However, what is distinctive here compared with synthesis techniques, like
Bird-Meertens Formalism [2] and calculational programming [12], is the necessarily strong interplay between coordination and expression transformation:
changes to box/wire configurations affect matches which in turn affect patterns
and results. A single rule application is not therefore just a *program migration*
from one representation to another, but hold more resemblance to a form of program rephrasing called *program refactoring* [6].

 Just as Hume integrates a finite state coordination language with a functional
transition control language, the work presented here draws on the twin traditions
of process network and functional program transformation. The coordination aspects of the rules have many similarities with those found in the box calculus for
Petri nets[5] as well as process calculi [1]. The control aspects resemble classic
functional programming techniques including curry/uncurry, fold/unfold [3] and
functional refactoring [14]. Hence, a full transformation can be seen as a program
translation, consisting of several program rephrasing steps.

 In principle the transformation proofs could have been achieved using (ob-
servational) bisimulations in a process algebra like CSP [11]. However, it is not
possible to achieve an adequate representation of Hume's rich expression layer
in a process algebra requiring the introduction of further formalism, for example
Schneider's B/CSP combination [18]. Here, we think a "lifted logic", like TLA,
that may be founded on any underpinning predicate formalism, is more appropriate.

 Previously, we have explored horizontal box integration in establishing informally that FSM-Hume actually is finite state [17]. Different strategies for general

formal verification of Hume programs are first discussed in [7]. TLA is first used to verify programs in [9], while Hierarchical Hume and linear recursion to box iteration with respect to scheduling are discussed in [8].

5.8   CONCLUSION AND FUTURE WORK

We have presented a first approach towards a box calculus for Hierarchical Hume programs, which introduces correct transformation by construction, formalized through structural operational semantics and TLA. We have then discussed rule derivation and the combination of rules into strategies, and presented the use of the calculus through two HW-Hume transformation examples.

Hierarchical Hume enables us to elide the potentially global impact of what should be localized program changes by providing a framework for the identification and isolation of distinct sub-systems within a program. Furthermore, the calculus supports the systematic transformation of program components through the introduction, modification, elimination, composition and separation of boxes and wires. A major strength of the calculus is that it combines changes to control aspects within boxes with those to coordination aspects between boxes.

Our work at the lowest, least expressive HW-Hume level has given us confidence in the calculus and allowed us to focus on the intricate properties of the coordination layer, which are the same for all Hume levels. Extending the calculus to the higher levels of Hume will mainly require an extension of the purely functional transformation rules, together with data refinement. This will allow us to tackle problems that have substantive behavioral and hence resource cost implications, like the recursion to iteration example previously discussed. We speculate that it may also be necessary to incorporate rules which are not behavior preserving on their own, but which can be combined into "correct" rules/strategies.

Our next step is to identify a sufficient set of rules which is adequate for the classes of transformations between and within levels that may be used to optimize resource use. The rules will be realized in the Isabelle theorem prover, which will require a deep embedding of at least the expression layer. A TLA layer will then be built on top of this embedding. In the longer term, we intend the calculus to be used from a graphical-based IDE for Hume. We will also explore how to minimize user-interaction in cost-oriented program development using *proof planning*[15, 4] heuristics to guide transformations.

ACKNOWLEDGMENTS

This work is supported by the EU FP6 EmBounded project, and Gudmund Grov is supported by a James Watt Scholarship. We would like to thank our colleagues Robert Pointon and Andrew Ireland for valuable discussions of transformation and Hierarchical Hume, and the anonymous TFP reviewers for their excellent comments.

A   SUMMARY OF PROOF RULES

A.1   Functions

Gen_Rules(rs)**:** Returns a *generalization* of rs. In patterns variables
    are replaced by '_' while the rest is unchanged. In expression everything
    but '$*$' is replaced by '_', and all function calls are removed.

get_box(B, bcs)**:** Returns box configuration with box id B from list bcs.

HeapLocs_Copy$([l_1, \cdots l_n], H_1, H_2)$**:** Returns a tuple $\langle [l'_1, \cdots l'_n], H'_2 \rangle$ holding
    a copy of $[l_1, \cdots l_n]$ of H_1 into H_2 and the updated H_2.

is_Blocked(B)**:** Holds if box B cannot be executed.

len(L)**:** Returns the length of list L.

mutually_exclusive(rs)**:** Holds if the patterns of rule set rs are mutually exclusive.

project$([(p_1 \rightarrow e_1), \cdots (p_n \rightarrow e_n)], [(p'_1 \rightarrow e'_1), \cdots (p'_m \rightarrow e'_m)])$**:** Pairwise comb-
    ines each pattern p_i and p'_j with e_i and e'_j where $i \in 1..n$ and $j \in 1..m$.

$L_1 @ L_2$**:** Concat list L_1 in front of list L_2.

A.2   Rules and Strategies

CaseE(B, i) **:** Moves case expression in match i of box B into B's rule set

CaseI(B, i, j) **:** Replaces match i to j in box B by a case-expression.

DupI(A, x, x', B, y, y') **:** Duplicates wire connecting x of box A and y of B,
    with wire names x' (of A) and y' (of B) respectively.

HCompE$(B, [i_1, \cdots, i_n], [o_1, \cdots, o_m], X, Y)$ **:** Horizontally de-composes box B
    into boxes X and Y, where X has inputs $[i_1, \cdots, i_n]$ and outputs $[o_1, \cdots, o_m]$.
    Y will have the inputs/output of B not in $[i_1, \cdots, i_n]/[o_1, \cdots, o_m]$.

HCompI(A, B, N)**:** Horizontally composes box A and box B into N.

HieE(B)**:** Replaces B with it's (only) child box.

HieI(B, N)**:** Replaces box B by N which only holds B.

IdE(B)**:** Eliminates identity box B.

IdI(B, v, N)**:** Introduces an identity box N to wire connected to v of box B.

MatchE(B, n)**:** Eliminates match n of box B.

MatchVarI(B, i, o)**:** Replaces constants in inputs i and output o by a variable.

Rename(A, N)**:** Renames box A to N.

Replace$([A_1, \cdots, A_n], [B_1, \cdots, B_m])$ **:** Replaces boxes $A_1, \cdots, A_n$ by $B_1, \cdots, B_m$.

ReplaceExpr(A, n, e) **:** The expression of match n of box A is replaced by e.

ThreadE(B, x, y) **:** Removes threading of through input x and output y of box B.

Unfold(B, n, f) **:** Unfolds function f in match n of box B.

VCompE$(B, N, [o_1, \cdots o_n], M, [i_1, \cdots i_n])$ **:** Vertically de-composes box B into
    two sequentially composed boxes N and M, where N has B's inputs and
    $[o_1, \cdots o_n]$ as outputs, and M has $[i_1, \cdots i_n]$ as inputs and B's outputs.

VRename(A, x, N)**:** Renames wire x of box A to N.

REFERENCES

[1] J. C. M. Baeten. A Brief History of Process Algebra. *Theoretical Computer Scisence*, 335(2-3):131–146, 2005.

[2] R. Bird and O. de Moor. *Algebra of Programming*. Prentice-Hall, 1997.

[3] R. Burstall and J. Darlington. A Transformation System for Developing Recursive Programs. *Journal of the ACM*, 24(1):44–67, January 1977.

[4] A. Cook, A. Ireland, G.J. Michaelson, and N. Scaife. Discovering Applications of Higher Order Functions Through Proof Planning. *Journal of Formal Aspects of Computing*, 17(1):38–57, 2005.

[5] R. Devillers, H. Klaudel, and R-C. Riemann. General Parameterised Refinement and Recursion for the M-net Calculus. *Theoretical Computer Science*, 300(1-3):259–300, May 2003.

[6] M. Fowler. *Refactoring: Improving the Design of Existing Code*. Addison-Wesley, August 1999.

[7] G. Grov. Verifying the Correctness of Hume Programs – An Approach Combining Algorithmic and Deductive Reasoning. In *Proceedings of the 20th IEEE/ACM International Conference on Automated Software Engineering (ASE-05)*, pages 444–447. ACM Press, 2005.

[8] G. Grov, R. Pointon, G. Michaelson, and A. Ireland. Preserving Coordination Properties when Transforming Concurrent System Components, 2007. under review for APLAS'07.

[9] K. Hammond, G. Grov, G. Michaelson, and A. Ireland. Low-Level Programming in Hume: an Exploration of the HW-Hume Level. In *International Conference on Implementation and Application of Functional Languages, Budapest, Hungary*, September 2006. To Appear in LNCS 4449.

[10] K. Hammond and G.J. Michaelson. Hume: a Domain-Specific Language for Real-Time Embedded Systems. In *Proc. Conf. Generative Programming and Component Engineering (GPCE '03)*, Lecture Notes in Computer Science. Springer-Verlag, 2003.

[11] C. A. R. Hoare. *Communicating Sequential Processes*. Prentice-Hall International, 1985.

[12] G. Hutton and J. Wright. Calculating an Exceptional Machine. In H-W. Loidl, editor, *Trends in Functional Programming Volume 5*, pages 49–64, 2006.

[13] L. Lamport. The Temporal Logic of Actions. *ACM Toplas*, 16(3):872–923, May 1994.

[14] H. Li and S. Thompson. A Comparative Study of Refactoring Haskell and Erlang Programs. In *Proceedings of 6th IEEE Workshop on Source Code Analysis and Manipulation, Philadelphia, USA*, September 2006.

[15] P. Madden. *Automated Program Transformation Through Proof Transformation*. PhD thesis, University of Edinburgh, 1991.

[16] Z. Manna. *Mathematical Theory of Computing*. McGraw-Hill, 1974.

[17] Greg Michaelson, Kevin Hammond, and Jocelyn Sérot. The Finite State-Ness of FSM-Hume. In *Trends in Functional Programming*, volume 4, pages 19–28. Intellect, 2004.

[18] S. Schneider and H. Treharne. CSP Theorems for Communicating B Machines. *Formal Asp. Comput*, 17(4), 2005.

[19] E. Visser. A Survey of Strategies in Rule-Based Program Transformation Systems. *Journal of Symbolic Computation*, 40(1):831–873, 2005. Special issue on Reduction Strategies in Rewriting and Programming.

Chapter 6

unreadTVar: Extending Haskell Software Transactional Memory for Performance

Nehir Sonmez[1][2], Cristian Perfumo[1][2], Srdjan Stipic[1][2], Adrian Cristal[1], Osman S. Unsal[1], Mateo Valero[1][2]

Abstract: As new trends in computer architecture lead towards shared-memory chip multiprocessors (CMP), the rules for programming these machines are significantly changing. In the search for alternatives to deadlock-prone lock-based concurrency protocols, Software Transactional Memory (STM) extensions to Haskell have provided an easy-to-use lock-free abstraction mechanism for concurrent programming, using atomically composed blocks operating on transactional variables. However, as in the case for linked structures, the composition of these atomic blocks require extra attention, as the transactional management might act too conservatively by keeping track of more variables than necessary, causing an overall decrease in performance. To remedy this situation, we have extended the Transactional Memory module of the Glasgow Haskell Compiler (GHC) 6.6 to support a construct that allows the removal of a transactional variable from the readset. Although this construct that we term unreadTVar, when not applied carefully, might put the strong atomicity guarantees of STM at risk, the experimentations done with linked lists and binary trees show that it can significantly improve execution time and memory usage when traversing transactional linked

[1]Barcelona Supercomputing Center, Barcelona/Spain;
E-mail:{nehir.sonmez,cristian.perfumo,srdjan.stipic,adrian.cristal, osman.unsal,mateo.valero}@bsc.es
[2]Computer Architecture Department – Universitat Politècnica de Catalunya

structures.

6.1   INTRODUCTION

Chip multiprocessors have arrived and are dominating the microprocessor market, demanding efficient use of parallelism and easier methods in programming shared-memory parallel architectures. In this era, traditional mechanisms such as lock-based thread synchronization, which are tricky to use and non-composable, are becoming less likely to survive. Meanwhile, the use of imperative languages that cause uncontrolled side effects is becoming questionable. Consequently, while strongly typed functional languages are attracting more attention than ever, lock-free Transactional Memory (TM) is a serious candidate to the future of concurrent programming. As Harris et al. state in their work [5], STM can be expressed elegantly in a declarative language, and moreover, Haskell's type system (particularly the monadic mechanism) avoids threads to violate the restrictions that a transactional scheme demands regarding the access to shared variables. This situation is more likely to happen under other programming paradigms, for example, as a result of access to memory locations through the use of pointers.

The Transactional Memory approach, which is inherited from database theory, allows programmers to specify transaction sequences that are executed atomically, ensuring that all operations within the block either complete as a whole, or automatically rollback as if they were never run. Atomic blocks simplify writing concurrent programs because when a block of code is marked atomic, the compiler and the runtime system ensure that operations within the block appear atomic to the rest of the system [6]. Transactional management of the memory can be implemented either in hardware (HTM) [9], or software (STM) [18]. As always, there is an intermediate point that incorporates both approaches, called Hybrid TM (HyTM) [1, 15]. TM schemes attempt to optimistically interleave and execute all transactions in parallel. A transaction is committed if and only if other transactions have not modified the section of the memory which its execution depended on. As a consequence, the programmer no longer needs to worry about deadlocks, manual locking, low-level race conditions or priority inversion [7].

In this paper, the following contributions are made:

- The problems related to synthetic but abundantly used linked structures which suffer from serious performance and memory problems when realized transactionally are investigated.

- By extending the Haskell STM with the `unreadTVar` operation, which removes transactional variables from the readset, a more efficient way of constructing the atomic blocks that operate on linked structures was provided. Although the idea has been previously implemented in imperative languages such as C, C++ and Java [19, 10], this is the first implementation of such a feature for a functional language, which also supports composability.

- Specifically, linked lists and binary trees were focused on in order to present absolute speedup results that show substantial increase in system performance using the proposed approach. Moreover, safety issues and potential downsides are discussed in detail.

The rest of this paper is organized as follows: In Section 6.2, the STM library of Concurrent Haskell is summarized, after which, in Section 6.3, an example case of linked structures, namely the singly linked list, is presented with an explanation of the problem of false conflict and the proposed solution. Section 6.4 introduces the new function: `unreadTVar`, demonstrates its implementation and its usage. Section 6.5, discusses performance results on linked lists and binary trees versus the potential safety issues and trade-offs. Conclusions are derived on Section 6.6.

6.2 BACKGROUND: STM IN CONCURRENT HASKELL

The Glasgow Haskell Compiler 6.6 [11] provides a compilation and runtime system for Haskell 98 [13], a pure, lazy, functional programming language. The GHC natively contains STM functions built into the Concurrent Haskell library [14], providing abstractions for communicating between explicitly forked threads.

6.2.1 The Monadic World

STM provides a safe way of accessing shared variables between concurrently running threads through the use of monads [2], having only I/O actions in the `IO` monad and STM actions in the `STM` monad. Programming using distinct STM and I/O actions ensures that only STM actions and pure computation can be performed within a memory transaction (which makes it possible to re-execute transactions), whereas only I/O actions and pure computations, and not STM actions can be performed outside a transaction. This guarantees that `TVars` cannot be modified without the protection of `atomically`, and thus separates the computations that have side-effects from the ones that are effect-free. Utilizing a purely declarative language for TM also provides explicit read/writes from/to mutable cells; memory operations that are also performed by functional computations are never tracked by STM unnecessarily, since they never need to be rolled back [5].

6.2.2 Transactional Execution with **TVars**

Threads in STM Haskell communicate by reading and writing transactional variables, or `TVars`. All STM operations make use of the `STM` monad, which supports a set of transactional operations, including allocating, reading and writing transactional variables, namely the functions `newTVar`, `readTVar` and `writeTVar`, respectively, as it can be seen on Table 6.1.

Transactions are started within the `IO` monad by means of the `atomically` construct. When a transaction is finished, it is validated by the runtime system that it was executed on a consistent system state, and that no other finished transaction may have modified relevant parts of the system state in the meantime [12]. In this case, the modifications of the transaction are committed, otherwise, they

Running STM operations	Transactional Variable Operations
`atomically::STM a->IO a`	`data TVar a`
`retry::STM a`	`newTVar::a->STM(TVar a)`
`orElse::STM a->STM a->STM a`	`readTVar::TVar a->STM a`
	`writeTVar::TVar a->a->STM()`

TABLE 6.1: Haskell STM Operations

are discarded. The Haskell STM runtime maintains a list of accessed transactional variables for each transaction, where all the variables in this list which were written are called the "writeset" and all that were read are called the "readset" of the transaction. It is worth noticing that these two sets can (and usually do) overlap.

Operationally, `atomically` takes the tentative updates and applies them to the `TVars` involved, making these effects visible to other transactions. This method deals with maintaining a per-thread transaction log that records the tentative accesses made to `TVars`. When `atomically` is invoked, the STM runtime checks that these accesses are valid and that no concurrent transaction has committed conflicting updates. In case the validation turns out to be successful, then the modifications are committed altogether to the heap.

6.2.3   Other STM Tools

STM Haskell also provides means for composable blocking. The `retry` function of the `STM` monad aborts the current atomic transaction, and re-runs it after one of the transactional variables that it read from has been updated. This way, the atomic block does not execute unless there is some chance that it can make progress, avoiding busy waiting by suspending the thread performing `retry` until a re-execution makes sense. Conditional atomic blocks or join patterns can be implemented with the `orElse` method. This statement can be used to form alternative execution paths [4]: i.e. in a `orElse` b, if a invokes a `retry`, then b is executed; if b also retries, the whole statement does. The expressiveness provided by these two functions reflect the programmer's intent more accurately by allowing the runtime to manage the execution of the atomic block more efficiently and intelligently [12].

STM is robust to exceptions and uses methods similar to the exception handling that GHC provides for the `IO` monad. The function `atomically` prevents any globally visible state changes from occurring if an exception is raised inside the atomic block [5].

6.3   PROBLEM STATEMENT

6.3.1   Lock-Free Linked Structures in Haskell

Linked structures such as lists, trees and graphs are simple but very useful mechanisms for modeling a wide range of abstractions in several application domains

```
data LinkedList =
    Start {nextN :: TVar LinkedList}
    | Node { val :: Int, nextN :: TVar LinkedList}
    | Nil
```

FIGURE 6.1: Data declaration for a transactional linked list in Haskell

such as operating systems and compiler design. A desirable feature of these structures when they attempt to exploit concurrency is that they should be able to be shared and accessed safely and concurrently by many different threads. For this reason, lock-free shared memory data structures have long been studied in imperative languages [3, 20, 10]. The data declaration of a transactional singly linked list, similar to [6], is shown on Figure 6.1. Here, a Haskell implementation that uses transactional variables which refer to the tail of the list is illustrated. A linked list is defined as a `Start` node that does not hold a value; (possibly) regular nodes holding a value and a transactional reference to the next node of the list; and `Nil`, the end of the list.

Figure 6.2 contains the code for a function that inserts an element in a sorted linked list of integers. The `readTVar` adds the current node to the readset, and by moving to the next node by reading its `TVar`, we are able to compare the two node values to see whether the insertion should take place in between. If this is the case, we create a new node, link it to the next node and write a `TVar` (inside the `newListNode` function), and then write the new link from the previous node to the new one by writing another `TVar`, as shown on line 8. In other words, list traversal can only be accomplished by reading `TVars`, and the links to and from the newly created node can only be applied by writing transactional variables.

6.3.2   The Large Readset Size Issue

Traversing a transactional linked structure (either to insert, delete or search an element) consists of reading as many transactional variables as the nodes that follow, i.e. a transaction to insert an element in the position n of a transactional linked list would have a readset with (n-1) elements at commit time. Given that n could be very large, some obvious questions arise: Is it necessary to collect all of the elements read by the transaction in the dataset? Is it possible to remove some of those variables that were read earlier in the traversal from the readset?

6.3.3   The Problem of "False Conflict"

As a consequence of the large readset size issue, the false conflict problem appears. Imagine a list with 1000 elements and two threads operating over it, with one transaction (*T1*) wanting to insert or delete some element in the very beginning of the list, and another one (*T2*) wanting to operate on another element close

```
1   insertListNode :: TVar LinkedList -> Int -> STM ()
2   insertListNode curTNode numberToInsert = do
3     { curNode <- readTVar curTNode
4     ; let nextNTNode = nextN curNode
5     ; let doInsertion nextNNode =
6         do
7         { newNode <- newListNode numberToInsert nextNNode
8         ; writeTVar nextNTNode newNode
9         }
10    ; nextNNode <- readTVar nextNTNode
11    ; case nextNNode of
12        Nil -> doInsertion nextNNode
13        Node {val=valnextNNode, nextN=nextNnextNTNode}->
14          do
15          {if (valnextNNode == numberToInsert)
16            then return ()
17            else if (valnextNNode > numberToInsert)
18              then doInsertion nextNNode
19              else do
20                {insertListNode nextNTNode numberToInsert}
21          }
22    }
```

FIGURE 6.2: Linked List Node Insertion

to the end of the list. In order to get to the position to operate on, *T2* should accumulate a significant number of variables in its readset (pointers up to the current
position). Now, if *T1* committed, one pointer near the beginning of the list (i.e. in
T2's readset) would be modified and as a result of this, *T1* would be rolled back.
This scenario can be seen in Figure 6.3.

It can be intuitively said that with this approach, the probability of conflicts
(and thus rollbacks) while inserting and deleting elements on a linked list is directly proportional to its length. To tackle this undesirable characteristic, it would
be nice to "forget" those elements in the readset that are far behind with respect
to the current position of the traversal. This approach, which was previously discussed by [9], and implemented on imperative languages by [3, 19] involves the
use of inverse functionality of reading a transactional variable, i.e. "unreading" it.
Thus, if we had not accumulated the variables in our readset indiscriminately, and
instead had kept a fixed-size readset that moves forward as the list is traversed, the
probability of conflicts would not have been as large as the length of the list [8].
The idea of avoiding false conflict with a fixed-size readset is depicted in Figure
6.4.

A smaller readset implies a fewer number of conflicts and aborts as discussed
in [17]. In the next section, we relax the constraints of STM to be able to have a
constant readset size on our linked structures, and thus we aim for a faster execution time.

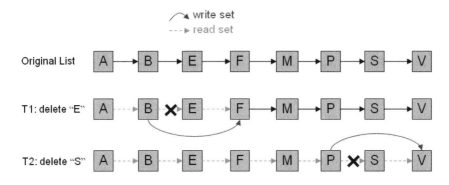

FIGURE 6.3: False Conflict

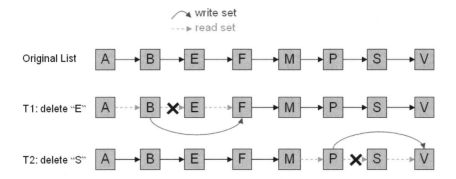

FIGURE 6.4: Avoiding False Conflict: *T1* and *T2* Operate on the List Concurrently

6.4 PROPOSED SOLUTION: `unreadTVar`

Since we are using Haskell to perform our tests on STM and its API defines `readTVar` as the function to read a transactional variable, we decided to call the function that "forgets" variables in the readset `unreadTVar`. The signature of this function is as follows:

```
unreadTVar :: TVar a -> STM ()
```

The semantics of `unreadTVar` x are:

- If x is not in the current transaction's readset, nothing happens.

- If x is both in the current transaction's readset and its writeset, nothing happens.

- If x only in the current transaction's readset, x is removed from it.

Recall that when a transaction *T1* reaches the commit phase, it has to check whether another committed transaction *Ti* has changed the value of any of the variables in *T1*'s readset, and if so, *T1* must rollback. Removing a variable from the readset means that the transaction will not look after it anymore. In other words, at commit time it does not matter at all if that variable has been modified by another transaction or not.

6.4.1   Implementation of `unreadTVar`

The implementation of `readTVar` was done by adding a function to the transactional library implemented in C (*STM.c*) and "plumbing" it through until making it available as a regular Haskell function in the *Conc.hs* file. This function traverses the dataset to identify the `TVar` to "unread" and to expulse it if it has only been read (i.e. no writes have been performed on it). The already existing infrastructure was almost completely suitable for the modification and apart from adding the new `unreadTVar` function, only one line of existing code had to be altered in a non-harmful way.

A dataset in Haskell STM is maintained in a linked list of so-called chunks [7]. Each chunk is a data structure that holds a limited number of transactional variable descriptors. When a chunk is full, another one has to be allocated and linked to the rest of the dataset to expand its capacity. Since the ordering of the variables within the set is not important, "unreading" was implemented by exchanging the last variable in the chunk with the unread one and decrementing the `nextFreePosition` index that refers to that chunk. Originally, the traversal of the dataset was done by reading all variables in each chunk except for the potentially incomplete one (the last one that has been inserted), in which case, the last variable to be examined was the (`nextFreePosition` - 1) st. The introduced modification consists of always traversing each chunk up to the last used position, because by adding the "unread" functionality, the variable that is "unread" can be in a chunk that is not the current one (last one that has been added), and thus causing incomplete chunks in the middle of the linked list of chunks. Finally when the transaction commits, all chunks are freed.

6.4.2   Using `unreadTVar`

As an example of the intended use, Figure 6.5 presents the modification that has to be done to increase the performance and the memory usage of the function previously shown in Figure 6.2. In this case, by using `unreadTVar`, the size of the readset varies between one and three elements on each iteration. Without `unreadTVar` use, the readset grows by one element on each iteration, and finally, in the extreme case of inserting or deleting the last element of the list, contains the whole set of elements of the list.

Furthermore, it is worth noticing that even with this approach, there is still a chance that two transactions that operate on elements that are far away from each other conflict, but this is quite unlikely to happen, i.e. the transaction on

```
19          else do
            { unreadTVar curTNode
20          ; insertListNode nextNTNode numberToInsert
            }
```

FIGURE 6.5: unreadTVar's Use in Linked List Node Insertion

the element that is closer to the beginning of the list must commit while the other transaction is traversing the same point of the list.

6.5 PERFORMANCE VERSUS SAFETY

6.5.1 Experimental Results

As pointed out above, having multiple transactions that operate on list elements that are far away from each other (with respect to traversal order) is a scenario that harms the performance of traditional linked structures because of the large number of rollbacks that will take place. To reproduce these settings, a program which forks two threads was created, where each of these threads atomically inserts and atomically deletes one element that is close to the beginning, and another one close to the end of a linked list. This way, the duration of each thread is the same on average, and there is a variety of (both long and short) transactions involved in the execution. Figure 6.6 summarizes the results of several such experiments concerning lists of different sizes, performed on an Intel 1.66 GHz dual-core machine with 1 GB of RAM and 2 MB shared L2 cache, running Linux. Two threads operate as described above, on the third element from the beginning and on the third from the end, with list sizes varying from 10 to 10,000.

As it can be seen, without using unreadTVar, the bigger the list, the more time it takes on average to operate on an element when the list has a considerably large size. This is because a bigger readset implies two overheads: The probability of re-execution because of rollbacks is greater, and on the other hand, commits are slower because there are more variables to check for conflicts [17]. Working with a small list, there is a high chance of conflict between transactions, no matter whether unreadTVar is used or not, causing the "U-shape" of the curves. As explained in Section 6.3.3, the probability of conflicts always increases with list size.

In order to investigate the scalability of unreadTVar, more experiments have been conducted on a four dual-core processor SMP server with Intel Xeon 5000 processors running at 3.0 GHz with 4MB L2 cache/processor and 16GB of total memory, where all of the reported results are based on the average of five executions. For the sake of variety regarding to the applications, binary trees were also analyzed in an analogous way to the linked list. The basic experiment consisted of 8000 operations on one shared data structure (i.e. either linked list or

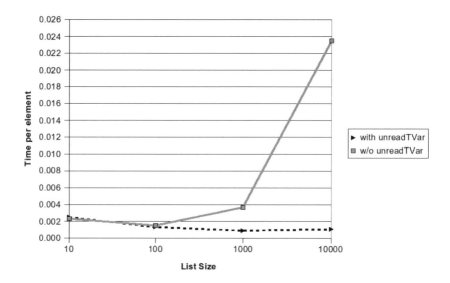

FIGURE 6.6: Time Taken per Element at Different List Sizes

binary trees), initially filled up only with even numbers to hold half of its capacity. Each operation was one atomic insertion of a random number and one atomic deletion of another one, both between 1 and 10000. The workload has been divided for multithreaded versions in such a way that the total number of operations performed for all threads is equal to 8000. For each data structure, three versions of the program were developed: a transactional version that uses the original STM library, another transactional version that uses the modified STM library to include the unreadTVar, and finally a sequential version implemented using IORefs. IORefs are analogous to TVars in the sense that both types of variables provide access to mutable memory cells, however; IORefs do not incorporate any synchronization mechanism. In Figures 6.7 and 6.8, the execution times are plotted for both data structures showing that:

- For both structures, the unreadTVar outperforms the original transactional library. Although more measurements might be needed on larger systems to confirm this, the results suggest that further performance improvements are possible beyond four dual-core processors.

- The unreadTVar version scales better for the linked list than the original STM approach. More number of cores would be needed to make a conclusion for the case of the trees.

- There is a breakpoint where the unreadTVar version starts showing absolute speedup. With eight cores, the unreadTVar version is 274% and 190% faster than the sequential IORef version for linked lists and binary trees respectively.

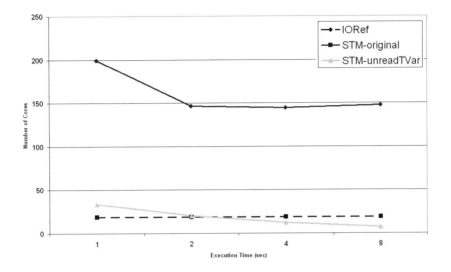

FIGURE 6.7: Scalability of unreadTVar on Linked Lists

- The regular transactional version is unable to show any absolute speedup even with 8 cores, compared to the sequential IOref version.

Based on the observations itemized above, unreadTVar turned out to be substantially faster than the original transactional version for transactions with a larger readset because it reduces the probability of conflicts and, therefore, rollbacks. The synthetic applications presented in this paper act as a proof of concept that the technique is useful in cases where linked structures are heavily utilized. For example, CCHR [16], a constraint solver developed in Haskell with TM as the parallel programming model, uses linked lists to write and read shared data that consists of the rules that the solver is trying to simplify.

6.5.2 Safety Issues

Imagine that we want to implement the function sum::LinkedList->STM Int that calculates the sum of all the elements in a linked list. Then, a subtle difference in the semantics will appear if one version that uses unreadTVar is compared to another one that does not use it. In the first case, there is a possibility that the calculation yields a number that represents the sum of a list that never existed. To see this, imagine that in time *t* when list traversal is around the middle of the list, one element *A* is deleted near the beginning of the list and by the time *t + 1*, another element *Z* is deleted around the end. Now, when the calculation of the sum is over, the value will be equal to the addition of the list containing the element in the beginning but without containing the one in the end, and actually such a list never existed. This condition could be valid or invalid depending on

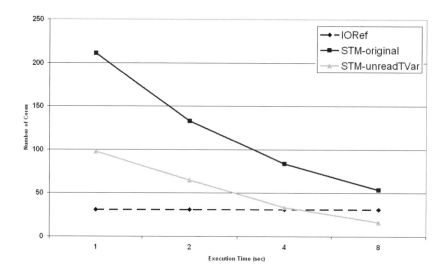

FIGURE 6.8: Scalability of `unreadTVar` on Binary Trees

the programmer's criteria. Figure 6.9 shows the list at time t, at time $t + 1$, with $A = 1$ and $Z = 9$ and the non-existent list seen by the *sum* function. So, by changing the strong semantic guarantees of STM, possible race conditions are introduced. Depending on the abort policy, if the readset is completely emptied, at that exact point there is no reason to rollback the transaction. Therefore, to comply with the semantics of the program and to avoid race conditions, the dangers of completely emptying the transaction's readset by using `unreadTVar` should be taken into account.

As a price for the performance improvement discussed previously, the safety promises of STM have been broken. Now the application has left the safe grounds and might behave inconsistently. This is the reason why while using `unreadTVar`,

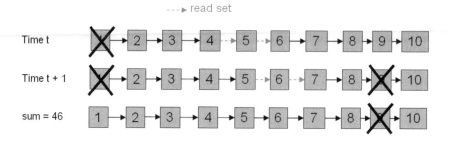

FIGURE 6.9: Calculation of the Sum of a List that Never Existed

```
module UnsafeSTM where
import GHC.Conc           -- The STM library
newtype UnsafeSTM a = STM a
unreadTVar :: TVar a -> UnsafeSTM ()
unsafeLiftSTM :: UnsafeSTM a -> STM a
```

FIGURE 6.10: The unsafeSTM module

the programmer has to be aware of these consequences and always has to keep an eye on the readset. As a light-weight approach to drawing a line between the safe and the unsafe world, a Haskell module called `UnsafeSTM` can be introduced (Figure 6.10). This module could be used alongside an unsafe lifting function to bring a computation into the (safe) STM monad. This would make it clear to the programmer that she is leaving the safe ground provided by Haskell's type system. Although with this method the syntax is made a little more complex, writing programs this way would also make it clearer at which points `unreadTVar` is usefully applied.

Since list insertion and deletion allow the use of `unreadTVar`, whereas calculating the list sum does not, the necessity of a criterion to decide whether to use the function or not arises. According to [10], this operation that does conflict reduction is "for designing shared pointer-based data structures such as lists and trees in which a transaction reads its way through a complex structure". The idea is that if it is necessary to have a snapshot of the linked structure that is being worked on, `unreadTVar` should not be used. On the other hand, if the programmer, during traversal, only cares about a smaller area around the current node and not the whole structure, then it is a candidate situation to allow forgetting objects. The authors of this paper call this "the snapshot criterion".

One transaction that uses `unreadTVar` can coexist in the same program with another that does not use it. However, in terms of composability, they can not be composed together safely inside the same atomic block, as the reduced readset that `unreadTVar` introduces might remove some variables that are useful for the other function to operate correctly. In other words, composing the sum function together with an insertion function that uses `unreadTVar` inside the same atomic block is a situation that must be refrained from.

Missing an opportunity for `unreadTVar` does not affect the original semantics of the program, however, adding too many could harm correctness. The `unreadTVar` could also be used on an already-complete program for fine-tuning the transactions for increased performance [19].

6.6   CONCLUSIONS

This paper introduced an efficient mechanism, the `unreadTVar`, to increase the performance of applications that use linked structures realized transactionally on Haskell. This was achieved by modifying the Haskell STM and adding the functionality of removing items from the readset of a transaction. Our results have shown consistency with the imperative versions of this functionality, where to the best of our knowledge, this was the first implementation for a functional language. We have provided performance comparisons run on actual hardware that showed substantial performance improvements due to the mechanism. The `unreadTVar` approach made two improvements to the implementation of transactional linked lists. First, by providing the transactions with a smaller dataset to work with, it significantly decreased the probability of having rollbacks. Second, since a smaller number of `TVars` had to be checked for consistency before committing, commits were made faster.

The most important drawback of using the `unreadTVar` is that it requires more care from the programmer. Since it is used for performance optimization, it requires the knowledge of exactly when and with which variable to use it. Specifically, as shown in the case in Figure 6.9, the usage does not apply for all sorts of operations that can be done with a linked structure, but preferably only the ones that fit the snapshot criterion. Although we attempted to add an extra level of security with the lifting function while using the `unreadTVar`, the approach might be more accurate with a compiler that is able to identify where to use it safely. Since compared to the sequential version, the original transactional version is unable to show any speedup even with 8 cores, approaches like the `unreadTVar` are necessary as significant ways of optimizing the performance of STM in Haskell.

ACKNOWLEDGEMENTS

This work is supported by the cooperation agreement between the Barcelona Supercomputing Center - National Supercomputer Facility and Microsoft Research, by the Ministry of Science and Technology of Spain and the European Union (FEDER funds) under contract TIN2004-07739-C02-01 and by the European Network of Excellence on High-Performance Embedded Architecture and Compilation (HiPEAC). The authors would like to thank Tim Harris, Eduard Ayguadé Parra, Roberto Gioiosa, Paul Carpenter, all at BSC-Nexus-I, Marco T. Morazán and the anonymous reviewers for all their helpful suggestions.

REFERENCES

[1] Peter Damron, Alexandra Fedorova, Yossi Lev, Victor Luchangco, Mark Moir, and Daniel Nussbaum. Hybrid transactional memory. *SIGOPS Oper. Syst. Rev.*, 40(5):336–346, 2006.

[2] Anthony Discolo, Tim Harris, Simon Marlow, Simon L. Peyton Jones, and Satnam Singh. Lock-free data structures using stm in haskell. In *Eighth International Symposium on Functional and Logic Programming (FLOPS)*, volume 3945 of *Lecture Notes in Computer Science*, pages 65–80. Springer, 2006.

[3] Keir Fraser. *Practical lock freedom*. PhD thesis, Cambridge University Computer Laboratory, 2003. Also available as Technical Report UCAM-CL-TR-579.

[4] Tim Harris, Adrian Cristal, Osman S. Unsal, Eduard Ayguade, Fabrizio Gagliardi, Burton Smith, and Mateo Valero. Transactional memory: An overview. *IEEE Micro*, 27(3), 2007.

[5] Tim Harris, Simon Marlow, Simon Peyton-Jones, and Maurice Herlihy. Composable memory transactions. In *PPoPP '05: Proceedings of the tenth ACM SIGPLAN symposium on Principles and practice of parallel programming*, pages 48–60, New York, NY, USA, 2005. ACM Press.

[6] Tim Harris and Simon Peyton-Jones. Transactional memory with data invariants. In *First ACM SIGPLAN Workshop on Languages, Compilers, and Hardware Support for Transactional Computing*, 2006.

[7] Tim Harris, Mark Plesko, Avraham Shinnar, and David Tarditi. Optimizing memory transactions. In *Proceedings of the ACM SIGPLAN Conference on Programming Language Design and Implementation*, pages 14–25. ACM Press, 2006.

[8] M. Herlihy. Course slides for cs176 - introduction to distributed computing: Concurrent lists, 2006.

[9] M. Herlihy and J. E. B. Moss. Transactional memory: Architectural support for lock-free data structures. In *Proceedings of theTwentiethAnnual International Symposium on Computer Architecture*, 1993.

[10] Maurice Herlihy, Victor Luchangco, Mark Moir, and William N. Scherer. Software transactional memory for dynamic-sized data structures. In *Proceedings of the 22nd Annual Symposium on Principles of Distributed Computing*, pages 92–101. ACM Press, 2003.

[11] http://www.haskell.org. Haskell official website.

[12] Frank Huch and Frank Kupke. Composable memory transactions in concurrent haskell. In *17th International Workshop on Implementation and Application of Functional Languages (IFL)*, 2005.

[13] Hal Daume III. Yet another haskell tutorial, 2004.

[14] Simon Peyton Jones, Andrew Gordon, and Sigbjorn Finne. Concurrent Haskell. In *Conference Record of POPL '96: The 23rd ACM SIGPLAN-SIGACT Symposium on Principles of Programming Languages*, pages 295–308, St. Petersburg Beach, Florida, 21–24 1996.

[15] Sanjeev Kumar, Michael Chu, Christopher J. Hughes, Partha Kundu, and Anthony Nguyen. Hybrid transactional memory. In *Proceedings of Symposium on Principles and Practice of Parallel Programming*, Mar 2006.

[16] Edmund S. L. Lam and Martin Sulzmann. A concurrent constraint handling rules implementation in haskell with software transactional memory. In *DAMP '07: Proceedings of the 2007 workshop on Declarative aspects of multicore programming*, pages 19–24, New York, NY, USA, 2007. ACM Press.

[17] Cristian Perfumo, Nehir Sonmez, Osman S. Unsal, Adrian Cristal, Mateo Valero, and Tim Harris. Dissecting transactional executions in haskell. In *TRANSACT 07*. Aug 2007.

[18] Nir Shavit and Dan Touitou. Software transactional memory. In *Proceedings of the 14th Annual ACM Symposium on Principles of Distributed Computing*, pages 204–213. ACM Press, 1995.

[19] Travis Skare and Christos Kozyrakis. Early release: Friend or foe? In *Workshop on Transactional Memory Workloads*. Jun 2006.

[20] Hakan Sundell. *Efficient and Practical Non-Blocking Data Structures*. PhD thesis, Department of Computing Science, Chalmers University of Technology, 2004.

Chapter 7

Property Directed Generation of First-Order Test Data

Fredrik Lindblad[1]

Abstract: Random testing is a powerful method for verifying program properties. However, as the complexity of the program and properties increases, writing customized input data generators quickly becomes necessary. We present a method for systematic generation of input data by lazy instantiation using metavariables and parallel partial evaluation of properties. This method is applied on specification based program verification. We claim that some program verification problems can be handled by systematic generation without the need of writing custom generators, and that some problems, for which writing generators is not a solution and random testing fails, are still simple enough for systematic generation. The system we present is related to narrowing and functional logic programming. It basically corresponds to needed narrowing but differs in the presentation and in some details of the parallel evaluation mechanism.

7.1 INTRODUCTION

One way to test a program is to write formal specifications for some aspects of its intended behavior. This enables automatic instead of manual testing, since the specifications can be used to assess whether a test succeeds or not. QuickCheck[5] is a popular tool for random testing of Haskell programs. Here, the program properties are expressed as boolean valued functions in Haskell itself.

As an example, imagine that we are representing binary search trees (BST) by ordinary binary trees and that we have implemented an operation, merge, which merges two BSTs. The precondition of merge should be that the two trees are really BSTs, i.e. the order of the elements is correct. We therefore implement a

---

[1]Department of Computer Science and Engineering, Chalmers University of Technology / Göteborg University, Gothenburg, Sweden, E-mail: frelindb@cs.chalmers.se

boolean function, `isBST`, which checks whether a tree is a BST. Next, we can state the property that, given two BSTs, the result of `merge` is again a BST:

```
prop t1 t2 = (isBST t1 && isBST t2) 'implies'
              isBST (merge t1 t2)
```

If non-specialized random testing is applied on this property, then most of the generated input trees will not be BSTs, since a less restrictive representation is used, namely general binary trees. Each time this happens, the implication is rendered effect-less. A lot of fruitless tests are thus performed. This problem can be overcome in QuickCheck by writing custom data generators, which narrow the generation and make the precondition fulfilled more frequently.

What we propose is to instead make more use of the precondition which has already been written, in this case `isBST`. This can be achieved by generating input data step-by-step while evaluating the functional description of the precondition. To gain the benefits from this, the search should be systematic rather than random. This way of searching for data is in itself not new. See the section on related work. But, to our knowledge, we contribute both in terms of some details of the system and in terms of its area of application.

In order to allow a property directed generation of data, we start from a small functional language with lazy evaluation and add *metavariables* (or *logical variables*). These are used as place holders for unknown parts of the data. During the search, the data is instantiated one step at a time, in an order in which it is required by the evaluation of the property. The search procedure is restricted to constructing first-order data structures. Consequently, metavariables can be seen as ordinary variables which are free, should this be more convenient to the reader.

Another addition with respect to a standard functional language is a possibility to perform *parallel evaluation*. This is useful in the presence of metavariables. For example, consider a predicate which is a conjunction of two other predicates, `p x = p1 x && p2 x`. Both `p1` and `p2` put restrictions on `x`. If (`&&`) is defined in the normal way, i.e. by looking at the arguments one at a time from left to right, we may have a situation where `x` is partially instantiated in such a way that, at this point, the value of (`p2 x`) is known to be `False`, whereas the value of (`p1 x`) is still unknown. Thus, by looking at both arguments in parallel, we might know something about the value of a function at an earlier stage and thereby reduce the search space. Of course, replacing the normal (`&&`) by a parallel version requires precaution in the presence of partial functions. This is discussed in section 7.4.6.

A key question is whether this property directed approach has an impact on the size of the search space substantial enough to be noticed in practice when applied on program verification problems. Later on we will claim that this is the case by presenting some examples.

7.2   RELATED WORK

7.2.1   Automatic Testing of Functional Programs

In the area of functional programming, *QuickCheck*[5] is a popular tool for testing. It is easy to adopt, since properties are written as normal boolean functions. A disadvantage of QuickCheck is that the properties are not taken into account while constructing input data. It was argued in the introduction that this sometimes makes the testing inefficient.

There is a another tool for testing Haskell code, called *SmallCheck*[11]. Like our approach, it is based on replacing random by systematic testing. But, like QuickCheck, it blindly generates data and then tests it. The main idea behind SmallCheck is that counter examples many times are small and that systematic generation can be better than random for various reasons, e.g. because it can find counter examples in the order of their size. Our approach is to some extent similar to that in SmallCheck, but adds some machinery to allow a more efficient systematic search.

7.2.2   Narrowing and Functional Logic Programming

The search algorithm we present can be seen as an instance of *narrowing*. More precisely, it falls within *lazy needed narrowing*[3] and is similar to *parallel weakly needed narrowing*[2]. In spite of this, we have chosen to refer to our system as *lazy instantiation*. This is not an attempt to neglect the relation to the results in the area of narrowing. Instead, since narrowing is so closely related to *rewriting*, whereas the system presented here is not, we considered it safer to use a different name.

Most recent narrowing techniques are based on compiling the rewrite rules into *definitional trees*[1]. Our system does not have rewrite rules, but merely case expressions. However, by combining our system with a functional language compiler which does the transformation from rewrite rules to case expressions, such as GHC, the result more or less amounts to needed narrowing. On the theoretical level, we believe that our presentation contributes in the way that, by avoiding rewrite rules, the system becomes relatively simple which helps focusing on the search algorithm.

The lazy, or needed, aspect of the system we present is indeed in principal not different from needed narrowing. But, on top of that we have added a notion of *parallel evaluation*. This addition is crucial for the performance in some of the examples presented towards the end. The parallel evaluation is also not a new concept in this context. It is related to *parallel narrowing*[2]. However, the resulting search algorithms are not quite the same. For example, in parallel narrowing the search might branch on instantiating different variables at the same point, whereas this is not possible in our version.

Using the terminology presented in [1], our system is intended to deal with *weakly orthogonal* programs, i.e. the rules may overlap provided that the functions are well-defined. This is normally enforced by stating that the right hand side of rules should be equal when they overlap. Note that we do not demand the right hand sides to be trivially equal, but merely that the results are the same at the end. This is the case with parallel addition, which is mentioned later on.

Narrowing techniques are used in *functional logic programming*. One important feature in functional logic programming languages, such as *Curry*[6, 7], is the possibility to write nondeterministic functions. Other features are *encapsulated search*[8] and *residuation*[6]. None of these are part of our system. The reason is simply that our focus is to apply narrowing techniques on plain functional programs, not to promote a different programming style by extending functional programming with logic programming features.

In *Curry* there is the notion of *concurrent conjunction*. The parallel evaluation in our system generalizes this. The semantics of concurrent conjunction is not documented in detail[7], so it is difficult to know if it is more similar to our approach or to that in [2]. Note that the *and*-construct in the operational semantics of Curry[6] deals with the scheduling of computations in the presence of residuation. It is not related to parallel evaluation in the sense which is discussed here.

7.3   STEP-BY-STEP EXAMPLES

Before giving a more precise definition of the system, let us look at a couple of toy examples in order to make the mechanism of the search clear. The first example involves the following definitions:

```
data N = Z                         Z       >  _      = False
       | S N                       (S x)   >  Z      = True
                                   (S x)   >  (S y)  = x > y
p :: [N] -> Bool
p []       = True                  False && _ = False
p (x:[])   = True                  True  && x = x
p (x:y:xs) = x > y && p (y:xs)
```

The boolean predicate p is defined over lists with elements in N, which denotes the natural numbers. The predicate contains all lists in which the numbers are strictly decreasing. Let us now use the principle of lazy narrowing (or lazy instantiation) in order to find such lists. First we apply the predicate to a metavariable, which serves as a placeholder for the currently unknown value.

$$p \; ?_1$$

Next we evaluate this expression lazily as far as possible. The evaluation gets stuck immediately because p does a case analysis on its argument, which is unknown. We say that $?_1$ is *blocking* the evaluation of the expression. Therefore we instantiate $?_1$ to one of its valid constructor forms, inserting fresh metavariables at the argument positions. Since $?_1 :: [N]$ we first guess $?_1$ to be the empty list.

$$?_1 := []$$

We then continue evaluating the expression. This gives us `True` which means we have found a solution to the search problem, namely a member of the predicate p. The correct list can be compiled by combining all instantiations we have currently made, in this case just a single one. But we want more solutions, so we carry on by undoing the last step. Hence we replace the previous instantiation by $?_1 := ?_2 : ?_3$, stating that we assume $?_1$ to be an arbitrary non-empty list. We continue the lazy evaluation with the new instantiation and arrive at

$$p\ (?_2 : ?_3).$$

According to the definition of p, $?_3$ is now the blocking metavariable. We therefore instantiate $?_3$, first to the empty list which again leads to a solution, namely $?_2 : [\,]$, which is in fact a class of valid instances. This of course corresponds to the fact that for lists of length one, the one element can have any value. Then we instantiate $?_3$ to a non-empty list, $?_3 := ?_4 : ?_5$. Now the evaluation stops at

$$?_2 > ?_4\ \&\&\ p\ (?_4 : ?_5),$$

with $?_2$ being the blocking metavariable, since both (`&&`) and (`>`) first look at their first argument. This time we have the constructors Z and S to choose from. Instantiating $?_2$ to zero makes the expression evaluate to `False`. Here we can see the main idea of narrowing, namely that by detecting failure before the data is fully instantiated, a whole class of instances can be disqualified as candidates in a single step. In this case all combinations of instances replacing $?_4$ and $?_5$ have been found to lead to non-solutions. If we instead instantiate $?_2$ to a non-zero number, $?_2 := S\ ?_6$, and continue a couple of steps in the same way, the reader can see that the next solution we encounter is $S\ ?_6 : Z : [\,]$. We could carry on in the same manner in order to find more solutions, but lets stop at this point.

The second example is very simple and is intended to illustrate the notion of parallel evaluation applied on boolean conjunction. We add the following definitions to the ones in the previous example.

```
q :: N -> Bool          odd Z = False
q x = odd x && S Z > x   odd (S Z) = True
                         odd (S (S n)) = odd n
```

We will search for members of the predicate q. We therefore start with the expression $q\ ?_1$. The predicate happen to have no elements, but the situation is still relevant, since the main point is to detect early failure whenever possible. But since (`&&`) first looks at its left argument, the search mechanism described in the previous example will end up generating an infinite sequence of odd numbers, only to find out that each of them is too large. Let us now redefine the boolean conjunction to be parallel.

```
False && _     = False
_     && False = False
True  && True  = True
```

These clauses should not be interpreted with the standard first-match semantics in mind. They rather express that whenever the first or the second argument evaluates to `False` the conjunction itself is also `False`. When performing a search with this parallel definition of (`&&`), we evaluate both arguments of any conjunction as far as possible. In this example it means that when $?_1$ has been instantiated to S $?_2$, the second conjunct will evaluate to `False` causing the search to terminate without regarding any instantiations of $?_2$.

In this example the subexpressions that were evaluated in parallel happened to be blocked by the same metavariable at all times. This may of course not be the case when we are dealing with non-linear data structures. In general there is a collection of blocking metavariables when doing parallel evaluation. How we deal with this will be discussed later on.

7.4   THE SYSTEM

Program verification as presented in the introduction readily generalizes to the problem of finding members of a decidable predicate expressed as a boolean function, p :: X -> Bool. In other words, we search for values x of type X such that (p x) computes to True. The presented system is restricted in such a way that X must be a first-order algebraic data type, just like for any standard narrowing strategy. Including higher-order types requires a more involved machinery. See the concluding section for a few comments about higher-order narrowing.

We start from a functional programming language with first-order non-recursive algebraic data types and case-expressions. To this we add *metavariables*, denoted by indexed question-marks, $?_i$, which allow step-by-step construction of values during search. A second extension is that, instead of an ordinary case expression, the language has a construction for *select-case* terms. This is simply a collection of normal case expressions which are evaluated in parallel. As soon as it is clear which branch to choose for one of the case expressions in a select-case term, that one is selected for further evaluation and all the others are discarded. The other case expressions can be safely discarded under the assumptions that the term is well-defined, i.e. all alternatives in a select-case term yield the same result. The feature of parallel case expressions is intended to allow symmetrical definitions of operators such as conjunction, as described in the introduction.

Recursive data types and functions are not part of the presentation. They can be thought of as infinite types and terms or as defined using meta-level fix-points. Recursive data types and functions are however part of the implementation. Recursive functions may cause non-termination in the same way as when executing functional programs normally. Recursive data types potentially make the search space infinite. This is handled simply by using iterated deepening.

After a more precise presentation of the syntax and the partial reduction of terms, we describe a simple search strategy for the problem stated above. This is followed by some preliminaries of proving the correctness of the search strategy. A proof of the correctness is not included. After that we give some notes on our implementation.

$$
\begin{array}{lcl}
\tau & ::= & \overline{c\,\overline{\tau}} \\
\end{array}
\qquad
\begin{array}{lcl}
\Gamma & ::= & \varnothing \\
& | & \Gamma[?_i : \tau]
\end{array}
$$

$$
\begin{array}{lcl}
t,u,v & ::= & x \\
& | & \text{select case } t \text{ of } \overline{br} \\
& | & c\,\overline{t} \\
& | & ?_i \\
& | & \text{blkd}_{\mathcal{M}}\, t
\end{array}
\qquad
\begin{array}{lcl}
\Delta & ::= & \varnothing \\
& | & \Delta[?_i = c\,\overline{t}] \\
\\
br & ::= & c\,\overline{x} \to t
\end{array}
$$

FIGURE 7.1: Types, terms, environments and closures

7.4.1 Syntax

Figure 7.1 presents the syntax. A bar over an entity denotes a list. Variables are denoted by x and constructor names by c. Types are denoted by τ. A type is a list of constructors where each constructor is followed by a list of its arguments' types. Types are represented by syntactic constructs, rather than declaring a many-sorted signature which is normally the case. The reason for this deviation is to be able to make the instantiation of a metavariable to the constructors of its type explicit in the search algorithm. Let $\mathcal{B}$ denote the type of booleans, $\mathcal{B} \equiv \{\texttt{true}, \texttt{false}\}$.

A term, denoted by t, u, v, is either a variable occurrence, a select-case term, a constructor application or a metavariable occurrence. Select-case terms consists of a list of ordinary case expressions. Each case expression has a list of branches, denoted by br. For the sake of simplicity, the patterns in the branches are restricted to the form $c\,\overline{x}$, i.e. a constructor followed by a list of variables. A constructor application is a constructor followed by a list of argument terms. The last term construction, $\texttt{blkd}_{\mathcal{M}}\, t$, is used internally by the algorithm and represents a term, t, whose further reduction is blocked by a set of metavariables, $\mathcal{M}$.

An environment, Γ, is a set of typing judgments for metavariables. A closure, Δ, is a set of binding judgments for metavariables. The right hand side of a binding judgment is restricted to be a constructor application. The judgment $\Gamma \vdash ?_i : \tau$ will be used to denote that $?_i$ is declared to be of type τ in Γ, whereas $\Gamma \nvdash ?_i$ means that $?_i$ is not declared in Γ, i.e. is a fresh metavariable. The judgment $\Delta \vdash ?_i = c\,\overline{t}$ means that $?_i$ is bound to $c\,\overline{t}$ in Δ, and $\Delta \nvdash ?_i$ expresses that $?_i$ is not bound in Δ.

7.4.2 Type Rules

We omit a formal presentation of type rules for terms in the language. They basically contain no surprises. However, an important detail is that we demand case expressions to have exactly one branch for each constructor in the data type. A reference implementation of the language and search algorithm has been written[9]. This also contains a type-checking algorithm.

We will use the notation $[x_1 : \tau_1, \ldots, x_n : \tau_n]\, t : \tau$ to denote the judgment that t is type correct and of type τ in the context where $x_1 : \tau_1, \ldots, x_n : \tau_n$.

$$\frac{t_i \twoheadrightarrow_\Delta c\,\overline{u} \quad \mathtt{pick}\ c\,\overline{u}\,\overline{br}_i = v \quad v \twoheadrightarrow_\Delta v'}{\mathtt{select}\ \overline{\mathtt{case}\ t\ \mathtt{of}\ \overline{br}} \twoheadrightarrow_\Delta v'}$$

$$\frac{\forall i.t_i \twoheadrightarrow_\Delta \mathtt{blkd}_{\mathcal{M}_i}\ t'_i}{\mathtt{select}\ \overline{\mathtt{case}\ t\ \mathtt{of}\ \overline{br}} \twoheadrightarrow_\Delta \mathtt{blkd}_{\bigcup_i \mathcal{M}_i}\ \mathtt{select}\ \overline{\mathtt{case}\ t'\ \mathtt{of}\ \overline{br}}}$$

$$\frac{}{c\,\overline{t} \twoheadrightarrow_\Delta c\,\overline{t}} \qquad \frac{\Delta \vdash ?_i = t}{?_i \twoheadrightarrow_\Delta t} \qquad \frac{\Delta \nvdash ?_i}{?_i \twoheadrightarrow_\Delta \mathtt{blkd}_{\{?_i\}}\ ?_i}$$

FIGURE 7.2: Term reduction

7.4.3   Term Reduction

We now turn to head reduction of terms, $t \twoheadrightarrow_\Delta t'$, in the presence of metavariables, presented in figure 7.2. The term which is reduced is assumed to be closed, i.e. all variable occurrences are bound by a variable on the left hand side of a surrounding case branch. It may on the other hand of course contain *meta* variable occurrences. A reduction is indexed by the closure in which it takes place. The idea is to reduce a term outside-in until a metavariable is encountered whose value is not known, i.e. is not bound by a binding judgment in the closure. The reduction of a term always produces either a constructor application or a blocked term.

When reducing a select-case term the presence of several alternative definitions is used to pick any one of them which allows the reduction to continue further. If the scrutinee term of one of the case expressions reduces to a constructor application, then, due to the restriction we imposed on the patterns, we know that the left hand side of one of its branches will match the term. The function `pick` is not described formally. It is assumed to, given a constructor, a list of terms and a list of branches, find the branch whose head on the left hand side matches the constructor and return the branch's body with the argument terms correctly substituted into it. The resulting term is then reduced. If, on the other hand, the scrutinees of all the case expressions reduce to a blocked term, then further reduction is postponed, and the select-case term itself is marked blocked by the union of the blocking metavariables.

A metavariable occurrence is reduced to its value if it has a binding judgment in the closure. Otherwise, the term is marked blocked by the meta variable itself.

We will now illustrate the two non-standard aspects of the reduction beginning with metavariables and blocked terms. Let us define a macro for boolean conjunction.

$$x \wedge y \equiv \mathtt{select}\ \mathtt{case}\ x\ \mathtt{of}\ \{\mathtt{true} \to y,\ \mathtt{false} \to \mathtt{false}\}$$

Next, assume we want to reduce $?_1 \wedge ?_2$ in a closure, Δ, not containing any binding judgments for $?_1$ or $?_2$. Expanding the macro we see that the scrutinee of the only case expression is $?_1$, and $?_1 \twoheadrightarrow_\Delta \mathtt{blkd}_{\{?_1\}}\ ?_1$. Since the scrutinee of the case expression reduces to a blocked term, we have $?_1 \wedge ?_2 \twoheadrightarrow_\Delta \mathtt{blkd}_{\{?_1\}}\ ?_1 \wedge ?_2$. Hence,

$$\text{init } t\ \tau \ = \ (\varnothing[?_1 : \tau], \varnothing, t')$$
$$\text{where} \quad t[x := ?_1] \twoheadrightarrow_\varnothing t'$$

$$\text{step } ?_i\ c_j\ (\Gamma, \Delta, t) \ = \ (\Gamma[\overline{?_k} : \overline{\tau}_j], \Delta', t')$$
$$\text{where} \quad \Gamma \vdash ?_i : c\,\overline{\tau}$$
$$\Gamma \nvdash \overline{?_k}$$
$$\Delta' = \Delta[?_i = c_j\ \overline{?_k}]$$
$$t \twoheadrightarrow_{\Delta'} t'$$

$$\text{search } (\Gamma, \Delta, \text{true}) \ = \ [\text{compose } \Delta\ ?_1]$$
$$\text{search } (\Gamma, \Delta, \text{false}) \ = \ []$$
$$\text{search } (\Gamma, \Delta, \text{blkd}_{\mathcal{M}}\ t) \ = \ \text{concatMap } (\backslash c_j \rightarrow \text{search } (\text{step } ?_i\ c_j\ (\Gamma, \Delta, t)))\ \overline{c}$$
$$\text{where} \quad ?_i \in \mathcal{M}$$
$$\Gamma \vdash ?_i : \overline{c\,\overline{\tau}}$$

$$\text{compose } \Delta\ ?_i \quad | \quad \Delta \vdash ?_i = c\,\overline{\imath} \ = \ c\ (\text{map } (\text{compose } \Delta)\ \overline{\imath})$$
$$\text{compose } \Delta\ ?_i \quad | \quad \Delta \nvdash ?_i \ \ = \ ?_i$$

FIGURE 7.3: Definitions of init, step, search and compose

the term was only partially reduced and blocked by $?_1$ to indicate that the lack of knowledge of this metavariable's value stopped the reduction from proceeding further. Moreover, if the term consists of nested case expressions, the blocking information is passed on to the top of the resulting term. For instance, applying the reduction rules we get $(?_1 \wedge ?_2) \wedge ?_3 \twoheadrightarrow_\Delta \text{blkd}_{\{?_1\}}\ (?_1 \wedge ?_2) \wedge ?_3$.

The other anomaly is the parallel evaluation following from the presence of the select-case construction. We can define a parallel, symmetrical version of the conjunction.

$$x \wedge_p y \equiv \text{select } \{\text{case } x \text{ of } \{\text{true} \rightarrow y, \text{ false} \rightarrow \text{false}\},$$
$$\text{case } y \text{ of } \{\text{true} \rightarrow x, \text{ false} \rightarrow \text{false}\}\}$$

Given the term $?_1 \wedge_p ?_2$, we see that the scrutinees of the two parallel case expression are $?_1$ and $?_2$ respectively. Both these reduce to blocked terms, $\text{blkd}_{\{?_1\}}\ ?_1$ and $\text{blkd}_{\{?_2\}}\ ?_2$, and the select-case term is consequently blocked by the union of the blocking metavariables. Thus $?_1 \wedge_p ?_2 \twoheadrightarrow_\Delta \text{blkd}_{\{?_1, ?_2\}}\ ?_1 \wedge_p ?_2$. In the case of parallel conjunction, if either of t and u reduces to false, then $t \wedge_p u$ will reduce to false.

7.4.4 Search Algorithm

Now assume that we have a term, t, and a type, τ, such that $[x : \tau]\ t : \mathcal{B}$. For this predicate over τ we want to find all elements, i.e. constructor terms, u, such that $t[x := u] \twoheadrightarrow \text{true}$.

A simple search algorithm is defined by the functions in figure 7.3. Given a predicate and its domain, i.e. a t and a τ, `init` produces the initial deduction state. The state consists of an environment, a closure and a partially reduced term. The initial term is based on t where the free variable is replaced by $?_1$, and the initial environment declares $?_1$ to be of type τ. The `step` function takes a metavariable, a constructor and a state. For that state, the closure is extended by a judgment binding the metavariable to an application of the desired constructor with fresh metavariables as arguments. The environment is extended by type judgments for the new metavariables and the term is re-reduced in the new closure. So, the search algorithm is based on elementary steps which refine the data by one constructor at a time.

Given an initial state, the `search` function does a depth first search by applying the step function recursively. Before each step, the term of the state is examined. There are three cases.

- If the term is `true`, a solution has been found and the value is constructed by calling the `compose` function. The constructed term may however contain uninstantiated metavariables, corresponding to parts of the data which the reduction did not depend on. Hence, in general, a solution is a term containing constructor applications and (uninstantiated) metavariables. We will call such a term a partial constructor term (PCT).

- If the term is instead `false`, a non-solution has been reached and the search is back-tracked.

- Finally, if the term is of the form $\text{blkd}_{\mathcal{M}}\ t$, then one of the blocking metavariables in $\mathcal{M}$, say $?_i$, is picked for refinement and the search is forked by one branch for each constructor of the metavariable's type.

For a pair, t and τ, $(\text{search }(\text{init } t\ \tau))$ will return a list of PCTs making the predicate true.

The presented algorithm is nondeterministic in the choice of the metavariable to refine when there are several metavariables blocking the term. The strategy for picking a blocking metavariable can certainly have a large impact on the size of the search space. A natural choice is to keep a collection of metavariables for refinement and add new ones for each new reduction of the term. The collection of pending metavariables can e.g. be either a queue or a stack. One could also think of using a priority queue and trying to design some heuristics for assigning priorities to metavariables. However, coming up with good and general such heuristics seems difficult. Using the stack approach is vastly superior for some special applications, but the queue seems better in most cases. It also has the advantage that it treats the metavariables in a fair way. This is important when dealing with recursive functions and data types. Since, when using a queue, all blocking metavariables will be refined sooner or later, some problems including recursive data types will generate a finite search space rather than infinite.

7.4.5   Correctness of the Search Algorithm

We have not proved the correctness of the presented algorithm. Nevertheless, we think that formulating it informally contributes to understanding the algorithm.

A first attempt to state the correctness is to claim that the search algorithm is sound if, for all constructor terms u in (search (init t τ)), we have $t[x := u] \twoheadrightarrow_{\varnothing}$ true. It is complete if the reverse holds. However, there are two details that require a more refined formulation of the correctness.

The first is that, due to the presence of select-case terms, users can write terms which are not well defined. A term may be evaluated to different values depending on which case expression is chosen in a select-case term which is not well defined. Hence, all we can hope for is that the constructor terms for which all the possible evaluation paths yields True are found. On the other hand, if the algorithm finds a PCT, we can only require that there exists one path leading to True. For predicates which can compute to both true and false for a fixed value, the soundness and completeness do not express anything. But, again, the nondeterminism in this language is only intended to give alternative definitions of well defined functions, such as a symmetric conjunction.

The second detail is that the algorithm returns PCTs, and not constructor terms. But constructor terms and PCTs can be related by saying that a PCT, t, *includes* a constructor term, u, if there is a metavariable substitution, Δ, such that $\Delta t = u$. In the case of completeness, the strongest we can claim is that for any constructor term, u, for which the predicate is true, the algorithm will find a PCT which includes u.

7.4.6   Implementation

We have implemented the presented system by writing a compiler and a runtime system executing the search algorithm. The compiler reads the GHC external core language. By using the GHC compiler to translate full Haskell into a smaller language, many features come for free, such as patterns and type classes. The features that we have added compared to the presented system are basically recursive data type and function definitions, as well as higher-order functions.

In the presented rules for term reduction, we chose to let the rule which blocks a select-case term not leave the blocking information in its subexpressions. This was in order to keep the presentation simple. But if this information is preserved, re-reduction of a term can be more economic. In the implementation, when a metavariable has been refined, only the parts of the term which are indeed blocked by that metavariable are re-evaluated.

The blocking metavariables are stored in a queue, as discussed above. Also, the search is parameterized by a search depth, which is in general needed when dealing with recursive data types. Iterated deepening is used to avoid infinite branching and to find small solutions before larger ones.

The examples which are presented in the next section and whose details are given in [9], were written for an older version of the implementation, which ac-

gp*n*	finite algebraic groups, *n* is size of group
hp*n*	leftist heaps, *n* is size of heap
gr*n*	directed, single edge graphs with paths from all to all edges, *n* is number of edges plus vertices
re*n*	regular expressions, checking an incorrect property, *n* is total number of constructors in generated data
ri*n*	valid pairs of type and term for reference implementation, *n* is number of constructors in type and term

TABLE 7.1: Abbreviations and descriptions of the examples

cepted only a subset of Haskell. Higher-order functions were e.g. not supported, so the source code may appear a bit clumsy.

When applying lazy instantiation on a Haskell program, one may want to replace e.g. normal boolean conjunction for its parallel counterpart in order to improve performance. But this influences the semantics of the program. A program can be written in such a way that the second argument of a conjunction or disjunction is partial sometimes, but not when the value of the first argument forces the computation of the second one. If a conjunction or disjunction is changed to compute the arguments in parallel, such partiality may be exposed. Partiality due to undefinedness is easily handled if the exception can be caught. An error in the second argument of a conjunction should simply yield False, since it must then be the case that the first argument eventually computes to this value, provided that the program is correct. Partiality due to non-termination cannot be handled in this way. It is up to the user to avoid changing functions to their parallel counterparts when non-termination may be exposed.

7.5 EXAMPLES

We will now present a few examples where the system has been used to systematically generate data. Table 7.1 gives a short presentation of the examples which are referred to in the figures of this section. The full examples can be found in [9].

In the first three examples, the measurement of the size of the data is customized rather than based on the depth of the search (number of constructors). This was done by adding a size predicate to the property. We represent the size by natural numbers implemented as a recursive data type. For non-linear data, such as trees, one needs to add the sizes of several sub terms. Using an ordinary addition function defined by recursion on one of the arguments can lead to a generation of much larger data than intended. We work around this by using the feature of parallel evaluation also for addition of recursively defined numbers. Using this, as soon as any part of a tree grows, the increase of the size is propagated to the top.

One of the purposes of the presented approach is to remove the necessity of writing custom generators is some cases. Adding customized size predicates may appear to go against this idea. The size predicates are however not very important for the performance. They are used in order to have a clear measure of how large a set of candidates has been covered. Note also in the example gp, that finite groups may be rather unrealistic as input data to a program. But it is an example where the parts of the data are highly interdependent. In such situations the impact of parallel conjunction is substantial.

In order to make the examples a bit more vivid to the reader, we will give some more details of a couple of them. The example hp is about leftist heaps with the rank stored in each node. The heaps are represented by trees with natural numbers both as ranks and elements in the nodes.

```
data RTree = Empty
           | Node Nat Nat RTree RTree
```

The predicate isHeap decides whether a tree is a leftist heap with the correct rank stored. It is defined in terms of three sub properties.

```
isHeap :: RTree -> Bool
isHeap x = wellRanked x >&< leftist x >&< hop x
```

The last conjunct is the heap order property. All three sub properties are defined recursively over the tree. The operator (>&<) is the parallel version of (&&). In order to control the size of the heaps, we use the following property to generate them.

```
prop :: Nat -> RTree -> Bool
prop size x = sizeRTree x <= size >&< eltSizeOk size x
              >&< isHeap x
```

The number of nodes is calculated by sizeRTree using the parallel addition mentioned above, while eltSizeOk makes sure the element in each node is smaller than the given size.

The result of running the system on the isHeap property with size 7 looks like this:

```
Empty
(Node 0 1 Empty Empty)
(Node 0 1 (Node 0 1 Empty Empty) Empty)
(Node 0 1 (Node 1 1 Empty Empty) Empty)
. . .
(Node 0 1 (Node 6 1 Empty Empty) Empty)
(Node 0 1 (Node 0 1 (Node 0 1 Empty Empty) Empty) Empty)
. . .
(Node 4 3 (Node 4 2 (Node 6 1 Empty Empty)
  (Node 5 1 Empty Empty)) (Node 4 2 (Node 4 1 Empty Empty)
  (Node 5 1 Empty Empty)))
. . .
```

The total number of solutions with size less or equal to 7 is 474620, which take around a second to find.

The other example we will look a bit more closely at, `re`, uses the following data type for regular expressions:

```
data RE = Sym Nat
        | Or RE RE
        | Seq RE RE
        | And RE RE
        | Star RE
        | Empty
```

Here the construction `And` is meant to denote the intersection between two regular expressions, whereas `Seq` stands for the concatenation of expressions. Symbols are represented by natural numbers. The function `accepts` checks whether a regular expression matches a list of symbols.

```
accepts :: RE -> [Nat] -> Bool
```

We add the auxiliary function `repInt` such that `repInt n k re` accepts between n and k sequences of symbols, where each sequence is accepted by `re`.

```
repInt :: Nat -> Nat -> RE -> RE
```

The search was run on the negation of the following property:

```
prop :: (Nat, Nat, RE, RE, [Nat]) -> Bool
prop (n,k,p,q,s) =
  (accepts (And (repInt n k p) (repInt n k q)) s)
  <==> (accepts (repInt n k (And p q)) s)
```

The left hand side of the equivalence says that the sequence, s, is accepted by both repeating p between n and k times, and by repeating q between n and k times. The right hand side claims that s is accepted by repeating the conjunction of p and q between n and k times. The property holds from right to left, but not the other way around, since the left hand side is less restrictive. The following counter example of this property is found after about one second using iterated deepening.

```
(2, 2, Or Empty (Seq (Sym 0) (Sym 0)), Sym 0, [0, 0])
```

The counter example exploits the fact that on the left hand side of the equivalence the repetitions of p and q need not be aligned. Finding this counter example is not tractable using QuickCheck.

7.5.1 Lazy Instantiation

Figure 7.4 shows a comparison between using the system, i.e. the property directed lazy instantiation, versus a blind enumeration, both in order to generate all possible test data up to the size indicated by the suffixed number in the chart. The

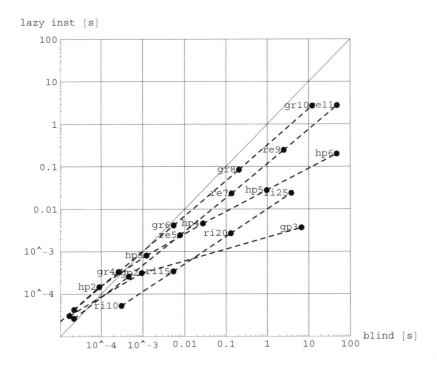

FIGURE 7.4: Lazy instantiation vs. blind enumeration

logarithm of the running times is used to fit several orders of magnitude into the same plot. If a point is to the right of the diagonal, lazy instantiation is faster than blind enumeration.

For some of the examples, lazy instantiation becomes noticeably faster as the size increases. The most successful ones are two to three orders of magnitude faster at the largest sizes included in the plot. For the less successful, the difference grows rather slowly with size. It is obvious that some applications are more suitable than others for lazy instantiation.

The main idea of our approach is to evaluate properties step-by-step while constructing the data. Hopefully this allows knowing the output of the predicate (True or False) when the data is still to large extent uninstantiated. In such situations it is clear that all further instantiations will result in the same output, since the evaluation does not depend on the uninstantiated parts. If the output is known at an early stage often enough, the resulting pruning of the search tree will be substantial and the speed gain of the enumeration will be noticeable.

The differences in how successful the method is compared to blind enumeration should be related to the degree of early failure of the problem. For problems where the constructed data is subject to non-structural inspection, large portions of the data must be instantiated before the answer is known. A typical example

parallel [s]

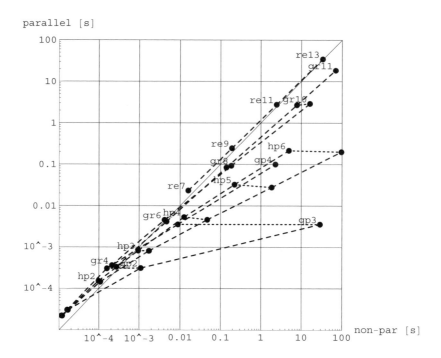

FIGURE 7.5: Non-parallel vs. parallel evaluation

is generating programs which are executed in the property. The regular expressions example could be characterized in this way. On the other hand, problems which basically inspect the constructed data following its structure recursively should exhibit high frequency of early failure. The heap example belongs to this category.

7.5.2   Parallel Evaluation

In figure 7.5, the comparison is between using and not using parallel versions of conjunction, disjunction and addition. In this plot there are additional lines, consisting of shorter dashes. These lines connect runs which only differ by the order of certain conjuncts in the properties.

We can see that for some examples there is a permutation of the conjuncts, for which the non-parallel evaluation search works equally well, or even slightly better than the parallel evaluation search. On the other hand, for some of them there are also permutations where non-parallel search is substantially worse than parallel. The fact that the short dashed lines are almost horizontal however shows that the parallel search is not sensitive to the order of conjuncts, as expected. Hence, the main advantage of parallel evaluation seems to be its robustness –

when used, one is not obliged to tweak the order of conjuncts in the property.

7.6   CONCLUSIONS AND FUTURE WORK

The presented examples indicate that using lazy instantiation, or narrowing techniques in general, rather than blind generate-and-test may improve the speed of enumerating constrained data considerably. We have not yet conducted a thorough comparison between our approach and a random testing tool, such as QuickCheck. However, what we have seen so far suggests that many examples which can be solved using our approach are not tractable with random testing unless custom generators are added. Also, for some problems, like the regular expressions example, writing generators does not apply or is too complicated, and random testing simply fails. This aside, not having to write custom generators is in our opinion already an improvement.

In a typical program verification situation, such as the one presented in the introduction, we have a choice. Either we generate input data meeting the precondition and, for each such input, test the consequent of the implication. Or, we try generating data which directly disproves the property, i.e. by involving the entire property in the search. One advantage of the latter is that this provides more guidance for the search. However, our experiments show that the effect of this extra guidance is very modest, at best increasing speed a few times. On the other hand, the former choice makes it possible to test programs written in another language, functional or non-functional. As long as the precondition is expressed in our system, a search can be performed that enumerates valid input data which can be exported to another language and used for testing.

Applying random testing directly on lazy instantiation does not make sense. A systematic search is necessary in order to benefit from the guidance. However, we have done some experiments on combining systematic and random search. The results show that this can sometimes lead to better performance and it would be interesting to look at this more closely.

One interesting improvement of the system is to make the algorithm continuously detect if the current problem separates into several independent subproblems. Consider e.g. a term such as $P(?_1) \wedge_p Q(?_2)$. Since the first and second conjunct depend on disjoint sets of metavariables, the problem could be divided in two. This way the instantiation of $?_1$ and $?_2$ would not be interleaved and the search space could shrink drastically. The situation appears e.g. when generating correct terms for some typed λ-calculus. A term is typically type correct if all its sub terms are correct. We have implemented a prototype of the general system which separates independent subproblems. It seems to have a large impact on this kind of problems. However, the prototype is very inefficiently implemented, so the actual running times currently differ only moderately.

Antoy and Tolmach have investigated achieving higher-order narrowing with first-order narrowing strategies [4]. Encoding higher-order terms in a first-order data type and applying narrowing on a higher-order proof checking algorithm can be seen as an attempt in the same direction.

The presented system does not cover generation of data containing primitives, such as characters or integers. In all the presented examples we use recursively defined natural numbers instead of integers. This seems to suffice in many cases since we often look for solutions containing small numbers. An investigation of extending narrowing with linear constraints is presented in [10].

To sum up, we have introduced a system named lazy instantiation which is closely related to parallel narrowing. There are however differences in the details of parallel evaluation which we believe can be important. Also, the presentation is in some sense as simple as possible for the intended application area. Hopefully it is accessible to persons who are familiar with functional programming, but not rewriting. We have argued that the system (and also narrowing in large) can successfully be applied on specification based program verification. Finally, we have given some empirical results that support this claim and show the impact of our notion of parallel evaluation.

REFERENCES

[1] S. Antoy. Evaluation strategies for functional logic programming. *Journal of Symbolic Computation*, 40(1):875–903, 2005.

[2] S. Antoy, R. Echahed, and M. Hanus. Parallel evaluation strategies for functional logic languages. In *Proc. Fourteenth International Conference on Logic Programming*, pages 138–152, Leuven, Belgium, July 1997. MIT Press.

[3] S. Antoy, R. Echahed, and M. Hanus. A needed narrowing strategy. *Journal of the ACM*, 47(4):776–822, July 2000.

[4] S. Antoy and A. Tolmach. Typed higher-order narrowing without higher-order strategies. In *4th Fuji International Symposium on Functional and Logic Programming (FLOPS'99)*, volume 1722, pages 335–350, Tsukuba, Japan, 11 1999. Springer LNCS.

[5] Koen Claessen and John Hughes. Quickcheck: a lightweight tool for random testing of haskell programs. In *ICFP '00: Proceedings of the fifth ACM SIGPLAN international conference on Functional programming*, pages 268–279, New York, NY, USA, 2000. ACM Press.

[6] M. Hanus. A unified computation model for functional and logic programming. In *Proc. 24st ACM Symposium on Principles of Programming Languages (POPL'97)*, pages 80–93, 1997.

[7] M. Hanus et al. Curry, an integrated functional logic language. http://www.informatik.uni-kiel.de/˜curry,/, 2006.

[8] M. Hanus and F. Steiner. Controlling search in declarative programs. In *Principles of Declarative Programming (Proc. Joint International Symposium PLILP/ALP'98)*, pages 374–390. Springer LNCS 1490, 1998.

[9] F. Lindblad. Source code for examples including reference implementation. http://www.cs.chalmers.se/˜frelindb/tfp_suppl.tar

[10] Wolfgang Lux. Adding linear constraints over real numbers to curry. In *FLOPS '01: Proceedings of the 5th International Symposium on Functional and Logic Programming*, pages 185–200, London, UK, 2001. Springer-Verlag.

[11] Colin Runciman.   Smallcheck: another lightweight testing library in haskell.
http://www.cs.york.ac.uk/fp/darcs/smallcheck/

Chapter 8

Designing a Generic Graph Library using ML Functors
– *Project Paper* –

Sylvain Conchon[1], Jean-Christophe Filliâtre[1], Julien Signoles[2]

Abstract: This paper details the design and implementation of OCAMLGRAPH, a highly generic graph library for the programming language OCAML. This library features a large set of graph data structures—directed or undirected, with or without labels on vertices and edges, as persistent or mutable data structures, etc.—and a large set of graph algorithms. Algorithms are written independently from graph data structures, which allows combining user data structure (resp. algorithm) with OCAMLGRAPH algorithm (resp. data structure). Genericity is obtained through massive use of the OCAML module system and its functions, the so-called *functors*.

8.1 INTRODUCTION

Finding a graph library for one's favorite programming language is usually easy. But applying the provided algorithms to one's own graph data structure or building undirected persistent graphs with vertices and edges labeled with data other than integers is likely to be more difficult. Figure 8.1 quickly compares several graph libraries according to the following criteria: number of graph data structures; purely applicative or imperative nature of the structures; and ability to apply the provided algorithms to a user-defined graph data structure. As one can notice, none of these libraries gives full satisfaction. This paper introduces

---

[1]LRI, Univ Paris-Sud, CNRS, INRIA Futurs (ProVal), 91893 Orsay, France,
E-mail: {Sylvain.Conchon,Jean-Christophe.Filliatre}@lri.fr
[2]CEA-LIST, Laboratoire Sûreté des Logiciels, 91191 Gif-sur-Yvette cedex, France,
E-mail: Julien.Signoles@cea.fr

	language	graph data structures	imperative / persistent[4]	generic algorithms
GTL [5]	C++	1	I	no
LEDA [13]	C++	2	I	no
BGL [2]	C++	2	I	yes
JDSL [4]	Java	1	I	yes
FGL [3, 9]	Haskell	1	P	yes
MLRisc [6]	SML	1	I	no
Baire [1][5]	OCAML	8	P/I	meaningless

FIGURE 8.1: Comparison with other graph libraries

OCAMLGRAPH[3], a highly generic graph library for the programming language OCAML [7], which intends to fulfill all these criteria.

OCAMLGRAPH introduces genericity at two levels. First, OCAMLGRAPH does not provide a single data structure for graphs but many of them, enumerating all possible variations (19 altogether)—directed or undirected graphs, persistent or mutable data structures, user-defined labels on vertices or edges, etc.—under a common interface. Secondly, OCAMLGRAPH provides a large set of graph algorithms that are written independently from the underlying graph data structure. These can then be applied naturally to the data structures provided by OCAML-GRAPH itself and also on user-defined data structures as soon as these implement a minimal set of functionalities.

Without proper parameterization, such a large set of variants may easily result in unmanageable code. We avoid this pitfall using the OCAML module system [12], which appears to be the tool of choice for this kind of meta-programming. The genericity of OCAMLGRAPH is indeed achieved through a massive use of OCAML functors. On one hand, they are used to avoid code duplication between the many variations of graph data structures, which is mandatory here due to the high number of similar but different implementations. On the other hand, they are used to write graph algorithms independently from the underlying graph data structure, with as much genericity as possible while keeping efficiency in mind.

This paper is organized as follows. Section 8.2 gives an overview of OCAML module system. Section 8.3 demonstrates the use of OCAMLGRAPH through an example. Section 8.4 exposes the design of the common interface for all graph data structures and explains how the code is shared among various implementations. Section 8.5 describes the algorithms provided in OCAMLGRAPH and how genericity is obtained with respect to the graph data structure. Finally Section 8.6 presents some benchmarks.

---

[3]OCAMLGRAPH is an open source library available at http://ocamlgraph.lri.fr/.

8.2 OVERVIEW OF OCAML MODULE SYSTEM

This section quickly describes the OCAML module system. Any reader familiar with OCAML can safely skip this section.

The module system of OCAML is a language by itself, on top of the core OCAML language, which only fulfills software engineering purposes: separate compilation, names space structuring, encapsulation and genericity. This language appears to be independent of the core language [12] and may be unfolded statically. It is a strongly typed higher-order functional language. Its terms are called *modules* or *structures*. They are the basic blocks in OCAML programs, that package together types, values, exceptions and sub-modules.

8.2.1 Structures

Modules are introduced using the `struct...end` construct and the (optional) `module` binding is used to give them a name. Outside a module, its components can be referred to using the *dot notation*: `M.c` denotes the component `c` defined in the module `M`.

For instance, a module packaging together a type for a graph data structure and some basic operations can be implemented in the following way:

```
module Graph = struct
  type label = int
  type t = (int × label) list array
  let create n = Array.create n []
  let add_edge g v1 v2 l = g.(v1) ← (v2,l)::g.(v1)
  let iter_succ g f v = List.iter f g.(v)
end
```

The type `Graph.t` defines a naïve graph data structure using adjacency lists with edges labeled with integers: a graph is an array (indexed by integers representing vertices) whose elements are lists of pairs of integers and labels (declared as an alias for the type `int`).

8.2.2 Signatures

The type of a module is called a *signature* or an *interface*[6] and can be used to hide some components or the definition of a type (then called an *abstract data type*). Signatures are defined using the `sig...end` construct and the (optional) `module type` binding is used to give them a name. Constants and functions are declared via the keyword `val` and types via the keyword `type`.

---

[4]An imperative graph is a mutable data structure where modifications are performed in-place, while a persistent graph is an immutable data structure; see, for instance, Okasaki's book [14] for more details about persistent data structures.

[5]The Baire library seems to be no longer available from the Internet.

[6]with the same meaning as in MODULA but not as in JAVA

For instance, a possible signature for the `Graph` module above, that hides the graph representation and the type of labels, could be the following:

```
module type GRAPH = sig
  type label
  type t
  val create : int → t
  val add_edge : t → int → int → label → unit
  val iter_succ :
    t → (int × label → unit) → int → unit
end
```

Restricting a structure by a signature results in another view of the structure. This is done as follows:

```
module G' = (G : GRAPH)
```

Since interfaces and structures are clearly separated, it is possible to have several implementations for the same interface. Conversely, a structure may have several signatures (hiding and restricting more or less components).

8.2.3 Functors

The functions of the module system are called *functors* and allow us to define modules parameterized by other modules. Then they can be applied one or several times to particular modules with the expected signature. The benefits of functors in software engineering are appreciated as soon as one has to parameterize a *set* of types and functions by another *set* of types and functions, in a sound way[7]. For instance, to implement Dijkstra's shortest path algorithm for any graph implementation where edges are labeled with integers, one can write a functor looking like:

```
module type S = sig
  type label
  type t
  val iter_succ :
    t → (int × label → unit) → int → unit
end

module Dijkstra (G : S with type label = int) =
  struct
    let dijkstra g v1 v2 = (* ... *)
  end
```

The `with type` annotation is used here to unify the abstract type `label` from the signature S with the type `int`. One may also notice that the signature S

---

[7]See, for instance, Norman Ramsey's *ML Module Mania* [15] as an example of a massive use of ML functors.

required for the functor's argument only contains what is necessary to implement the algorithm. However, we can apply the functor to any module whose signature contains *at least* S i.e. is a *subtype* of S.

Functors are also first-class values, i.e they can be passed as arguments to other functors. Finally, it is possible to aggregate signatures or modules using the include construct which can be näively seen as a textual inclusion.

8.3 MOTIVATING EXAMPLE

To illustrate the use of OCAMLGRAPH, we consider a Sudoku solver based on graph coloring. The idea is to represent the Sudoku grid as an undirected graph with 9×9 vertices, each vertex being connected to all other vertices on the same row, column and 3×3 group. Solving the Sudoku is equivalent to 9-coloring this graph. Figure 8.2 displays the sketch of a solution to this problem using OCAMLGRAPH[8]. There are four steps in this code:

1. We choose a graph data structure for our Sudoku solver: it is an imperative undirected graph with vertices labeled with pairs of integers (the cells coordinates) and unlabeled edges. In this structure, vertices are also equipped with integer marks, that are used to store the assigned colors.

2. We create the Sudoku grid and fill it with the initial constraints.

3. We obtain a coloring algorithm for our graph data structure.

4. We solve the Sudoku problem by 9-coloring the graph.

This code is almost as efficient as a hand-coded Sudoku solver: on average, a Sudoku puzzle is solved in 0.2 seconds (on a Pentium IV 2.4 GHz). The remainder of this paper goes into more details about the code above.

8.4 SIGNATURES AND GRAPH DATA STRUCTURES

Managing many variants of graph data structures without proper parameterization results into unmanageable code. Here we show how we factorized the OCAML-GRAPH implementation to avoid such pitfall. Section 8.4.1 describes the common sub-signatures shared by all graphs. Section 8.4.2 details their various implementations.

8.4.1 Sharing Signatures for All Graphs

All graph data structures share a common sub-signature G for observers. Two other signatures distinguish the modifiers for persistent and imperative graphs, respectively.

The common signature G includes an abstract type t for the graph datatype and two modules V and E for vertices and edges respectively. The signature for E

---

[8]Full source code for the Sudoku example is given in appendix A.

```
module G = Imperative.Graph.Abstract
              (struct type t = int × int end)

let g = G.create ()

let () =
  ... add vertices to g with G.add_vertex,
      edges with G.add_edge and initial
      constraints (20 lines of code) ...

module C = Coloring(G)

let () = C.coloring g 9
```

FIGURE 8.2: A Sudoku solver using OCAMLGRAPH

always includes a type `label` which is instantiated by the singleton type `unit` for unlabeled graphs. Modules V and E both implement the standard comparison and hashing functions so that graph algorithms may easily construct data structures containing vertices and edges. G also includes usual observers such as functions to iterate over vertices and edges, which are massively used in graph algorithms. The common signature looks like:

```
module type G = sig
  type t
  module V : sig type t ... end
  module E : sig
    type t
    type label
    val label : t → label
    ...
  end
  val iter_vertex : (V.t → unit) → t → unit
  val iter_succ : (V.t → unit) → t → V.t → unit
  ...
end
```

We distinguish the signature P for persistent graphs from the signature I for imperative graphs, since the modifiers do not have the same type in both:

```
module type P = sig
  include G
  val empty : t
  val add_vertex : t → V.t → t
  val add_edge : t → V.t → V.t → t
```

```
  ...
end
module type I = sig
  include G
  val create : unit → t
  val add_vertex : t → V.t → unit
  val add_edge : t → V.t → V.t → unit
  ...
end
```

8.4.2   19 Graph Data Structures in 1000 Lines of Code

OCAMLGRAPH provides 19 graph data structures, which include all the possible combinations of the following four criteria:

1. *directed* or *undirected* graph;

2. *labeled* or *unlabeled* edges;

3. *persistent* or *imperative* data structure; and

4. *concrete* or *abstract* type for vertices.

The last point requires some explanations. Vertices are always labeled internally with the value provided by the user. Accessing this value depends on the choice of concrete or abstract vertices. Concrete vertices allow unrestricted access to their value. Abstract vertices hide their value inside an abstract data type. The former allows a more immediate use of the data structure and the latter a more efficient implementation. In particular, imperative graphs with abstract vertices can be equipped with integer mutable marks, which are used in our Sudoku solver.

A functor is provided for each data structure. It is parameterized by user types for vertex labels and possibly edge labels. These functors[9] are displayed in Figure 8.3 as square boxes mapping signatures of input modules (incoming plain edges) to the signature of the graph module (outgoing plain edges). Of these, 8 functors exist in both directed and undirected versions. Input signatures ANY_TYPE, ORDERED_TYPE_DFT and COMPARABLE define the user types for vertices and edges labels. For instance, functor AbstractLabelled from Imperative.Graph takes as arguments two modules of signatures ANY_TYPE and ORDERED_TYPE_DFT respectively and produces a module implementing signature IM. This signature extends signature I with mutable marks, as indicated by the dashed edge from IM to I. Three other implementations complete the set of graph data structures, namely ConcreteBidirectional for graphs with an efficient access to predecessors, and Matrix.(Graph, Digraph) for graphs implemented as adjacency matrices. For efficiency reasons, these three implementations do not offer the same combination of criteria as the previous ones.

---

[9]The signatures of all these functors are available at http://ocamlgraph.lri.fr/doc/.

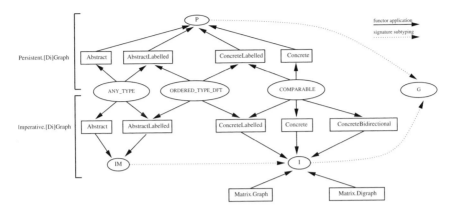

FIGURE 8.3: OCAMLGRAPH data structures components

Several functors are used internally to avoid code duplication among the functors presented in Figure 8.3. For instance, a functor adds labels to unlabeled graphs; another one encapsulates concrete vertices into an abstract data type; etc. Putting it all together, the code size for the nineteen graph data structures is about 1000 lines. This is clearly small enough to be easily maintained. In Section 8.6 we will show that this code is also quite efficient.

The graph data structure for our Sudoku solver is simply an imperative undirected graph with abstract vertices labeled with pairs of integers and unlabeled edges. It is obtained as:

```
module G = Imperative.Graph.Abstract
               (struct type t = int × int end)
```

8.5 GENERIC ALGORITHMS

This section introduces the second use of functors in OCAMLGRAPH: generic programming of graph algorithms.

8.5.1 Decoupling Algorithms and Graph Data Structures

As demonstrated in Section 8.4, our library provides many graph data structures. It makes it necessary to factorize the code for graph algorithms that operate on these structures. Again, functors provide a nice encoding of generic algorithms.

The basic idea when coding an algorithm is to focus only on the required operations that this algorithm imposes on the graph data structure. Then this algorithm can be expressed naturally as a functor parameterized by these operations. These operations usually form a subset of the operations provided by OCAMLGRAPH graph data structures. In a few cases, the algorithm requires specific operations that are independent of the graph data structure. In such a case, the specific operations are provided as an additional functor parameter.

Such a "functorization" of algorithms has two benefits: first, it allows to add quickly new algorithms to the library, without duplicating code for all data structures; secondly, it allows the user to apply an existing algorithm on his own graph data structure. Note that on the latter case the user is responsible for fulfilling the requirements over the functor parameters (which are available from OCAML-GRAPH documentation).

8.5.2   Example: Depth-First Traversal

We illustrate the generic programming of graph algorithms on the particular example of depth-first prefix traversal (DFS). To implement DFS, we need to iterate over the graph vertices and over the edges leaving a given vertex. If we do not assume any kind of marks on vertices, we also need to build a data structure to store the visited nodes. We choose a hash table for this purpose and thus we require a hash function and an equality over vertices. Thus the minimal input signature for the DFS functor is as follows:

```
module type G = sig
  type t
  module V : sig
    type t
    val hash : t → int
    val equal : t → t → bool
  end
  val iter_vertex : (V.t → unit) → t → unit
  val iter_succ : (V.t → unit) → t → V.t → unit
end
```

The DFS algorithm is then implemented as a functor with an argument of signature G. The result of functor application is a module providing a single function dfs to traverse a given graph while applying a given function on all visited vertices:

```
module Dfs(G : G) :
  sig val dfs : (G.V.t → unit) → G.t → unit end
```

To implement this functor, we first instantiate OCAML's generic hash tables on graph vertices:

```
module Dfs(G : G) = struct
  module H = Hashtbl.Make(G.V)
```

Then we can implement the traversal. The following code uses a hash table h to store the vertices already visited and an explicit stack stack to store the vertices to be visited (to avoid the possible stack overflow of a recursive implementation). Function G.iter_vertex is used to start a DFS on every vertex. The DFS itself is performed in function loop using G.iter_succ:

```
let dfs f g =
  let h = H.create 65537 in
  let stack = Stack.create () in
  let push v =
    if not (H.mem h v) then
    begin H.add h v (); Stack.push v stack end
  in
  let loop () =
    while not (Stack.is_empty stack) do
      let v = Stack.pop stack in
      f v;
      G.iter_succ push g v
    done
  in
  G.iter_vertex (fun v → push v; loop ()) g
end
```

Beside this simple algorithm, OCAMLGRAPH provides other kinds of traversals (breadth-first, postfix, etc.) and more efficient implementations when the graph data structure contains mutable marks on vertices.

8.5.3   Example: Graph Coloring

As a second example, we present a graph coloring algorithm used in our Sudoku solver. For the purpose of our algorithm, we require the presence of get and set operations on integer marks associated to vertices. We use these marks to store the color assigned to each vertex. We also need iterators over vertices and successors. Thus the minimal signature for a graph data structure used in our graph coloring algorithm is the following:

```
module type GM = sig
  type t
  module V : sig type t ... end
  module Mark : sig
    val get : V.t → int
    val set : V.t → int → unit
  end
  val iter_vertex : (V.t → unit) → t → unit
  val iter_succ : (V.t → unit) → t → V.t → unit
end
```

OCAMLGRAPH already provides implementations for such a signature. This is the case for the graph data structure used in our Sudoku solver. Then the graph coloring algorithm is implemented as the following functor:

```
module Coloring(G : GM) : sig
  val coloring : G.t → int → unit
end
```

It provides a single function `coloring` which colors a given graph with a given number of colors. Some marks may contain initial constraints. The implementation of this coloring algorithm is given in appendix B. To complete our Sudoku solver, we simply need to apply the above functor on our graph module `G`:

```
module C = Coloring(G)
```

If `g` contains the Sudoku graph, and assuming that the initial constraints are set in `g` marks, solving the Sudoku amounts to 9-coloring graph `g`:

```
C.coloring g 9
```

8.5.4 Building Graphs

In Section 8.4.1, we have shown that persistent and imperative graphs have creation functions with different signatures. However, as we have written algorithms in a generic way, we may want to build graphs in a generic way, that is independently of the underlying data structure. For instance, we may want to implement graph operations (such as union, transitive closure, etc.) or to build some classic graphs (such as the full graph with *n* vertices, the de Bruijn graph of order *n*, etc.) or even random graphs. In all these cases, the persistent or imperative nature of the graph is not really significant but the signature difference disallows genericity.

To solve this issue, we introduce a module `Builder`. It defines a common interface for graphs building:

```
module type S = sig
  module G : Sig.G
  val empty : unit → G.t
  val copy : G.t → G.t
  val add_vertex : G.t → G.V.t → G.t
  val add_edge : G.t → G.V.t → G.V.t → G.t
  val add_edge_e : G.t → G.E.t → G.t
end
```

It is immediate to realize such a signature for persistent or imperative graphs:

```
module P(G : Sig.P) : S with module G = G
module I(G : Sig.I) : S with module G = G
```

It is important to notice that for imperative graphs the values returned by the functions `add_vertex`, `add_edge` and `add_edge_e` are meaningless.

Therefore, it is easy to write a generic algorithm that builds graphs. First we write a generic version as a functor taking a module of signature `Builder.S` as argument:

```
module Make(B : Builder.S) = struct ... end
```

and then we can trivially provide two variants of this functor for both persistent and imperative graphs, with the following two lines:

```
module P(G : Sig.P) = Make(Builder.P(G))
module I(G : Sig.I) = Make(Builder.I(G))
```

Thus the use of the module `Builder` is entirely hidden from the user point of view.

8.6 BENCHMARKS

Surprisingly, we could not find any standard benchmark for graph libraries. In order to give an idea of OCAMLGRAPH efficiency, we present here the results of a little benchmark of our own. We test four different data structures for undirected graphs with unlabeled edges, that are either persistent (P) or imperative (I) and with either abstract (A) or concrete (C) vertices. In the following, these are referred to as PA, PC, IA and IC, respectively. All tests were performed on a Pentium 4 2.4 GHz.

We first test the efficiency of graph creation and mutation. For that purpose, we build cliques of V vertices (and thus $E = V(V+1)/2$ edges since we include self loops). Then we repeatedly delete all edges and vertices in these graphs. Figure 8.4 displays the creation and deletion timings in seconds up to $V = 1000$ (that is half a million edges). The speed of creation observed is roughly 100,000 edges per second for imperative graphs. The creation of persistent graphs is slower but within a constant factor (less than 2). Deletion is twice as fast as creation. Regarding memory consumption, all four data structures use approximately 5 machine words (typically 20 bytes) per edge.

Our second benchmark consists in generating graphs corresponding to 2D mazes and traversing them using depth-first and breadth-first traversals. Given an integer N, we build a graph with $V = N^2$ vertices and $E = V - 1$ edges. Figure 8.5 displays the timings in seconds for various values of N up to 600 (i.e. 360,000 vertices). The observed speed is between 500,000 and 1 million traversed edges per second.

We also tested the adjacency matrix-based data structure. Creation and deletion are much faster in that case, and the data structure for a dense graph is usually much more compact (it is implemented using bit vectors). However, the use of this particular implementation is limited to unlabeled imperative graphs with integer vertices. The above benchmarks, on the contrary, do not depend on the nature of vertices and edges types. Thus they are much more representative of OCAMLGRAPH average performances.

8.7 CONCLUSION

We presented OCAMLGRAPH, a highly generic graph library for OCAML providing several graph data structures and graph algorithms. Algorithms are written independently from graph data structures, which allows combining user data structure (resp. algorithm) with OCAMLGRAPH algorithm (resp. data structure). To our knowledge, there is no library for any applicative language as generic

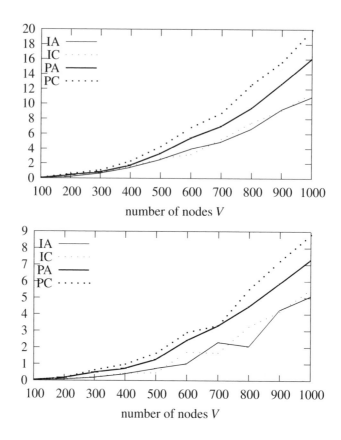

FIGURE 8.4: Benchmarks creation (top) and deletion (bottom)

as OCAMLGRAPH. This genericity is obtained using OCAML module system
and especially its functors which allow sharing large pieces of code and provide clear separation between data structures and algorithms. The same level
of genericity could probably be achieved using Haskell's multi-parameter type
classes [8, 16, 11]. Regarding imperative languages, graph libraries are rarely as
generic and never provide as many different data structures.

Since its first release (Feb. 2004), the number of OCAMLGRAPH users has
been increasing steadily and several of them contributed code to the library. Some
of them provided new graph data structures (e.g. ConcreteBidirectional)
and others new algorithms (e.g. minimal separators). It clearly shows the benefits
of a generic library where data structures and algorithms are separated.

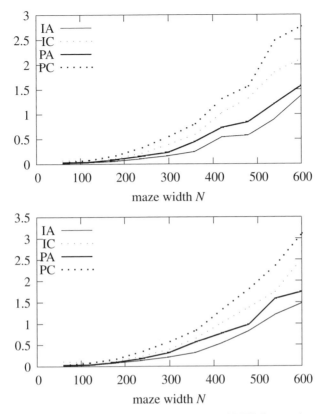

FIGURE 8.5: Benchmarks DFS (top) and BFS (bottom)

ACKNOWLEDGEMENTS

We would like to thank the anonymous reviewers for their helpful comments. We already improved the implementation of OCAMLGRAPH following one of the reviewer suggestions (generalizing mutable marks from integer to arbitrary types).

A   SIMPLE SUDOKU SOLVER USING OCAMLGRAPH

Below is the full listing for a Sudoku solver using OCAMLGRAPH, as described in this paper. This program reads the Sudoku problem on standard input and prints the solution on standard output.

```
open Graph

(* We use undirected graphs with nodes containing
   a pair of integers (the cell coordinates in
   0..8 x 0..8). *)
```

```
module G = Imperative.Graph.Abstract
                (struct type t = int * int end)

(* The Sudoku grid = a graph with 9x9 nodes *)
let g = G.create ()

(* We create the 9x9 nodes, add them to the graph
   and keep them in a matrix for later access *)
let nodes =
  let new_node i j =
    let v = G.V.create (i, j) in G.add_vertex g v; v
  in
  Array.init 9 (fun i -> Array.init 9 (new_node i))

let node i j = nodes.(i).(j)

(* We add the edges: two nodes are connected whenever
   they can't have the same value *)
let () =
  for i = 0 to 8 do for j = 0 to 8 do
    for k = 0 to 8 do
      if k <> i then G.add_edge g (node i j) (node k j);
      if k <> j then G.add_edge g (node i j) (node i k);
    done;
    let gi = 3 * (i / 3) and gj = 3 * (j / 3) in
    for di = 0 to 2 do for dj = 0 to 2 do
      let i' = gi + di and j' = gj + dj in
      if i' <> i || j' <> j then
        G.add_edge g (node i j) (node i' j')
    done done
  done done

(* We read the initial constraints from standard input *)
let () =
  for i = 0 to 8 do
    let s = read_line () in
    for j = 0 to 8 do match s.[j] with
      | '1'..'9' as ch ->
        G.Mark.set (node i j) (Char.code ch - Char.code '0')
      | _ -> ()
    done
  done

(* We solve the Sudoku by 9-coloring the graph g *)
module C = Coloring.Mark(G)
let () = C.coloring g 9

(* We display the solution *)
let () =
```

```
for i = 0 to 8 do
  for j = 0 to 8 do
    Format.printf "%d" (G.Mark.get (node i j))
  done;
  Format.printf "\n";
done;
Format.printf "@?"
```

B   GRAPH COLORING IMPLEMENTATION

Below is the code of the graph coloring functor introduced in Section 8.5.3 and used to write the Sudoku solver. The code uses a simple backtracking algorithm which performs a breadth-first traversal of the graph and successively tries each color for each visited vertex. To be able to backtrack during the traversal we use persistent cursors [10] provided by another OCAMLGRAPH functor, namely Traverse.Bfs. A persistent cursor is created with function start, the visited element is obtained with function get and the cursor is moved to the next element with function step. The latter returns a new cursor, contrary to usual cursors which are modified in-place, thus allowing backtracking.

```
module Coloring(G : GM) = struct
  module Bfs = Traverse.Bfs(G)

  exception NoColoring

  let coloring g k =
    (* assign color i to vertex v, if possible,
       and raise NoColoring otherwise *)
    let try_color v i =
      G.iter_succ
        (fun w ->
          if G.Mark.get w = i then raise NoColoring)
        g v;
      G.Mark.set v i
    in
    (* traversal of g using persistent cursor iter *)
    let rec iterate iter =
      let v = Bfs.get iter in
      for i = 1 to k do
        try try_color v i; iterate (Bfs.step iter);
            assert false
        with NoColoring -> ()
      done;
      G.Mark.set v 0; raise NoColoring
    in
    try iterate (Bfs.start g); assert false
```

```
with Exit -> ()
```

```
end
```

Note that the actual implementation in OCAMLGRAPH is slightly more complex since it uses Kempe's linear-time simplification (vertices of degree less than k are repeatedly removed and pushed on a stack, then the backtracking algorithm above is performed and finally vertices initially removed are popped from the stack and colored).

REFERENCES

[1] Baire. http://www.edite-de-paris.com.fr/~fpons/Caml/Baire/.

[2] BGL - The Boost Graph Library. http://www.boost.org/libs/graph/doc/.

[3] FGL - A Functional Graph Library. http://web.engr.oregonstate.edu/~erwig/fgl/.

[4] The Data Structures Library in Java. http://www.cs.brown.edu/cgc/jdsl/.

[5] The Graph Template Library. http://infosun.fmi.uni-passau.de/GTL/.

[6] The MLRISC System. http://cs1.cs.nyu.edu/leunga/www/MLRISC/Doc/html/INTRO.html.

[7] The Objective Caml language. http://caml.inria.fr/.

[8] D. Dreyer, R. Harper, and M. M. T. Chakravarty. Modular type classes. In *POPL*, 2007.

[9] Martin Erwig. Inductive graphs and functional graph algorithms. *Journal of Functional Programming*, 11(5):467–492, 2001.

[10] Jean-Christophe Filliâtre. Backtracking Iterators. Research Report 1428, LRI, Université Paris-Sud, January 2006. http://www.lri.fr/~filliatr/ftp/publis/enum-rr.ps.gz.

[11] Oleg Kiselyov. Applicative translucent functors in Haskell, 2004. At http://www.haskell.org/pipermail/haskell/2004-August/014463.html.

[12] Xavier Leroy. A modular module system. *Journal of Functional Programming*, 10(3):269–303, 2000.

[13] Kurt Mehlhorn and Stefan Nher. Leda: a platform for combinatorial and geometric computing. *Commun. ACM*, 38(1):96–102, 1995.

[14] Chris Okasaki. *Purely Functional Data Structures*. Cambridge University Press, 1998.

[15] Norman Ramsey. ML Module Mania: A Type-Safe Separately Compiled, Extensible Interpreter. In *ACM SIGPLAN Workshop on ML*, 2005.

[16] Stefan Wehr. *ML Modules and Haskell Type Classes: A Constructive Comparison*, November 2005. Submitted for publication and available at http://www.stefanwehr.de/diplom.

Chapter 9

Hop Client-Side Compilation

Florian Loitsch[1], Manuel Serrano[1]

Abstract: Hop is a new language for programming interactive Web applications. It aims to replace HTML, JavaScript, and server-side scripting languages (such as PHP, JSP) with a unique language that is used for client-side interactions and server-side computations. A Hop execution platform is made of two compilers: one that compiles the code executed by the server, and one that compiles the code executed by the client. This paper presents the latter.

In order to ensure compatibility of Hop graphical user interfaces with popular plain Web browsers, the client-side Hop compiler has to generate regular HTML and JavaScript code. The generated code runs roughly at the same speed as hand-written code. Since the Hop language is built on top of the Scheme programming language, compiling Hop to JavaScript is nearly equivalent to compiling Scheme to JavaScript. SCM2JS, the compiler we have designed, supports the whole Scheme core language. In particular, it features proper tail recursion. However complete proper tail recursion may slow down the generated code. Despite an optimization which eliminates up to 40% of instrumentation for tail call intensive benchmarks, worst case programs were more than two times slower. As a result Hop only uses a weaker form of tail-call optimization which simplifies recursive tail-calls to while-loops.

The techniques presented in this paper can be applied to most strict functional languages such as ML and Lisp.

SCM2JS can be downloaded at http://www-sop.inria.fr/mimosa/personnel/Florian.Loitsch/scheme2js/. It is also distributed along with Hop which can be found at http://hop.inria.fr.

---

[1]Inria Sophia Antipolis, 2004 route des Lucioles - BP93, F-06902 Sophia Antipolis, Cedex, France, E-mail: {florian.loitsch, manuel.serrano}@inria.fr

9.1   INTRODUCTION

Hop [15] is a new functional language designed for programming Web 2.0 applications. It is tuned for programming interactive graphical user interfaces for the Web. A Hop application executes simultaneously on two computers: one for computing the logic of the application, which we refer to as the *server* or *broker* (conforming to existing practice [13]) and one for running the graphical user interface, which is henceforth denoted as the *client*. The Hop execution model is distributed but a Hop program is made of one unique source code. Inside that code, a syntactic construction introduces server code, another one specifies client code. Compiling a Hop program involves two different compilation processes. The server code is compiled to native code by a compiler that has already been described in various papers [14, 12]. The client code is compiled to JavaScript, which is the imposed language for programming graphical user interfaces on the Web. Indeed, JavaScript is the only language that is supported by all major Web-browsers. Hop is an extension to the Scheme programming language [6] and this compilation is therefore mostly equivalent to a Scheme-to-JavaScript translation.

9.1.1   Main Contributions

From a practical point of view the main contribution of this work is the creation of SCM2JS, a fully functional efficient Scheme-to-JavaScript compiler. According to our observations, the Scheme compliant version with proper tail-recursion generates code that is at most 2.5 times slower than hand-written JavaScript code, but with incomplete (but usually sufficient) support for tail-recursion the compiled code is on par with hand-written code. The latter compilation mode is used in Hop and hence suitable for daily work.

From a technical point of view we suggest improvements to existing tail call techniques. Proper tail recursion does not exist in JavaScript and must hence be coded by hand. We advertise the use of JavaScript's `this`-keyword to adapt existing trampoline techniques so they become compatible with existing JavaScript code (Section 9.5.1). We also propose an optimization to the tail recursion mechanism that allowed us to remove 40% of the tail call instrumentation in some benchmarks (Section 9.5.2).

9.1.2   Organization of the paper

We start by giving an overview of Hop in Section 9.2. Section 9.3 then shows how SCM2JS compiles Scheme's core language to JavaScript. In Section 9.4 we discuss function compilation. This specifically includes our `while` transformation for recursive loop functions. This transformation always improves performance. The compilation of the remaining tail calls is presented in Section 9.5. This transformation has no impact on most benchmarks but, in the worst case, can slow down the execution by more than a factor of 2. Section 9.6 shows the results of our benchmarks. Related work is discussed in Section 9.7. We finally conclude this paper in Section 9.8.

Our compiler supports first-class continuations, but their compilation is too complex and extensive to fit into this paper and will be the subject of another publication.

9.2   HOP

In this section we briefly present the Hop programming language by an example (Section 9.2.1). A more thorough description and a discussion of its virtues compared to other Web-programming languages can be found in [15]. Once Hop has been introduced, we can then enumerate the main characteristics of the client code compilation (Section 9.2.2).

9.2.1   Hop at a glance

The Hop server associates URLs to programs. Hence, in order to start a Hop program one has to direct his Web browser to one of these URLs. This starts the execution of the program on the server. In general, web based programs are event-based, and implement the following pattern: the program is started and it élaborates a response which is sent to the client. That response is usually made of a data structure implementing an HTML element representing the graphical user interface. Once the client has received its graphical user interface it interacts with the user and, when necessary, invokes other services on the server.

The code snippet in Figure 9.1 shows a small Hop program that mimics the famous *Google suggest* application: given the first characters of the entered search term popular completions are proposed.

```
1:  (let ((def (<DIV> "")) 
2:       (svc (service (w) 
3:               (<P> (sql-exec db 
4:           "SELECT * FROM dict WHERE (prefix=~a)" w))))) 
5:  (<HTML> (<INPUT> :onkeyup 
6:              ~(innerHTML-set! $def ($svc this.value))) 
7:          "The definitions are:" def)) 
```

FIGURE 9.1: Google suggest written in Hop.

When this program is invoked the server will start creating an HTML-page as response. This page (starting at line 5) contains a <DIV> area (bound to the variable def) and a text field, which will react on onkeyup-events. During this elaboration stage the callback functions is compiled to JavaScript, and the complete page is then sent to the client. There, a change to the input-field triggers the callback, which updates the def-element. The update happens in two steps.

First the service[2] `svc` of line *2* is called with the input-field's value (accessible through `this.value`), and, as second step, the visible text of `def` is replaced by the result returned by the server (`(innerHTML-set! $def ...)`). The function `svc` executes a database query to find all words that with the given prefix. Note that (except for the database query) both server and client are written in (extended) Scheme, and that switching from one to the other can be done using only one character. Client code is introduced by a ~ (tilde) and one can escape back to server-code using $. This construct strongly resembles Scheme's *quasiquotes* in that $ escaped expressions are already evaluated during construction before sending the page to the client. During that elaboration stage the reference to `def` is transformed to JavaScript code retrieving the `div`, and the service is transformed into a server call. The example in Figure 9.2 further demonstrates this property.

```
1: (let* ((x 0)
2:        (svc (service () (set! x 1))))
3:   (<HTML>
4:     (<BUTTON> :onclick ~(begin ($svc) (alert $x)))))
```

FIGURE 9.2: The service-call will not change the transmitted x-value.

Since the elaboration of this site has replaced x with its actual value 0, the modification in the service has no effect on the client side and the alert shows 0. Even though the service-call in line *4* modifies the variable x the program will alert 0. During elaboration of the site, `(alert $x)` had already been replaced by `(alert 0)` and the modification in the service is not transmitted to the client anymore.

One should note that while server code and client code are expressed in the same language they are intended for different purposes. The server code can access all resources of the server computer. In particular, it can access the file system, the network interfaces, or it can execute long lasting CPU intensive computations. However, it is not knowledgeable of any characteristics of the graphical user interface that are only known to the client code. The client code, on the other hand, knows everything about the graphical user interface but, for security reasons, has no access to other resources. This dichotomy between server code and client code is reflected by two different APIs that are available to the server and to the client. In conclusion: *(i)* Hop is a functional language built on top of the Scheme programming language with which it shares most of its syntax. *(ii)* Server code and client code are expressed in the same language. *(iii)* The tilde sign ~ introduces client code and the dollar sign $ inside client code escapes back to server code. *(iv)* A *service* is a function defined on the server (Figure 9.1, line *2*) that can be invoked from the client (Figure 9.1, line *6*). *(v)* Finally service invocations in-

---

[2]The `service` form creates a function that can be invoked by both client and server code, but executes always on the server.

volve transmitting and receiving complex values that can be any compound data structure.

9.2.2   Compiling Hop client code: the SCM2JS compiler

```
1: (define (server-info)
2:     (string-append (host-name) " " (date)))
3: (<HTML> (<BUTTON> :onclick ~(f $(server-info)))
4:           (<SCRIPT> ~(define (f val) (alert val))))
```

FIGURE 9.3: Hop program example.

We have developed a compiler, named SCM2JS, which was needed to compile Hop client code to JavaScript. Hop server code is compiled by another compiler and in Figure 9.3 only the expressions starting with ~ in line *3* and line *4* are hence of interest. Hop extracts these lines and sends the list of expression to SCM2JS. As can be seen, Hop client side code resembles Scheme. In fact Hop client code is a superset of IEEE Scheme [6] with one exception: it does not support exact arithmetic. Most Hop extensions consist of additional library functions or new syntactic forms that are macro-expanded before the compilation takes place. The example however demonstrates some additional difficulties: SCM2JS has to deal with server objects (the call to the server, $(server-info), is server-code and has to be treated as a black box), out-of-order compilation (the function f is defined in a line following the first use of f), and the use of dynamically bound variables (like alert).

When compiling Hop client code SCM2JS allows unbound variables, and both symbol-related difficulties are hence avoided. Server objects are straightforward to implement and, these requirements dealt with, Hop client-side compilation is mostly equivalent to a Scheme-to-JavaScript compilation. In consequence, all the techniques presented in this paper would equally apply to a pure Scheme-to-JavaScript compiler. By extension, most of the material presented here could also be useful for compiling other strict functional languages (e.g. ML) to JavaScript. In the rest of this paper we will indiscriminately use the terms "Hop client code" or "Scheme" for denoting the input language of SCM2JS.

Hop client code compilation has to fulfill two requirements:

- CPU intensive parts of Hop programs are executed on servers. However, in order to let GUIs be as reactive as possible it is important to make the Hop client code as efficient as possible. We consider it of prime importance to guarantee that Hop imposes no performance penalty in comparison with traditional Web development kits whose client code is implemented in JavaScript. That is, the performance of compiled Hop client code must be on par with equivalent handwritten JavaScript code. We consider performance as a potential issue even though we have noticed tremendous differences in performance

depending on the hardware architecture and the JavaScript interpreter used for
testing. For instance, we have found that, under similar conditions, Firefox
executed our benchmarks nearly ten times faster than Safari. Safari is nevertheless a popular browser which tends to demonstrate that most users are
not paying much attention to performance. Developers, on the other hand, are
more concerned with performance, and noticeable slower client side code is
not acceptable.

- Scheme and JavaScript must be tightly integrated. That is, all global bindings
  should be easily accessible from both languages, and data structures must be
  usable indifferently in both languages. Function calls should always have the
  same syntax, independently of where the targets are.

9.3   CORE COMPILATION

This section introduces the compilation of the Scheme core language. Function
compilation and proper tail call handling are discussed in Sections 9.4 and 9.5.
JavaScript has been inspired by Scheme, and both languages are hence similar in
many respects. Like Scheme, JavaScript treats functions as first class citizens and
uses automatic memory management. SCM2JS is hence freed from the burden of
implementing closures or a garbage collector. Moreover, many Scheme constructs
(in particular closures) can be naturally mapped to semantically equivalent Java-
Script counterparts. Most transformations are as simple as transforming an array
to a list. Variable argument functions, for instance, use arrays to pass the variables
in JavaScript, but expects lists in Scheme. A compiled variable argument function
simply copies the members of the given array into a list.
Despite the similarities, compiling Scheme to JavaScript can not be accomplished
by a mere source-to-source transformation. Peculiar JavaScript scoping rules[3] and
the demand for optimizations require the construction of a true abstract syntax
tree.
JavaScript and Scheme do not share the same data types, either. JavaScript, for
instance, does not have any list data type, so SCM2JS compiles Scheme lists to
instances of a new class `sc_Pair` which is part of the SCM2JS runtime system.
In fact only Scheme's booleans, procedures and numbers (to a certain extent[4])
are semantically compatible with their respective counterparts in JavaScript. The
remaining types either behave differently or do not have any corresponding Java-
Script type:

- JavaScript strings are, contrary to Scheme strings, immutable. This restriction is not very limiting and users often prefer the ease of interfacing with

---

[3] A variable declaration inside a function is valid for the whole function. This is true
even when the declaration is after the first use. As a consequence it is not possible to
create cheap scopes inside functions.

[4] JavaScript numbers are floating point only. Scheme usually offers exact numbers
(integers) too.

JavaScript over a truly Scheme-conforming string implementation. Depending on a compiler flag SCM2JS can either directly compile Scheme strings to JavaScript strings (thereby simplifying the interface between JavaScript and Scheme code), or translate Scheme strings to JavaScript objects of class `sc_String`. Instances of this class represent mutable strings by holding one of JavaScript's immutable strings and transparently replacing it when necessary.

- Symbols are mapped to JavaScript strings. If SCM2JS is configured for mutable strings, then JavaScript strings are unused and hence free to use as symbols (which are also immutable). Otherwise Scheme strings and symbols are both compiled to JavaScript strings, and symbols are prefixed by a special unused Unicode character in order to distinguish them from strings.

- Pairs and characters are both compiled to JavaScript objects (respectively of class `sc_Pair` and `sc_Char`). The empty list is represented by `null`.

- Vectors are mapped to JavaScript `Arrays`.[5]

Due to the high level of JavaScript many standard optimizations are difficult to implement within SCM2JS. It is, for instance, not easy to take advantage of a typing pass. JavaScript itself is dynamically typed and does not offer any means to annotate variables with typing information. The lack of a `goto` statement too, rules out other common optimizations [9]. On the other hand, the optimizations that are still applicable can have a big impact on performance. For instance, our inlining pass (modeled after [12]) was able to cut the execution time of some benchmarks in half. Inlining library functions (like +, −, etc.) proved to be even more important. Our benchmarks were up to 25 times faster with this optimization enabled. Other optimizations include hoisting of constant assignments (especially function creations) or constant propagation.

9.4 FUNCTION COMPILATION

Scheme procedures and JavaScript functions are very similar and a naïve compilation would be straightforward. Scheme, however, makes more extensive use of procedures than JavaScript. In particular, it promotes the use of tail-recursive functions as loops. Using recursive tail calls as loops is only possible if they do not consume any stack (called "proper tail recursion"). Currently all important JavaScript interpreters are known not to perform tail call optimization. They abort after a predefined maximum function call depth and SCM2JS hence needs to handle tail calls by itself. A loop optimization pass transforms most recursive tail calls into loops. It is presented in the remainder of this Section. An optional transformation (Section 9.5) limits the call stack size for the remaining tail calls.

---

[5]Despite being called "Array", this data-type is an object and consists, like all JavaScript objects, of a hashtable.

In Scheme nearly all loops are implemented as recursive tail calls. Figure 9.4a demonstrates an example program with a common loop pattern. Parts enclosed into $<$ and $>$ are not important for our discussion and may represent any valid Scheme expression.

```
(let loop ((x 0)
           (y 0))
  (if <test>
      <body1>
      (begin
        <body2>
        (loop
          (* x 2)
          (+ x 1)))))
```

(a) a common Scheme loop pattern.

```
var x = 0, y = 0;
while (true) {
  if (<test>) {
    <body1>;
  } else {
    <body2>;
    var tmp = x;
    x = x * 2;
    y = tmp + 1;
    continue;
  }
  break;
}
```

(b) unoptimized

```
var x = 0, y = 0;
while (!<test>) {
  <body2>;
  y = x + 1;
  x = x * 2;
}
<body1>;
```

(c) optimized

FIGURE 9.4: Unoptimized and optimized `while` compilation of a common Scheme loop pattern.

Whenever SCM2JS encounters a tail call to the surrounding function it compiles this pattern into a `while` loop as in figure 9.4b and c. Note that the optimized version reorders the loop-variable assignment to avoid the temporary variable (which is compliant to Scheme's specification).

Such näive source-to-source translations are only sufficient as long as loop variables are not captured or not mutated. As the transformation reuses loop variables during each iteration explicit closure handling becomes necessary. For instance, in the following code the variable x is captured by an anonymous function at each iteration:

```
(let loop ((x 1))
  (store! (lambda () x))
  (set! x (* x 2))
  (loop (+ x 1)))
```

As the previous transformation hoists loop variables outside the loop, all anonymous functions would now share the same x.

In JavaScript, locally declared variables are visible within the whole function body as if they had been declared at the beginning of the function. The declaration of a new variable within the `while` body would hence deliver the same result.

SCM2JS solves the problem by pushing a new frame on the call stack (thus creat-

```
 1: var x = 1;                          var x = 1;
 2: while (true) {                      while (true) {
 3:   var stor = new Object();            var stor = new Object();
 4:   stor.x = x;                         stor.x = x;
 5:   store(function(stor_) {             with(stor) {
 6:       return function() {               var tmp_fun =
 7:         return stor_.x;                   function() {return x;};
 8:       };                                x *= 2;
 9:     }(stor));                           store(tmp_fun);
10:   stor.x *= 2;                        }
11:   x = stor.x + 1;                     x = stor.x + 1;
12: }                                   }
```

FIGURE 9.5: Explicit closure allocation with anonymous functions on the left
and with on the right.

ing an artificial scope). This can be accomplished by either invoking a function,
or by pushing an object onto the stack (using the JavaScript with statement).
Both techniques are implemented in SCM2JS (they can be selected with a compiler flag). Figure 9.5 shows the result of both approaches. An object is allocated
in line 3, which will hold the captured variables. In line 5 the storage object
is pushed onto the stack. In the first case an anonymous function is executed.
The parameter stor is thereby copied and the capturing function (created in line
6) hence captures a local stor_-object. In the second case JavaScript's with
statement pushes the stor object on the stack itself. The fields contained within
stor consequently become local variables for the enclosed statements. The capturing function saves the stack during its creation and hence holds a reference to
the pushed object. In both approaches the use of x in line 7 references now a
different x for each generated function.

The impact on the performance is largely dependent on the source-program and
the target browser. Some artificial benchmarks (executed under the same conditions as our other benchmarks in Section 9.6) revealed that under Firefox a very
short loop, like in our example, is the worst case and is respectively 17 (with
technique) and 28 (anonymous function technique) times slower than the same
version without explicit closure handling. Under Opera and Konqueror the impact is less noticeable (about 3 times slower for with and 4-6 times slower with
anonymous functions). However, this programming pattern is rare enough not to
impact the performance of most programs (and none of our benchmarks).

9.5   TAIL CALLS

It is well known that tail calls [2] can be implemented without stack consumption
when the execution platform supports goto. In the example of Figure 9.6 the
calls at line 3, and 7 are both tail calls and could be implemented with a goto if

compiled to assembly.

```
1: function even(x) {
2:    if (x === 0) return true;
3:    else return odd(x-1);
4: }
5: function odd(x) {
6:    if (x === 0) return false;
7:    else return even(x-1);
8: }
9: is2even = even(2);
```

FIGURE 9.6: A simple tail call intensive program.

In languages without `goto`, such as JavaScript, most[6] tail calls can be transformed into `while` loops (as in Section 9.4). Our example shows that this is not always possible and there exist two other popular techniques to achieve proper tail recursion for the remaining tail calls. The first technique, due to Henri Baker [1], requires the program to be transformed into Continuation Passing Style (henceforth CPS) first. Function invocations allocate frames on the stack which are used as the first generation of a generational garbage collector. Whenever the stack reaches the stack limit a garbage collection is performed, and the program restarts with an empty stack. CPS however is expensive in JavaScript and we therefore used the second technique, *trampolines*[16], in our compiler.

In the rest of this section we briefly present a naïve version of trampolines. Section 9.5.1 discusses a more efficient version of trampolines developed for the Funnel compiler [11] and our modification to make this technique compatible with native JavaScript calls. Section 9.5.2 then presents our tail call optimization.

Trampolines avoid tail calls by passing the target of tail calls to the caller waiting for the result of the currently running function. It is then the caller's task to invoke the received function (which itself could return another trampoline closure). The code in Figure 9.7 presents a trampoline version of the previous `even/odd` example. The omitted `odd` function would be similar to the `even` function.

At each tail call a new closure is allocated and returned (line *3*). The caller in line *5* then needs to restart potential trampoline-closures. In this basic form trampolines are expensive. Each tail call needs to create a closure and non tail calls have to test for trampoline closures within a `while` loop.

9.5.1 Efficient trampolines

A more efficient version of trampolines has been proposed by the authors of the Funnel-to-Java compiler [11]. They trade space for speed: instead of returning

---

[6]Except for `even/odd` and `ewal` all other benchmarks were tail-call free after the `while` transformation.

```
1: function even(x) {
2:   if (x === 0) return true;
3:   else return new Trampoline(odd, x-1);
4: }
5: res_or_tramp = even(2);
6: while (res_or_tramp instanceof Trampoline)
7:   res_or_tramp = res_or_tramp.restart();
8: is2even = res_or_tramp;
```

FIGURE 9.7: Even/Odd with trampolines.

after each tail call, a constant number c of consecutive tail calls are allowed. Once this limit is reached a special exception (which we will call "tail-exception") containing a trampoline for the not-yet executed call is returned. After the c frames have been popped the counter is reset to zero and the trampoline closure is invoked. If the limit is not reached (either the function returns or reaches a non tail call), then the execution continues normally without removing the frames. Setting c to 1 is hence equivalent to the näive trampoline technique. A higher value yields faster programs, but consumes more memory. According to their experiments a value of 40 seemed to be a good compromise.

SCM2JS's tail call handling resembles this technique in that it allows more than one consecutive tail call. Our implementation differs in the way the call counter is passed to functions. When the counter is passed as supplementary parameter it breaks the call convention, and interfacing with existing code becomes difficult. The näive use of global variables has its problems too: library functions do not modify the global variables, and instrumented functions would wrongly ignore them. Take, for instance, the code in Figure 9.8, where lib_f is a library function that comes from an existing JavaScript library and tail_f is an instrumented function that might throw a tail-exception.

```
1: function lib_f(f) {
2:   f(); // non-tail call
3:   remaining_code;
4: }
5: function tail_f() {
6:   /* tail-calls other tail-calling functions   */
7:   /* and will eventually reach the tail-limit. */
8: }
9: lib_f(tail_f);
```

FIGURE 9.8: Library-function calling a tail-calling function.

lib_f does not modify the global variables, and tail_f has hence no idea of the existence of the remaining continuation on the stack (the `remaining_code` of `lib_f`). `tail_f` will tail-call another tail-calling function, and execution will eventually reach the imposed limit `c`. At this moment a tail-exception is thrown. `lib_f` however does not know how to handle this exception and will simply ignore it. The continuation of `lib_f` is lost.

SCM2JS has adopted a solution to this problem that relies on JavaScript's method invocation protocol. JavaScript does not make any distinction between functions and methods. Any function can be used as method (as in `obj.f()`) or as a function (`f()`). In the first case the function `f` is a member of the object `obj` and executed as method. In the latter case `f` is simply invoked as function. Whenever a function is invoked as method, the keyword `this` points to the object as part of which it was executed (in our example `obj`). If a function is executed as simple function (and not method), then `this` points to the *global object* which contains all global variables.

Generally the `this` object is unused in functions that are not invoked as methods. SCM2JS therefore can use it as a container for the counter value. The call target is stored as a field in a unique object `TAIL_OBJECT` and then executed as a method call. The field `calls` of `TAIL_OBJECT` represents the tail-call counter `c`.

The (simplified) code in Figure 9.9 presents our technique on the transformed version of the previous example. At the beginning of the function the counter variable `sc_tailCalls` is initialized with the tail call counter stored in the tail object. The important data of the tail-object is thus saved, and the tail-object is free to be reused for other tail-calls.

For each tail call, the function first tests if it was called as tail call (line *6*). If the test succeeds, another test (line *7*) determines if `MAX_TAIL_CALLS` (our `c`) consecutive tail calls have been executed. If the limit has been reached a trampoline has to be returned (line *8*). If the limit has not yet been reached then the counter is incremented (line *10*), and the target is called as method (line *12*). No type check is necessary as the result would be returned verbatim indifferently of its type. If the procedure was not called as target of a tail call (line *14*), then it resets the counter to 1 and handles potential trampoline closures. The result of the tail call (line *17*) is tested (line *18*), and according to the result either restarted or simply returned. The `restart` method of the trampoline is responsible for restarting any potential further trampoline closures.

As the tail-object is reused for every tail-call, we must put tail-calls into A-Normal form [5]. Otherwise another function might change the counter-value of the tail-object after line *10* or line *15*.

Note that the non tail calls (like the one in line *25*) are not modified, and that tail calls (line *12*, and *17*) are compatible with all JavaScript functions that do not access `this`. Functions that use the `this` object are methods and usually attached to some object. Method calls, however, are never instrumented (not even in tail position) and are hence free to use the `this` variable.

```
 1: function even(x) {
 2:    var sc_tailCalls = TAIL_OBJECT.calls;
 3:    // nonTailCall();
 4:    if (x === 0) return true;
 5:    else {
 6:       if (this === TAIL_OBJECT) {
 7:          if (sc_tailCalls == MAX_TAIL_CALLS) {
 8:             return new Trampoline(odd, [x-1]);
 9:          } else {
10:             TAIL_OBJECT.calls = sc_tailCalls + 1;
11:             TAIL_OBJECT.f = odd;
12:             return TAIL_OBJECT.f(x-1);
13:          }
14:       } else {
15:          TAIL_OBJECT.calls = 1;
16:          TAIL_OBJECT.f = odd;
17:          var sc_tailTmp = TAIL_OBJECT.f(x-1);
18:          if (sc_tailTmp instanceof Trampoline)
19:             return sc_tailTmp.restart();
20:          else
21:             return sc_tailTmp;
22:       }
23:    }
24: }
25: is2even = even(2);
```

FIGURE 9.9: SCM2JS's optimized implementation of trampolines.

9.5.2   Acyclic trampoline optimization

Chain-calls that do not finish in a cycle are compiled to direct calls without trampoline instrumentation. As such they do not test against the limit c anymore and may exceed the c consecutive tail calls. As the chain does not end in any cycle the number of supplementary calls is however bounded by the length of this chain. Figure 9.10 illustrates the idea. In this example there are three tail call sites (line 4, 5, and 7). Furthermore the tail call chain len-print → approx-print → my-print does not end in a cycle. All three call locations are hence not instrumented. We have developed a static analysis that detects tail-call chains and potential cycles in them. When the analysis proves the absence of cycles, functions are not instrumented. Applied to the example of Figure 9.10, it successfully eliminates all instrumentation for the given functions.

If len-print is the cth consecutive call in a tail-call chain then it should return a trampoline, but without the instrumentation it continues tail calling, thus exceeding the limit. The "damage" is however limited as there is only one other tail call afterwards. In the worst case the program hence exceeds the given limit c by 2 (the length of the chain).

```
1:  (define (my-print msg) (print msg) msg)
2:  (define (approx-print val)
3:      (if (< val 10)
4:          (my-print "small")
5:          (my-print "big")))
6:  (define (len-print l)
7:    (approx-print (length l)))
```

FIGURE 9.10: Chain of tail-calls reaching a non-tail-call.

As this optimization is done at compile time it is not possible to determine all call targets, and some tail calls keep the trampoline instrumentation even though they can not reach any cycle. In our tail call intensive benchmark 40% of all tail calls have been simplified by this optimization.

Our experiments show that the cost for proper tail recursion is largely program-dependent. Most tail calls are loops (which are already handled by the `while` transformation) and programs tend to have few remaining tail calls. More than 80% of our benchmarks were tail-call free after the `while` transformation. Typical tail-call intensive programs however suggest a slow down of about 1.5, and extreme cases (like the `even/odd` example) run at most 2.5 times slower.

9.6 BENCHMARKS

To evaluate the performance of SCM2JS and trampolines we ran several benchmarks under two Internet browsers: Firefox 2.0.0.2 and Opera 9.10 build 521. All benchmarks were run on an Intel Pentium 4 3.40GHz, 1GB, running Linux 2.6.20. Each program was run 5 times, and the minimum time was collected. The time measurement was done by a small JavaScript program itself. Any time spent on the preparation (parsing, precompiling, etc.) was hence not measured.

Our first test measured the performance of SCM2JS generated code compared to handwritten JavaScript code. We wrote our benchmarks both in JavaScript and Scheme and then compared the execution time of the JavaScript version with the time of the compiled Scheme version. Figure 9.11a presents the ratio of the Java-Script time by the execution time of the compiled program. A value of 1.0 represents the reference time of the handwritten JavaScript code. Any value lower (resp. higher) than 1.0 means that the compiled Scheme code ran faster (resp. slower) than this code. SCM2JS fares quite well in this comparison. The compiled code generally approaches the reference value of 1.0. The good performance in `bague`, `fib`, `quicksort` and `even/odd` can be explained by our inlining pass, the bad value in `Nested` by the nature of this benchmark. `Nested` consists (as the name suggests) of several nested loops incrementing a counter in the most nested loop. The `while` loops themselves are minimal and any additional expression slows down the program. The JavaScript version `while(e--){...}` is up to 1.7 times faster than the generated version `while(e>0){...   --e;}`.

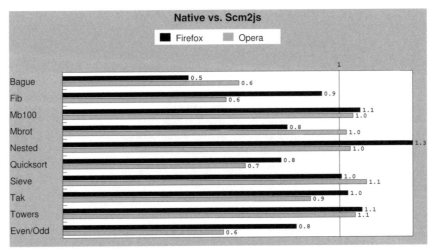

(a) Compiled Scheme relative to handwritten JavaScript files, which are the 1.0 mark. Lower is better.

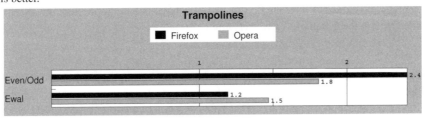

(b) Trampolined code relative to compiled code with the trampoline flag disabled, which are the 1.0 mark. Lower is better.

FIGURE 9.11: SCM2JS code interpreted by Firefox and Opera.

Figure 9.11b shows the performance penalties introduced by trampolines. As SCM2JS is able to prove that none of the previous benchmarks but even/odd contains any cyclic tail calls (at least after the while transformation), enabling or disabling proper tail-recursion has no effect on the generated code. Their performance would have been equal to 1, and we therefore do not print their results. We added another benchmark (ewal), which implements a meta circular Scheme interpreter that executes an iterative version of fact. The program uses many anonymous functions and tail calls and is hence a good candidate for this test. The extreme case even/odd is at most 2.5 times slower. The more realistic ewal is only about 1.7 times slower.

Although we think that code size is usually insignificant compared to the size of images that are sent with web-pages, we compared the size of the produced code with hand-written JavaScript and the original Scheme code. As we do not have a JavaScript version of the ewal program we used the original Scheme code as reference for this benchmark. All major web-browsers accept gzipped files and

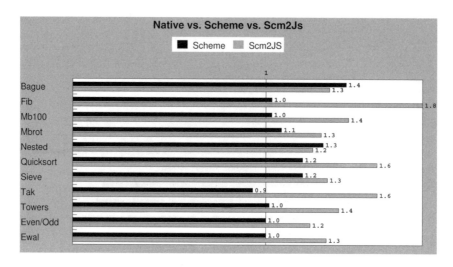

FIGURE 9.12: Code size comparison of handwritten JavaScript code, Scheme source, and SCM2JS produced code. All files have been compressed. JavaScript file size are the 1.0 mark. Lower is better.

we therefore only show the results for compressed files in Figure 9.12. The chart shows that even without trampolines SCM2JS produced code is usually bigger than the equivalent JavaScript code. This can be explained by inlining and other optimizations. When trampolines are enabled (not visible in the chart) then the even/odd and ewal programs are respectively 2 and 1.3 times bigger than without trampolines.

9.7 RELATED WORK

Related work can be classified into three categories: projects that run Scheme in Web-browsers, projects that use JavaScript as compilation target and projects that propose to unify client and server development.

There are many attempts to run Scheme and Lisp like languages on the client side. Contrary to SCM2JS these projects are either interpreters or they change the semantics of the input-language to match the semantics of JavaScript. For instance, ParenScript[10] (a compiler of a Lisp like language to JavaScript) keeps the distinction between statements and expressions from JavaScript. As such the do construct (compiled to JavaScript's while statement) can not be used at an expression location, and it does not return any value. Examples for interpreters are jsScheme[18] and Little Scheme[4].

JavaScript is a high-level language and hence not well suited as a compilation target. However, due to the ubiquity of JavaScript, such compilations have become more and more attractive.

Google[7] compiles Java to JavaScript. Java's object model can be simulated with

JavaScript's prototype object model, and both share many common constructs (with identical syntax). Java is statically typed and permits many optimizations that are infeasible in highly dynamic languages like JavaScript and Scheme. The compilation from Java to JavaScript hence seems to be a good choice for efficient code. Powerful features like higher order functions and variable argument functions are however lost in the process. Due to the different nature of Java and JavaScript it is necessary to use the JSNI (JavaScript Native Interface) to interface with existing JavaScript code.

Script#[8] and NeoSwiff[17] both compile C# to JavaScript and face hence the same difficulties and share the same advantages as the Google Java compiler.

All these compilers greatly simplify the development of Web projects, but still separate client and server development. In particular the communication between client and server is still complicated.

Links[3] eliminates this boundary. Links, a typed language, uses annotations to force the execution of functions on either the server or the client, but allows the execution of non-annotated functions on either side. When calls pass the client-server boundary they are transparently compiled to xml-http-requests. The client-side portion of a program written in Links is transformed to a CPS JavaScript, which breaks the call-convention with standard JavaScript functions. It is not yet optimized for speed and runs one to two orders of magnitude slower than SCM2JS.

9.8 CONCLUSION

In this paper we have presented SCM2JS, a Scheme to JavaScript compiler. Our work shows that such a compiler is feasible and can be efficient. We discussed the compilation of proper tail calls, one of the major differences between the two languages. The `while` transformation we presented compiles a large percentage of tail recursive calls into cheap `while` iterations (8 out of our 10 benchmarks were tail-call free after this optimization), and the trampoline implementation takes care of the rest. Proper tail-recursion is expensive though, and even though our optimization removed the costly instrumentation for up to 40% of affected functions worst case examples exhibited a slowdown of a factor two.

We modified existing tail-call techniques so that strict compatibility with existing JavaScript code is preserved. It is thus possible to interface easily with existing JavaScript libraries. Also SCM2JS generates efficient code. We therefore achieved both of our initial requirements for this compiler: good integration with JavaScript and good performance. The integration of SCM2JS into Hop (the framework which motivated the creation of SCM2JS) opened the door for a single language for Web programming. As Hop itself is a variant of the Scheme language it is now possible to write client-code and server-code of sophisticated web applications exclusively in Scheme.

REFERENCES

[1] H. Baker. CONS Should Not CONS Its Arguments, Part II: Cheney on the M.T.A <1>. SIGPLAN *Notices*, 30(9):17–20, September 1995.

[2] W. Clinger. Proper Tail Recursion and Space Efficiency. In *Conference on Programming Language Design and Implementation*, June 1998.

[3] Ezra Cooper, Sam Lindley, Philip Wadler, and Jeremy Yallop. Links: Web programming without tiers. submitted to ICFP 2006, 2006.

[4] Douglas Crockford. Little scheme. http://www.crockford.com/javascript/scheme.html.

[5] Cormac Flanagan, Amr Sabry, Bruce F. Duba, and Matthias Felleisen. The essence of compiling with continuations. In *Conference on Programming Language Design and Implementation*, volume 28(6), pages 237–247. ACM Press, New York, June 1993.

[6] IEEE Std 1178-1990. *IEEE Standard for the Scheme Programming Language*. Institute of Electrical and Electronic Engineers, Inc., New York, NY, 1991.

[7] Google Inc. Google web toolkit. http://code.google.com/webtoolkit/.

[8] Nikhil Kothari. Script#. http://projects.nikhilk.net/Projects/ScriptSharp.aspx.

[9] S. Muchnick. *Advanced Compiler Design & Implementation*. Morgan Kaufmann, 1997.

[10] Manuel Odendahl and Edward Marco Baringer. Parenscript. http://parenscript.org.

[11] M. Schinz and M. Odersky. Tail call elimination of the Java Virtual Machine. In *Proceedings of Babel*, Florence, Italy, September 2001.

[12] Manuel Serrano. Inline expansion: *when* and *how*? In *Int. Symp. on Programming Languages, Implementations, Logics, and Programs*, pages 143–147, Southampton, UK, September 1997.

[13] Manuel Serrano. The HOP Development Kit. In *Invited paper of the Seventh* ACM SIGPLAN *Workshop on Scheme and Functional Programming*, Portland, Oregon, USA, September 2006.

[14] Manuel Serrano and Marc Feeley. Storage use analysis and its applications. In *ICFP*, pages 50–61, Philadelphia, Penn, USA, May 1996.

[15] Manuel Serrano, Erick Gallesio, and Florian Loitsch. Hop, a language for programming the web 2.0. In *Dynamic Languages Symposium*, Oregan, USA, October 2006.

[16] D. Tarditi, A. Acharya, and P. Lee. No assembly required: Compiling Standard ML to C. *ACM Letters on Programming Languages and Systems*, 2(1):161–177, 1992.

[17] GlobFX Technologies. Neoswiff. http://www.globfx.com/products/neoswiff/.

[18] Alex Yakovlev. jsScheme. http://alex.ability.ru/scheme.html.

Chapter 10

Constructing Correct Circuits: Verification of Functional Aspects of Hardware Specifications with Dependent Types

Edwin Brady[1], James McKinna[1], Kevin Hammond[1]

Abstract: This paper focuses on the important, but tricky, problem of determining provably correct program properties *automatically* from program source. We describe a novel approach to constructing correct low-level programs. By using modern, full-spectrum *dependent types*, we are able to give an explicit and checkable link between the low-level program and its high-level meaning. Our approach closely links programming and theorem proving in that a type correct program is a constructive proof that the program meets its specification. It goes beyond typical *model-checking* approaches, that are commonly used to check formal properties of low-level programs, by building proofs over abstractions of properties. In this way, we avoid the state-space explosion problem that bedevils model-checking solutions. We are also able to consider properties over potentially infinite domains and determine properties for potentially infinite programs. We illustrate our approach by implementing a carry-ripple adder for binary numbers.

[1] School of Computer Science, University of St Andrews, St Andrews, Scotland,
E-mail: eb, james, kh@dcs.st-and.ac.uk

10.1 INTRODUCTION

Type theories based on *dependent types* [19, 8] have received significant interest in the functional programming community, promising enhanced mechanisms for expressing correctness properties for functional programs. Where conventional types express a program's meaning, *dependent types* allow types to be predicated on values, *so expressing a more precise meaning*. This allows the programmer both to write programs and to verify specifications within the same framework. *Simply because a program typechecks*, we obtain a *free theorem* [27] that the program conforms to its specification. In this paper, we will show how dependent types allow the relationship to be maintained explicitly between high-level data structures and their concrete representations.

To illustrate our approach we develop a simple program modeling a realistic circuit: a binary *carry-ripple adder*, in which the type of a binary number embeds the decoding function to natural numbers so that the type of binary addition expresses that it must correspond to addition on natural numbers. This program is implemented using IVOR [5], an interactive theorem prover for a *strongly-normalizing* dependent-type theory[2], which we call TT, embedded as a Haskell library. The main contributions of this paper are:

- We show how dependent types allow low-level constructions (such as bits, binary numbers and adder circuits) to be given types which express their high level meaning. Low level programs built from these constructions then reflect their high level meaning in their type, giving a program which is *correct by construction* [1], without the need for costly *model-checking* or similar apparatus.

- We give a realistic example of programming with dependent types. The advantage of using dependent types for our example program (or indeed any program where we require strong guarantees) is that dependent types link the proof and the program in a machine checkable manner. Proving correctness by hand is an error prone process; any error in a machine checkable proof will be caught by the typechecker.

Although there has been significant theoretical interest in dependent types, the number of practical examples has been highly limited to date ([17] is a notable exception). By developing such an example in this paper, we hope to demonstrate a wider range of applicability for dependent types than has hitherto been considered, and so to help convince any still-wavering functional programmers of the potential merits of a dependently typed approach.

Our approach is similar to *program extraction* [23, 18], or proving a specification in a theorem prover such as COQ [9] or Isabelle [22]. However, our emphasis is different in that we treat the program as the prior notion rather than the proof. By giving a precise type the program *is* the proof of the specification. We are thus able to write clear, concise programs without type annotations (other than the

---

[2]i.e. one where evaluation of all programs terminates without error.

top level type of each function), and with occasional explicit proof terms where required.

We find this approach greatly assists the construction of correct functional programs. It allows us to concentrate on the program itself and add details of proofs where necessary for well-typedness. helping to achieve the hitherto elusive general promise of ease-of-reasoning that was identified by John Hughes in his seminal 1984 paper "Why Functional Programming Matters" [15].

10.1.1 Programming with Dependent Types

In a dependently typed language such as TT, we can parameterize types over *values* as well as other types. We say that TT is a *full-spectrum* dependently typed language, meaning that *any* value may appear as part of a type, and types may be computed from any value. For example, we can define a "lists with length" (or vector) type; to do this we first declare a type of natural numbers to represent such lengths:

$$\underline{\text{data}} \quad \mathbb{N} : \star \quad \underline{\text{where}} \quad 0 : \mathbb{N} \quad | \quad s : \mathbb{N} \to \mathbb{N}$$

This declaration is written using GADT [24] style syntax. It declares three constants, $\mathbb{N}$, 0 and s along with their types, where $\star$ indicates the type of types. Then we may make the following declaration of vectors; note that ε only targets vectors of length zero, and $x{::}xs$ only targets vectors of length greater than zero:

$$
\begin{aligned}
\underline{\text{data}} \quad &\text{Vect} : \star \to \mathbb{N} \to \star \quad \underline{\text{where}} \\
&\quad \varepsilon \quad : \text{Vect } A\, 0 \\
| \quad &(::) \quad : A \to (\text{Vect } A\, k) \to (\text{Vect } A\, (s\,k))
\end{aligned}
$$

The type of Vect : $\star \to \mathbb{N} \to \star$ indicates that it is predicated on a type (the element type) and a natural number (the length). When the type includes explicit length information like this, it follows that a function over that type will express the invariant properties of the length. For example, the type of the program **vPlus**, which adds corresponding numbers in each vector, expresses the invariant that the input vectors are the same length as the output. The program consists of a type declaration (introduced by <u>let</u>) followed by a pattern matching definition:

$$
\begin{aligned}
\underline{\text{let}} \quad &\textbf{vPlus} : (\text{Vect } \mathbb{N}\, n) \to (\text{Vect } \mathbb{N}\, n) \to (\text{Vect } \mathbb{N}\, n) \\
&\textbf{vPlus} \quad \varepsilon \quad\quad \varepsilon \quad\quad \mapsto \varepsilon \\
&\textbf{vPlus}\, (x{::}xs)\, (y{::}ys) \quad \mapsto (x + y){::}(\textbf{vPlus}\, xs\, ys)
\end{aligned}
$$

Unlike in a simply typed language, we do not need to give error handling cases when the lengths of the vectors do not match; the typechecker verifies that these cases are impossible.

A key advantage of being able to index types over values is that it allows us to link *representation* with *meaning*. In the above example, the only part of the list's meaning we consider is its length — in the rest of this paper we will consider more detailed examples.

10.1.2   Theorem Proving

The dependent type system of TT also allows us to express properties directly. For example, the following heterogeneous definition of equality, due to McBride [20], is built in to TT:

$$\underline{\mathsf{data}} \quad (=) : (A : \star) \to (B : \star) \to A \to B \to \star \quad \underline{\mathsf{where}}$$
$$\mathsf{refl} : (a : A) \to (a = a)$$

Note that since the range of a function type may depend on previous arguments, it is possible to bind names in the domain, as with refl's domain $a : A$ here. This declaration states that two values in two different types may be equal, but the only way to construct a proof, by reflexivity, is if the two values really *are* equal. For convenience, we use an infix notation for the $=$ type constructor and leave the parameters A and B implicit. Since equality is a datatype just like $\mathbb{N}$ and Vect, we can write programs by pattern matching on instances of equality, such as the following program which can be viewed as a proof that s respects equality:

$$\underline{\mathsf{let}} \quad \mathbf{resp\_s} : (n = m) \to (\mathsf{s}\,n = \mathsf{s}\,m)$$
$$\mathbf{resp\_s}\,(\mathsf{refl}\,n) \;\mapsto\; \mathsf{refl}\,(\mathsf{s}\,n)$$

The type of this function implicitly abstracts over all n and m. It is implemented by pattern matching on the first argument, of type $n = m$. The only way to construct such a value is from $\mathsf{refl}\,n : n = n$, therefore to complete the definition it is sufficient to construct a proof of $\mathsf{s}\,n = \mathsf{s}\,n$.

We can use the equality type to perform equational reasoning on programs — a term of type $P\,x$ can be transformed to $P\,y$ if we have a proof of $x = y$, using the following function:

$$\underline{\mathsf{let}} \quad \mathbf{repl} : (x : A) \to (y : A) \to (x = y) \to (P : A \to \star) \to P\,x \to P\,y$$
$$\mathbf{repl}\,x\,y\,(\mathsf{refl}\,x)\,P\,p \;\mapsto\; p$$

Using this function (and an interactive theorem prover such as IVOR to assist in applying it correctly), we can build explicit and machine checkable proofs of any desired property, e.g. commutativity and associativity of addition.

In this paper, we will implement a carry-ripple adder for binary numbers, using inductive families to maintain a strong link between binary numbers and the natural numbers they represent. We will use these theorem proving techniques to construct proofs that addition of binary numbers corresponds to addition of unary natural numbers.

10.2   BINARY NUMBER REPRESENTATION

In this section we develop some primitive constructions which we will use to build a correct by construction binary adder. *Correct by construction* means that the fact that the program typechecks is a guarantee that it conforms to the specification given in the type. We use the word "correct" in a very strong sense; the totality of the type theory guarantees that a program will yield a result conforming to the specification in *all* cases.

10.2.1 Natural Number Arithmetic

We predicate binary numbers on their decoding as a $\mathbb{N}$, which means that binary addition must correspond to natural number addition. Addition is defined inductively, as an infix function $+$, as follows:

$$\underline{\text{let}} \quad (+) : \mathbb{N} \to \mathbb{N} \to \mathbb{N}$$
$$0 \quad + y \mapsto y$$
$$(\mathsf{s}\,k) + y \mapsto \mathsf{s}\,(k + y)$$

Multiplication can be defined similarly. It is straightforward to show several properties of these definitions in TT itself using IVOR's rewriting tactic (implemented via the **repl** function in section 10.1.2), e.g. the following are functions giving proofs of commutativity and associativity respectively:

comm_plus : $(x : \mathbb{N}) \to (y : \mathbb{N}) \to (x + y = y + x)$
assoc_plus : $(x : \mathbb{N}) \to (y : \mathbb{N}) \to (z : \mathbb{N}) \to ((x + y) + z = x + (y + z))$

By proving these properties, and showing that binary addition is equivalent to natural number addition by indexing binary numbers by the corresponding $\mathbb{N}$, we get these properties for free on binary numbers.

We briefly illustrate theorem proving in dependent type theory by showing a proof term for **comm_plus** above. Let us assume the following two lemmas (both simple to prove):

plus_0 : $(n : \mathbb{N}) \to (n = n + 0)$
plus_s : $(n, m : \mathbb{N}) \to (\mathsf{s}\,(m + n) = m + (\mathsf{s}\,n))$

The definition of plus gives rise to reduction rules which can be exploited by the typechecker; it is defined by pattern matching on the first argument, so an expression $a + b$ can always be reduced if a is constructor headed. The above lemmas give rewrite rules for the situation where b is in constructor form by a is not. Then **comm_plus** can be written as a recursive pattern matching function, making use of the **repl** function for equational reasoning:

$$\textbf{comm\_plus} \quad 0 \quad m \mapsto \textbf{plus\_0}\,m$$
$$\textbf{comm\_plus}\,(\mathsf{s}\,k)\,m \mapsto \textbf{repl}\,(\mathsf{s}\,(m + k))\,(m + (\mathsf{s}\,k))\,(\textbf{plus\_s}\,m\,k)$$
$$(\lambda a : \mathbb{N}.\,\mathsf{s}\,(k + m) = a)$$
$$(\textbf{resp\_s}\,(\textbf{comm\_plus}\,k\,m))$$

In the recursive case, **repl** is used to rewrite the type — it changes the type from $\mathsf{s}\,(k + m) = m + (\mathsf{s}\,k)$ to $\mathsf{s}\,(k + m) = \mathsf{s}\,(m + k)$. Then we can apply the function recursively (we think of this as applying the induction hypothesis) to the proof that equality respects successor given in section 10.1.2.

In practice, since the typechecker can construct several arguments to **repl** automatically, since it knows the types we are rewriting between, we will write applications of **repl** in the following way, eliding all but the rewriting lemma to be applied and the value to be returned:

$$\textbf{comm\_plus}\ \ 0\ \ m\ \ \mapsto\ \textbf{plus\_0}\,m$$
$$\textbf{comm\_plus}\,(s\,k)\,m\ \ \mapsto\ \textbf{repl}\,(\textbf{plus\_s}\,m\,k)\,(\textbf{resp\_s}\,(\textbf{comm\_plus}\,k\,m))$$

10.2.2 Bit Representation

The simplest building block of a binary number is the bit; in a traditional simply typed programming language we might represent this as a boolean. However, since we are interested in preserving meaning throughout the whole computation, we express in the type that bits on their own represent either zero or one:

<u>data</u>   Bit : $\mathbb{N} \to \star$ <u>where</u>   O : Bit 0 | I : Bit 1

For readability we will use traditional notation for numbers and arithmetic operators, except in pattern matching definitions; e.g. we write I : Bit 1 rather than I : Bit (s 0).

We will also need to add pairs of bits, which will result in a two bit number. It is convenient to represent bit pairs in their own type, with the corresponding decoding:

<u>data</u>   BitPair : $\mathbb{N} \to \star$ <u>where</u>
    bitpair : Bit b → Bit c → BitPair $(2 \times b + c)$

10.2.3 A Full Adder

Various algorithms can be used to adding n-bit binary numbers in hardware. Whichever we choose, the required primitive operation is a **full adder**. A full adder is a circuit which adds three binary digits, producing two digits (a sum, and the carry value). Three inputs, l, r and c_{in} are combined into two outputs, s and c_{out}:

$$s\ \ =\ \ (l\,\text{xor}\,r)\,\text{xor}\,c_{in}$$
$$c_{out}\ \ =\ \ (l\,\text{and}\,r)\,\text{or}\,(r\,\text{and}\,c_{in})\,\text{or}\,(c_{in}\,\text{and}\,l)$$

It is well known that this is a correct model of a full adder. It is straightforward to check by hand by constructing a truth table for the three inputs l, r and c_{in}. Using dependent types, we can let the machine check that we have a correct implementation with respect to the desired behavior. In this section we give two implementations of the full adder: firstly, a simple definition by pattern matching; and secondly, a definition implementing the above calculation through logic gates.

Simple Definition

We model this circuit with the following function, **addBit**, with the type guaranteeing that the resulting bit representation decodes to the sum of the inputs. Our definition is simply a lookup table enumerating all of the possibilities; typecheck-ing of this is fully automatic since the types of the left and right hand side of each equation are identical and any reduction of $+$ required at the type level is on constructor headed arguments.

<u>let</u>   **addBit** : $\text{Bit}\,c \rightarrow \text{Bit}\,x \rightarrow \text{Bit}\,y \rightarrow \text{BitPair}\,(c+x+y)$
  addBit O O O $\mapsto$ bitpair O O
  addBit O O I $\mapsto$ bitpair O I
  addBit O I O $\mapsto$ bitpair O I
  addBit O I I $\mapsto$ bitpair I O
  addBit I O O $\mapsto$ bitpair O I
  addBit I O I $\mapsto$ bitpair I O
  addBit I I O $\mapsto$ bitpair I O
  addBit I I I $\mapsto$ bitpair I I

Lower Level Operations

Any definition of **addBit** which satisfies the above type is guaranteed by con-struction to be a correct implementation. We can therefore model a full adder by modeling the required hardware operations (and, or and xor), then combining them to produce a full adder, i.e.:

  andGate : $\text{Bit}\,x \rightarrow \text{Bit}\,y \rightarrow \text{Bit}\,(\textbf{and}\,x\,y)$
  orGate : $\text{Bit}\,x \rightarrow \text{Bit}\,y \rightarrow \text{Bit}\,(\textbf{or}\,x\,y)$
  xorGate : $\text{Bit}\,x \rightarrow \text{Bit}\,y \rightarrow \text{Bit}\,(\textbf{xor}\,x\,y)$

Since bits are indexed over their interpretation as natural numbers, we need to provide the meaning of each of these operations on natural numbers as well as the operation itself. We treat zero as false, and non-zero as true. For example, to model an and gate, we first define the corresponding function over $\mathbb{N}$:

<u>let</u>   **and** : $\mathbb{N} \rightarrow \mathbb{N} \rightarrow \mathbb{N}$
  and $(\text{s}\,x)\,(\text{s}\,y)$ $\mapsto$ 1
  and 0 y $\mapsto$ 0
  and x 0 $\mapsto$ 0

Then an and gate modeling the behavior of Bits can be implemented:

  andGate I I $\mapsto$ I
  andGate O y $\mapsto$ O
  andGate x O $\mapsto$ O

The or and xor operations are implemented similarly. With these definitions, we can implement **addBit** as a combination of logic gates, given the earlier defi-nitions of the sum and carry outputs:

<u>let</u>   **addBit** : Bit c → Bit x → Bit y → BitPair $(c+x+y)$
    addBit $l\,r\,c_{in}$
        ↦ <u>let</u> c_{out} = **orGate** (**orGate** (**andGate** $l\,r$)(**andGate** $r\,c_{in}$)) (**andGate** $c_{in}\,l$)
            s = **xorGate** (**xorGate** $l\,r$) c_{in}
                <u>in</u> bitpair $c_{out}\,s$

We can be sure this is a correct implementation, because the typechecker verifies that the *meaning* of the pair of output bits is correct with respect to the meaning of the inputs. A small amount of theorem proving is required to help the type
checker; case analysis on each input c, x and y verifies that the types of the left
and right hand sides are always equal. We read the type as a specification that,
given bits with numeric meanings c, x and y, the output pair has numeric meaning
$c+x+y$.

10.2.4 Number Representation

There are two possibilities for a binary representation built on Bits — either left
or right-biased. A number is a list of bits; the choice determines whether a new bit
value b is added at the most significant end (changing a value n to $2^{width} \times b + n$),
or at the least significant end (changing a value n to $2 \times n + b$). As TT types, the
choices are:

1. Left-biased; adding most significant bit:

    <u>data</u>   Number : $\mathbb{N} \to \mathbb{N} \to \star$ <u>where</u>
            none   : Number 0 0
        | bit   : Bit b → Number *width val* →
                        Number $(1 + width)$ $(2^{width} \times b + val)$

2. Right-biased; adding least significant bit:

    <u>data</u>   NumberR : $\mathbb{N} \to \mathbb{N} \to \star$ <u>where</u>
            noneR   : NumberR 0 0
        | bitR   : NumberR *width val* → Bit b →
                        NumberR $(1 + width)$ $(2 \times val + b)$

Which we choose has important consequences. Not only does it affect how
the binary adder is written (and which algorithms are simplest to implement), but
also how we show the correspondence with addition on $\mathbb{N}$.
    Number is indexed over its width (i.e. the number of bits) as well as its de-
coding. As well as helping to compute the decoding, this allows us to specify the
effect an operation has on a number's width — e.g. addition of two n-bit numbers gives an n-bit number with carry, multiplication of two n-bit numbers gives
a $2 \times n$-bit number.

10.2.5 Number Equivalence

The representation we choose, Number or NumberR has a significant effect on how we show equivalence between binary and unary functions. Each models a list of bits, but we may find some functions easier to construct in one setting than another. In fact, we can show that the two representations are equivalent and hence interchangeable using the fact that we have indexed the binary representation over its decoding as a $\mathbb{N}$. It suffices to implement the following functions:

> <u>let</u>   **leftToRight** : Number $w\,val$ → NumberR $w\,val$
> <u>let</u>   **rightToLeft** : NumberR $w\,val$ → Number $w\,val$

We do not need to show that the composition of these two functions is the identity function. The property in which we are interested is that translating between representations preserves the decoding. Since the type expresses that decoding is preserved, we know that composition of **leftToRight** and **rightToLeft** gives a binary number with the same meaning as the original.

To illustrate this, we will show how to implement **leftToRight**. The simplest method in general is to provide functions to construct a NumberR with the same indices as the constructors for Number:

> **nonerL** : NumberR 0 0
> **bitrL** : Bit bv → NumberR $w\,val$ → NumberR $(1+w)\,(2^w \times bv + val)$

Implementing **nonerL** is straightforward, using the constructor noneR. For **bitrL**, we must show how to add a most significant bit to a right-biased number, where the bitR constructor adds the least significant bit. We might expect the following definition to work, simply pushing the bit to be added, b, through recursive calls:

> <u>let</u>   **bitrL** : Bit bv → NumberR $w\,val$ → NumberR $(1+w)\,(2^w \times bv + val)$
>   **bitrL** b noneR   ↦ bitR noneR b
>   **bitrL** b (bitR $n\,b_l$) ↦ bitR (**bitrL** $b\,n$) b_l

However, as it stands, this does not typecheck. We need to do a little extra manipulation of the types, since the type of the bitR constructor does not reflect the fact that the new bit is added as the high bit. The expected return type of the recursive case is:

> NumberR $(2+w)\,(2^{1+w} \times bv_l + (2 \times nv + bv))$

nv is the decoding of n, and bv_l the decoding of b_l. However, the type we get from the construction with bitR is:

> NumberR $(2+w)\,(2 \times (2^w \times bv_l + nv) + bv)$

It is easy to see, by simple algebraic manipulation, that the two expressions are equivalent. In order to convince the typechecker, however, we need an extra lemma which converts the return type we have into the return type we need for the value we wish to construct:

> **bitrL_lemma** : $(2^{1+w} \times bv_l + (2 \times nv + bv)) = (2 \times (2^w \times bv_l + nv) + bv)$

This lemma can be applied using **repl**; the correct definition of **bitrL** is:

<u>let</u>   **bitrL** : Bit bv → NumberR $w\,val$ → NumberR $(1+w)\,(2^w \times bv + val)$
  bitrL b noneR $\mapsto$ bitR noneR b
  bitrL b (bitR $n\,b_l$) $\mapsto$ **repl bitrL_lemma** (bitR (**bitrL** $b\,n$) b_l)

Implementing **bitrL_lemma** is also through equational reasoning with **repl**. IVOR has a library of useful theorems about addition and multiplication to assist with this; such a function could in many cases be constructed via the Omega decision procedure [25]. Having implemented **nonerL** and **bitrL**, the definition of **leftToRight** is a straightforward application of these functions.

<u>let</u>   **leftToRight** : Number $w\,val$ → NumberR $w\,val$
  leftToRight none $\mapsto$ **nonerL**
  leftToRight (bit $b\,n$) $\mapsto$ **bitrL** $b\,n$

The implementation of **rightToLeft** proceeds similarly, pushing the bit to be added through recursive calls and rewriting types through equational reasoning where required. Rewriting types in this way is a common pattern when implementing functions indexed by arithmetic operations, and it is therefore vital to have the support of a theorem proving environment in which the types can *direct* the implementation.

Having implemented these definitions, we are free to choose either representation for any function, and in practice we are likely to choose the representation which yields the more straightforward proofs.

For our adder, we choose the left-biased representation. Although it looks slightly more complex, in that the value depends on the number's width as well as the bit value, its main practical advantage is that it leads to a slightly simpler definition of full binary addition, with correspondingly simpler algebraic manipulations in order to prove correspondence with $\mathbb{N}$ addition.

10.2.6 Carry

The final part of the representation pairs a number with a carry bit. In order to deal with overflow, our addition function over n-bit numbers will give an n-bit number and a carry bit. This also means that n-bit add with carry can be implemented recursively in terms of $n-1$-bit add with carry, with easy access to the carry bit resulting from the recursive call.

<u>data</u>   NumCarry : $\mathbb{N} \to \mathbb{N} \to \star$ <u>where</u>
  numcarry : Bit c → Number $width\,val$ →
              NumCarry $width$ $(2^{width} \times c + val)$

10.3 A CARRY RIPPLE ADDER

We can now define an arbitrary width binary addition with carry function, **addNumber**. We can choose between several implementations of this, e.g. carry-ripple, or carry lookahead. However, because the type of the function precisely expresses its *meaning* (namely, that it implements addition on binary numbers corresponding to natural number addition), we can be sure that any type-correct implementation is equivalent to any other. The type of **addNumber** is as follows:

$$\underline{\text{let}} \quad \textbf{addNumber} \; : \; \text{Number } width \, x \rightarrow \text{Number } width \, y \rightarrow \text{Bit } c \rightarrow$$
$$\text{NumCarry } width \, (x + y + c)$$

10.3.1   First Attempt

We will define a carry ripple adder. This is a simple algorithm — to add two n-bit numbers, first add the least significant ($n - 1$-bit) numbers, then add the most significant bits with the carry resulting from the recursive addition. We would like to define **addNumber** as follows:

$$\textbf{addNumber} \quad \text{none} \quad \text{none} \quad carry \; \mapsto \; \text{numcarry } c \, \text{none}$$
$$\textbf{addNumber} \; (\text{bit } bx \, nx) \, (\text{bit } by \, ny) \, carry$$
$$\mapsto \; \underline{\text{let}} \, \text{numcarry } carry_0 \, rec \; = \; \textbf{addNumber} \, nx \, ny \, carry$$
$$\underline{\text{let}} \, \text{bitpair } carry_1 \, s \; = \; \textbf{addBit} \, bx \, by \, carry_0$$
$$\underline{\text{in}} \, \text{numcarry } carry_1 \, (\text{bit } s \, rec)$$

Although this *looks* like a correct implementation of add with carry, unfortunately it does not typecheck as written. The problem is similar to that encountered in our definition of **leftToRight** in Section 10.2.5, but more complex. Let us examine the types of the left- and right-1hand sides of the recursive case. We have:

$$bx \; : \; \text{Bit } bxv$$
$$by \; : \; \text{Bit } byv$$
$$nx \; : \; \text{Number } w \, nxv$$
$$ny \; : \; \text{Number } w \, nyv$$
$$carry \; : \; \text{Bit } c$$
$$\text{bit } bx \, nx \; : \; \text{Number } (1 + w) \, (2^w \times bxv + nxv)$$
$$\text{bit } by \, ny \; : \; \text{Number } (1 + w) \, (2^w \times byv + nyv)$$

Here, bxv, byv, nxv and nyv are the decodings of the bits and numbers, and w is the width of the numbers in the recursive call. The type of the left hand side is:

$$\textbf{addNumber} \, (\text{bit } bx \, nx) \, (\text{bit } by \, ny) \, carry$$
$$: \; \text{NumCarry} \, (1 + w) \, ((2^w \times bxv + nxv) + (2^w \times byv + nyv) + c)$$

Typechecking the right hand side proceeds as follows. We first check the type of the recursive call:

$$\textbf{addNumber} \, nx \, ny \, carry \; : \; \text{NumCarry} \, w \, (nxv + nyv + c)$$

From the recursive call, we obtain the sum of the lower bits and a carry flag by pattern matching the result against numcarry $carry_0$ rec. Assuming that $carry_0$ has type Bit c_0 and rec has type Number w $nrec$, we get:

$$\text{numcarry } carry_0 \, rec \; : \; \text{NumCarry} \, w \, (2^w \times c_0 + nrec)$$

The decodings c_0 and rec are introduced by the pattern matching against numcarry, and we can infer that $(2^w \times c_0 + nrec) = (nxv + nyv + c)$. Given this, we can check the type of adding the top bits:

> **addBit** $bx\, by\, carry_0$: BitPair $(bxv + byv + c_0)$
> bitpair $carry_1\ s$: BitPair $(2 \times ns + c_1)$

Again, ns and c_1 are introduced by pattern matching and we can infer that $(2 \times ns + c_1) = (bxv + byv + c_0)$. Finally, the result of the function is checked as follows:

> numcarry $carry_1$ (bit $s\, rec$) : NumCarry $(1 + w)\, (2^{1+w} \times c_1 + (2^w \times ns + nrec))$

For typechecking to succeed, we need to know that $(2^w \times c_1 + (2^w \times ns + nrec))$ and $((2^w \times bxv + nxv) + (2^w \times byv + nyv) + c)$ are convertible, in order to unify the type of the left hand side with the type of the right hand side. Unfortunately, we cannot expect this to happen automatically — it requires the typechecker to do some automatic equational reasoning given the equalities inferred by the pattern matching <u>let</u> bindings.

10.3.2   A Correct Carry Ripple Adder

Although our definition appears correct, the type of the second clause does not quite work automatically. We need to provide an explanation, in the form of a checkable proof using equational reasoning with **repl** as described in Section 10.1.2, that the values in the left- and right-hand sides of the pattern clause can be converted to each other. We write a helper function which makes the dependencies explicit in its type. We will write **addNumber** as follows:

> **addNumber**   none   none $carry$ $\mapsto$ numcarry c none
> **addNumber** (bit $bx\, nx$) (bit $by\, ny$) $carry$
> $\mapsto$ **bitCase** $carry\, bx\, by\, nx\, ny$ (**addNumber** $nx\, ny\, carry$)

The purpose of **bitCase** is to convert the type we want to give for the right hand side to the type required by the typechecker. In practice, this is where we do the theorem proving required to show the correctness of binary addition.

> <u>let</u>   **bitCase** : Bit c $\rightarrow$ Bit bxv $\rightarrow$ Bit byv $\rightarrow$
>   Number $w\, nxv$ $\rightarrow$ Number $w\, nyv$ $\rightarrow$
>   NumCarry $w\, (nxv + nyv + c)$ $\rightarrow$
>   NumCarry $(1 + w)\, ((2^w \times bxv + nxv) + (2^w \times byv + nyv) + c)$

The advantage of writing the definition in this way, passing the result of the recursive call to **addNumber** in to **bitCase**, is that the dependencies between the decodings of the numbers are maintained. To write **bitCase**, we follow a method similar to that for writing **bitlR** in Section 10.2.5; i.e. separate the construction of the data and the rewriting of the type through equational reasoning. Constructing the data involves adding the most significant bits, and appending the resulting bit pair to the result of the recursive call. We implement this with the following helper:

$$\underline{\text{let}} \quad \textbf{bitCase}' \; : \; \mathsf{BitPair}\, bv \rightarrow \mathsf{Number}\, w\, val \rightarrow$$
$$\mathsf{NumCarry}\, (w+1)\, (2^w \times bv + val)$$
$$\textbf{bitCase}' \, (\mathsf{bitpair}\, b\, c)\, num \; \mapsto \; \textbf{repl}\,\textbf{bitCase}'\textbf{p}\, (\mathsf{numcarry}\, b\, (\mathsf{bit}\, c\, num))$$

We use the **bitCase'p** lemma to rewrite the type so that the numcarry constructor can be applied. **bitCase'p** has the following type, as is easy to show by equational reasoning:

$$\textbf{bitCase}'\textbf{p} \; : \; (2^w \times (val + 2 \times cv) + bv) = (2^{w+1} \times cv + (2^w \times val + bv))$$

Finally, we observe that **bitCase** is easier to write if we rewrite the type so that the argument and return type include the common subterms $nxv + nyv + c$, since we can then treat this subterm as atomic. We also lift the common subterm 2^w, to give:

$$\underline{\text{let}} \quad \textbf{bitCase2} \; : \; \mathsf{Bit}\, c \rightarrow \mathsf{Bit}\, bxv \rightarrow \mathsf{Bit}\, byv \rightarrow$$
$$\mathsf{Number}\, w\, nxv \rightarrow \mathsf{Number}\, w\, nyv \rightarrow$$
$$\mathsf{NumCarry}\, w\, (nxv + nyv + c) \rightarrow$$
$$\mathsf{NumCarry}\, (1 + w)\, (2^w \times (bxv + byv) + (nxv + nyv + c))$$

The types are now in a form where the helper **bitCase'** can be applied directly:

$$\textbf{bitCase2}\, carry\, bx\, by\, nx\, ny\, (\mathsf{numcarry}\, carry_0\, val)$$
$$\mapsto (\textbf{bitCase}'\, (\textbf{addBit}\, bx\, by\, carry_0)\, val)$$

bitCase itself is written by rewriting the type to be in a form usable by **bitCase2**, using a suitable lemma **bitCaseRewrite**:

$$\textbf{bitCase}\, carry\, bx\, by\, nx\, ny\, val$$
$$\mapsto \textbf{repl}\,\textbf{bitCaseRewrite}(\textbf{bitCase2}\, carry\, bx\, by\, nx\, ny)$$

The **bitCaseRewrite** lemma simply expresses the equality between the indices in the types of **bitCase** and **bitCase2** and allows conversion between the two:

$$\textbf{bitCaseRewrite} \; : \; ((2^w \times bxv + nxv) + (2^w \times byv + nyv) + c) =$$
$$(2^w \times (bxv + byv) + (nxv + nyv + c))$$

This function has required us to break down the construction of the number into its component parts: adding the upper bits; making a recursive call; and gluing the results together. Each step has required some fairly simple equational reasoning to convert the decoding of the numbers and bits into the required type; the required lemmas can be implemented by a series of rewrites using **repl**. The full development, as an IVOR script constructing a TT program, is available online[3].

Since TT is a language of total functions, we can be confident that the above definition will always terminate. This is an important consideration, since part of guaranteeing the correctness of a function is the guarantee that it will yield a result for *all* type-correct inputs, not just a subset.

Although extra work is needed at the type level to show that the decodings of the binary numbers are consistent in the implementation of **bitCase**, the *computational* content is the same as our first attempt at defining **addNumber**. The

---

[3]http://www.dcs.st-and.ac.uk/\%7Eeb/CarryRipple

decoding and length data appear only at the type level, so need not be stored at runtime [7]. As a result, any function such as **repl** which merely manipulates the indices of a type can be replaced by the identity function at runtime, as shown in [4]. What remains is the computational content, i.e. just the bit manipulation.

10.3.3 Properties of addNumber

Since binary numbers are indexed over the natural numbers, and **addNumber** is correspondingly indexed over natural number addition, we should expect it to have corresponding properties. However, we do not have to prove these properties separately, but rather make use of properties we have already proved for $\mathbb{N}$. To do this, we make use of the following lemma:

> <u>let</u>   **numCarryUnique** : $(x : \mathsf{NumCarry}\,w\,val) \rightarrow$
> $(y : \mathsf{NumCarry}\,w\,val) \rightarrow (x = y)$

This lemma states that any two representations which decode to the same $\mathbb{N}$ are equal, and is implemented by structural decomposition of x and y — it is clear, looking at the indices of each constructor, that at each stage only one representation is possible.

Then the proof of commutativity of **addNumber** (setting the carry bit to zero for simplicity) is written as follows, using a lemma to expose the natural number addition in the type and rewriting it with **comm_plus**:

> <u>let</u>   **commAddNumberAux** : $(x : \mathsf{NumCarry}\,w\,(lv + rv) + 0) \rightarrow$
> $(y : \mathsf{NumCarry}\,w\,(rv + lv) + 0) \rightarrow$
> $(x = y)$
> **commAddNumberAux** $x\,y$
> $\mapsto$ **repl** (**comm_plus** $lv\,rv$) (**numCarryUnique** $x\,y$)

This function rewrites the type of x of using **comm_plus** to swap lv and rv, then uses **numCarryUnique** to show that the numbers x and y must be equal because their decodings are equal. It is possible to apply **numCarryUnique** only after rewriting the type of x with **comm_plus** so that it is the same as the type of y. We finish the proof of commutativity by applying the above lemma:

> <u>let</u>   **commAddNumber** : $(l : \mathsf{Number}\,w\,lv) \rightarrow (r : \mathsf{Number}\,w\,rv) \rightarrow$
> (**addNumber** $l\,r\,\mathsf{O} = $ **addNumber** $r\,l\,\mathsf{O}$)
> **commAddNumber** $l\,r$ $\mapsto$ **commAddNumberAux** (**addNumber** $l\,r\,\mathsf{O}$)
> (**addNumber** $r\,l\,\mathsf{O}$)

We have shown that **addNumber** is commutative without having to look at its definition at all — just using the properties of the function which gives its meaning. Indeed, *any* implementation of **addNumber** with the same type can be substituted into this proof. The main difficulty is rewriting the types to a form to which the natural number proofs can be applied.

10.3.4   Incremental Development

Writing a program such as **addNumber** requires us to be aware of the required type of each subterm, and the type of each operation we wish to apply. As we can see by examining the implementation of **bitCase** and its helper operations, such manipulation is difficult to manage by hand, even for relatively simple properties such as the correctness of **addNumber**. We therefore consider it essential that a practical dependently typed language allows the programmer to develop a program interactively (as with EPIGRAM [21] or theorem proving systems such as COQ [9]), rather than the traditional approach of submitting a monolithic program to a compiler.

10.4   RELATED WORK

The most closely related approach of which we are aware is the reFL^{ect} [11] language for verifying hardware circuit designs. Like reFL^{ect}, we are able to verify programs in the language TT itself. Unlike reFL^{ect}, however, we do not implement a theorem prover in TT, but rather use an interactive development system (IVOR) to construct well typed TT programs. The soundness of the system as a whole then relies solely on the soundness of the TT typechecker. This is a key advantage of our approach, since we rely only on the correctness of a checker for a standard and well understood type theory (similar to COQ [9] or EPIGRAM's ETT [8]) rather than external software.

Herrmann's approach [14] is also related to our own in that he constructs high level combinators to generate very specific low level code. He uses meta-programming (in Template Haskell) to generate type and size correct circuit designs, where size errors are caught by the Haskell type checker. We have previously studied correct hardware implementation in HW-Hume [12], which uses high level functional notation to implement low level concepts, but requires external tools (e.g. a model checker) to prove correctness properties. A closely related approach, similarly separating high level description from the low level code, is to use multi-stage programming [10]. A multi-stage language allows specialization of high level generic abstractions to specific instances, preserving type information between stages. A similar approach has been applied to generate high-performance parallel programs [13]. We are extending our approach with dependently typed multi-stage programming [6] — since the types encode correctness properties, specialization of a dependently typed program preserves these correctness properties, and we hope to adapt this method to generate hardware descriptions, e.g. via Lava [3], a Haskell-embedded domain specific language for describing circuits.

10.5   CONCLUSION

We have described an approach to constructing correct software with dependent types, and given a specific application area which can benefit from this approach, namely modeling of hardware circuits. The example we have presented — a binary adder — is relatively straightforward, but illustrates the important concepts behind our approach; namely that each data structure is explicitly linked with its high level meaning (in the case of binary numbers, their decoding as a $\mathbb{N}$). Writing the program proceeds largely as normal, with the additional requirement that we insert rewriting lemmas to preserve well-typedness, and with the benefit that any properties of the original, simpler definition are properties of the low level definition for free, such as our commutativity proof **commAddNumber**. The need to insert rewriting lemmas to show that our definition respects the original natural number implementation is the main cost of our approach. We believe this to be a small price to pay for guaranteed correctness. A part of our approach which we therefore consider *vital* to its practicality is the use of *type-directed* program development — when writing **bitCase**, for example, it is convenient to be able to see the required type for the right hand side of a pattern clause and do the equational reasoning *interactively*.

An alternative approach may be to use Haskell with Generalized Algebraic Data Types [24] (GADTs). GADTs allow limited properties of data types to be expressed by reflecting values at the type level. However, the kind of equational reasoning we need to implement **bitCase** is likely to be very difficult. Other weaker dependent type systems, such as sized types [16] or DML [28] allow types to be parameterized over numbers, but require an external constraint solver which does not allow the user directed equational reasoning required for **bitCase**.

Circuits are usually designed with respect to three views; behavior, structure and geometry. In a circuit description language such as VHDL or Haskell embedded domain specific language for circuit design such as Lava [3], it is possible to describe these views. Here, we have described the *behavioral* view and shown it to be correct through the type system. We hope to apply multi-stage programming with dependent types [26, 6] to transform programs between these views and generate hardware descriptions from high level programs such as **addNumber**.

The method could be used to verify more complex operations on a CPU, for example, multiplication, or in conjunction with program generation techniques and a hardware description language such as Lava or Wired [2] to develop correct by construction FPGA configurations In future, we plan to explore multi-stage programming techniques [10, 13, 6], possibly in combination with Lava, Wired or HW-Hume, to generate correct code.

ACKNOWLEDGEMENTS

We would like to thank Christoph Herrmann for his comments on an earlier draft, and the anonymous reviewers for their helpful suggestions. This work is generously supported by EPSRC grant EP/C001346/1, and by EU Framework VI Grant IST-2004-510255, funded under the FET-Open programme.

REFERENCES

[1] P. Amey. Correctness by Construction: Better can also be Cheaper. *CrossTalk: the Journal of Defense Software Engineering*, pages 24–28, March 2002.

[2] E. Axelsson and K. Claessen M. Sheeran. Wired: Wire-aware circuit design. In *CHARME 2005*, 2005.

[3] P. Bjesse, K. Claessen, M. Sheeran, and S. Singh. Lava: Hardware design in Haskell. In *Proc. ICFP '98*, 1998.

[4] Edwin Brady. *Practical Implementation of a Dependently Typed Functional Programming Language*. PhD thesis, University of Durham, 2005.

[5] Edwin Brady. Ivor, a proof engine. In *Proc. Implementation of Functional Languages (IFL 2006)*, volume 4449 of *LNCS*. Springer, 2007. To appear.

[6] Edwin Brady and Kevin Hammond. A Verified Staged Interpreter is a Verified Compiler. In *Proc. ACM Conf. on Generative Prog. and Component Engineering (GPCE '06), Portland, Oregon*, 2006.

[7] Edwin Brady, Conor McBride, and James McKinna. Inductive families need not store their indices. In Stefano Berardi, Mario Coppo, and Ferruccio Damiani, editors, *Types for Proofs and Programs 2003*, volume 3085, pages 115–129. Springer, 2004.

[8] James Chapman, Thorsten Altenkirch, and Conor McBride. Epigram reloaded: a standalone typechecker for ETT. In *TFP*, 2005.

[9] Coq Development Team. The Coq proof assistant — reference manual. http://coq.inria.fr/, 2001.

[10] J. Eckhardt, R. Kaibachev, E. Pašalíc, K. Swadi, and W. Taha. Implicitly Heterogeneous Multi-Stage Programming. In *Proc. 2005 Conf. on Generative Programming and Component Engineering (GPCE 2005)*, Springer-Verlag LNCS 3676, 2005.

[11] J. Grundy, T. Melham, and J. O'Leary. A Reflective Functional Language for Hardware Design and Theorem Proving. *J. Functional Programming*, 16(2):157–196, 2006.

[12] K. Hammond, G. Grov, G. J. Michaelson, and A. Ireland. Low-Level Programming in Hume: an Exploration of the HW-Hume Level. Submitted to IFL '06, 2006.

[13] Christoph A. Herrmann. Generating message-passing programs from abstract specifications by partial evaluation. *Parallel Processing Letters*, 15(3):305–320, 2005.

[14] Christoph A. Herrmann. Type-sensitive size parametrization of circuit designs by metaprogramming. Technical Report MIP-0601, Universität Passau, February 2006.

[15] John Hughes. Why functional programming matters. Technical Report 16, Programming Methodology Group, Chalmers University of Technology, November 1984.

[16] John Hughes, Lars Pareto, and Amr Sabry. Proving the correctness of reactive systems using sized types. In *Proceedings of the 23rd ACM SIGPLAN-SIGACT symposium on Principles of programmin*, pages 410–423, 1996.

[17] Xavier Leroy. Formal certification of a compiler back-end. In *Principles of Programming Languages 2006*, pages 42–54. ACM Press, 2006.

[18] Pierre Letouzey. A new extraction for Coq. In Herman Geuvers and Freek Wiedijk, editors, *Types for proofs and programs*, LNCS. Springer, 2002.

[19] Zhaohui Luo. *Computation and Reasoning – A Type Theory for Computer Science.* International Series of Monographs on Computer Science. OUP, 1994.

[20] Conor McBride. *Dependently Typed Functional Programs and their proofs.* PhD thesis, University of Edinburgh, May 2000.

[21] Conor McBride. Epigram: Practical programming with dependent types. Lecture Notes, International Summer School on Advanced Functional Programming, 2004.

[22] Tobias Nipkow, Lawrence C. Paulson, and Markus Wenzel. *Isabelle/HOL - A proof assistant for higher order logic*, volume 2283 of *LNCS*. Springer-Verlag, March 2002.

[23] Christine Paulin-Mohring. *Extraction de programmes dans le Calcul des Constructions.* PhD thesis, Paris 7, 1989.

[24] Simon Peyton Jones, Dimitrios Vytiniotis, Stephanie Weirich, and Geoffrey Washburn. Simple Unification-Based Type Inference for GADTs. In *Proc. ICFP '06: 2006 International Conf. on Functional Programmin g*, 2006.

[25] William Pugh. The Omega Test: a fast and practical integer programming algorithm for dependence analysis. *Communication of the ACM*, pages 102–114, 1992.

[26] W. Taha. A Gentle Introduction to Multi-stage Programming, 2003. Available from `http://www.cs.rice.edu/~taha/publications/journal/dspg04a.pdf`.

[27] P. Wadler. Theorems for free! In *Proc. 4th Int. Conf. on Funct. Prog. Languages and Computer Arch., FPCA'89, London, UK, 11–13 Sept 1989*, pages 347–359. ACM Press, New York, 1989.

[28] Hongwei Xi. *Dependent Types in Practical Programming.* PhD thesis, Department of Mathematical Sciences, Carnegie Mellon University, December 1998.